THE JOY OF PREACHING

THE JOY OF PREACHING

Phillips Brooks

INTRODUCTION BY
WARREN W. WIERSBE

KREGEL PUBLICATIONS
Grand Rapids, Michigan 49501

The Joy of Preaching, by Phillips Brooks. Foreword and biographical introduction by Warren W. Wiersbe. © 1989 by Kregel Publications, a division of Kregel, Inc. P. O. Box 2607, Grand Rapids, MI 49501. All rights reserved.

Cover Design: Brian Fowler

Library of Congress Cataloging-in-Publication Data

Brooks, Phillips, 1835-1893.
  [Lectures on Preaching]
  The joy of preaching / by Phillips Brooks; foreword and biographical introduction by Warren W. Wiersbe.
       p.   cm.
  Reprint. Originally published: Lectures on preaching.
London: H. R. Allenson, 1895.
  Bibliography: p.

  1. Preaching. I. Title.
BV4211.B7   1989   251—dc20   89-2549
                                                  CIP

ISBN   0-8254-2276-0 (pbk.)

1 2 3 4 5 Printing/Year 93 92 91 90 89

Printed in the United States of America

CONTENTS

Foreword by Warren W. Wiersbe 7

Phillips Brooks: A Preacher of Truth and Life
    by Warren W. Wiersbe 9

1. The Two Elements in Preaching 23
2. The Preacher Himself 45
3. The Preacher in His Work 67
4. The Idea of the Sermon 91
5. The Making of the Sermon 113
6. The Congregation 137
7. The Ministry for Our Age 159
8. The Value of a Human Soul 183

Appendices 199
1. The Teaching of Religion 201
2. The Fire and the Calf 225

FOREWORD

"Why should a preacher ministering in the Space Age read lectures on preaching that were delivered over a century ago?"

I was asked that question by several puzzled students when I assigned this book as one of the texts for a seminary homiletics course. It wasn't long before they understood why I chose it: *Phillips Brooks deals with the essential principles of preaching—principles that never change.* In fact, it is my conviction that everything useful written on homiletics in America in the last century is in one way or another a footnote to Phillips Brooks.

No matter what books on preaching you have read, whether they be ancient or modern, you must read what Brooks said if your training in sermon preparation is to be complete. But don't just read these lectures—digest them, assimilate them, and let his approach to homiletics become second nature to you.

Then you will experience what Phillips Brooks would want all ministers of the Word to experience: The joy of preaching!

WARREN W. WIERSBE

PHILLIPS BROOKS:
A Preacher of Truth and Life

by Warren W. Wiersbe

"Preaching is the communication of truth by man to men
. . . [it] is the bringing of truth through personality."

That is perhaps the most famous definition of preaching
found anywhere in American homiletical literature. It was
given at Yale University by Phillips Brooks on Thursday,
January 11, 1877, as the famous Boston preacher opened the
sixth series of the well-known "Lyman Beecher Lectures on
Preaching," better known today as "The Yale Lectures on
Preaching."[1]

Funded by a $10,000 grant from Henry N. Sage of Brooklyn,
the lectureship was inaugurated in 1871 by Lyman Beecher's
son, Henry Ward Beecher, the ministerial monarch of
Plymouth Congregational Church in Brooklyn. Beecher gave
the lectures the first three years, John Hall the fourth, and
William M. Taylor the fifth.

For the most part, the Yale lecturers have presented
interesting and helpful material over the years; and some of
the series have become classics. But I personally feel that

---

1. For the best surveys of the speakers and their lectures, see *The Heart of the
Yale Lectures*, by Batsell Barrett Baxter (Macmillan, 1947; reprint, Baker Book House,
1971); and *The Royalty of the Pulpit*, by Edgar DeWitt Jones (Harper, 1951). Baxter
ends with the 1943-44 series by G. Bromley Oxnam, and Jones with the 1948-49
series by Leslie Weatherhead.

most of what has been written on homiletics in America since 1871 is in one way or another a footnote to Phillips Brooks. That is why his lectures are so important to the preacher who wants to understand and apply the basic principles of the art and craft of preaching.[2]

Using Brooks' own definition as a guide, I want to examine the *personality* of the lecturer and then the *truth* that he preached. I think this is the best way to get acquainted with the man and his ministry, and thus be better prepared to appreciate his lectures and learn from them.

The Man

Phillips Brooks was born in Boston, Massachussetts, on December 13, 1835, with the kind of New England ancestry that almost predestined him to greatness. His father was descended from the famous Puritan preacher John Cotton (1585-1652); and his mother's family, after whom he was named, produced several leading ministers and laymen, among them John, Samuel, and William Phillips who helped to found and fund the famous Phillips Academies in Exeter and Andover, Massachusetts. Lewis O. Brastow wrote that Phillips Brooks was "the consummate flower of nine generations of cultured Puritan stock,"[3] and he was right.

His mother had a strong spiritual influence on the family; four of her six sons became preachers. When the Congregational church the family attended became too Unitarian for her, Mrs. Brooks quietly withdrew and united with St. Paul's Episcopal Church on Tremont Street. Soon her husband followed her. This was a significant move, for the new pastor, Alexander H. Vinton, was a devoted evangelical who taught his people the Word of God. Phillips Brooks grew up in an atmosphere of Bible preaching, devotional fervor, and practical service to others. By the time he went to college, he knew at least 200 hymns by heart.

When he graduated from Harvard University in 1855, Brooks was not certain what vocation to pursue; so he

---

2. After studying the entire Yale series exhaustively, Jones concluded that "Phillips Brooks' lectures, in sheer nobility of utterance, stand up as no other single volume in the series" (*The Royalty of the Pulpit*, p. 23).

3. Brastow, Lewis O., *Representative Modern Preachers* (New York: George H. Doran, 1904), p. 195. Brastow was Professor of Practical Theology at Yale from 1885 to 1907, so he would have known Phillips Brooks personally.

accepted a teaching position at the Boston Latin School, his alma mater. When he taught the younger students, he was quite happy in the classroom. When the older boys were assigned to him, however, he began to break down and could not adequately handle the discipline problems. Along with this, he was unable to get along with the headmaster, who was quite rough and unyielding. It was too much for the sensitive young man, and he resigned from the school in February, 1856. The headmaster told him, "I have never known any man who fails in teaching to succeed in anything else."

Thoroughly discouraged, Brooks counseled with President Walker of Harvard and Dr. Vinton, his own pastor; and both men urged him to enter the ministry. Brooks had never been confirmed in the Episcopal church, and he was even confused about his own conversion! In the days that followed, he solved his spiritual problems and surrendered to God in a "commitment that was so complete that no other experience was ever able to reduce it to second place in his life."[4]

The last week of October, 1856, Brooks quietly left Boston for Alexandria, Virginia, where he entered the Virginia Theological Seminary. A Yankee in the Southland, he had problems adjusting to a different kind of society; and he was deeply disturbed by what he saw of slavery. He also had problems accepting the careless lifestyle of some of his fellow students, men who prayed piously in chapel but ignored their studies and came to class unprepared.

Unfortunately, at that time the faculty was weak and the classes uninspiring; so Brooks gave himself to wide reading and independent study. Breadth of outlook was always characteristic of him, and he sought to learn all he could from whatever sources were available. To him, all truth was God's truth; and he was fearless in his quest. His friend and successor as Bishop of Massachusetts, William Lawrence, wrote, "He had no patience with that man or church who

---

4. Albright, Raymond W., *Focus on Infinity: A Life of Phillips Brooks* (New York: Macmillan, 1961), p. 34. This is one of the best modern biographies of Brooks and should be read along with Alexander V. G. Allen's *Life and Letters of Phillips Brooks.* A two-volume edition was published in 1900 by E. P. Dutton, New York, and an abridged edition in 1907. However, Albright had access to previously unpublished material, and he writes with the advantage of historical perspective. Except for the fact that Albright thinks that Spurgeon's middle initial is *W*, not *H* (p. 112), the book is accurate in details and filled with insights into the life and ministry of a great preacher.

was timidly asking of present thought, 'Is it orthodox?' The vital question was, 'Is it true?'"[5]

Brooks graduated from the seminary on July 1, 1859, and was properly ordained by William Meade, Bishop of Virginia. He was invited to serve the Church of the Advent in Philadelphia, with the possibility of becoming rector. The first few weeks on the field were difficult, and he was not sure he wanted to stay. He had to prepare two sermons, a lecture, and a Bible study each week and still carry on the expected pastoral and parish ministries. But gradually he developed a balanced schedule that kept him going successfully the rest of his life. He once told Lyman Abbott that he never knew what it was to be tired![6]

Phillips Brooks stood 6 feet 4 inches tall and at one time weighed nearly 300 pounds. (At his funeral, the casket was so heavy that one of the young Harvard pallbearers almost fell into the grave!) He was a delight to every hostess because he loved to eat, and he ate with such exuberance. He used large quantities of sugar and enjoyed iced drinks, especially the carbonated kind; and he often drank five glasses of water at a meal. In spite of his mother's pleas, he smoked all of his life. He especially enjoyed cigars. His idea of relaxation was "nothing in the world but plenty of books and time and tobacco."[7]

Brooks never married, a decision he called the greatest mistake of his life. He loved children and frolicked with them at every opportunity. He walked rapidly and loved to drive fast horses, and he was an incurable traveler. Nearly every other summer he would visit Europe, and he journeyed as far as the Holy Land (where he wrote "O Little Town of Bethlehem") and Japan, quite a feat in those days.

He had a keen sense of humor, although it does not show up in his printed sermons. When asked whether he believed a whale *really* swallowed Jonah, he replied, "There was no difficulty. Jonah was one of the minor prophets."

On November 18, 1861, Brooks resigned his ministry at the Church of the Advent to become rector of Holy Trinity

---

5. Lawrence, William, *Phillips Brooks: A Study* (Boston and New York: Houghton Mifflin Co., 1903), pp. 28-29. This is an address Dr. Lawrence gave at Trinity Church, Boston, in commemoration of the tenth anniversary of Brooks' death, January 23, 1903.

6. Abbott, Lyman, *Silhouettes of My Contemporaries* (Garden City, New York: Doubleday, Page and Co., 1922), p. 242.

7. Albright, *Focus on Infinity: A Life of Phillips Brooks*, p. 197.

Church, Philadelphia. The Civil War was in progress; in fact, on the day of Brooks' resignation, the Provisional Government of the Confederate States of America convened its fifth session in Richmond, Virginia. The times were difficult.

Without encouraging bigotry or partisan politics, Brooks took a courageous stand against slavery and did all he could to encourage the preservation of the Union. He and fellow minister Albert Barnes (author of *Barnes' Notes on the New Testament*) persuaded the mayor to allow the clergy to work on the defenses of the city. When the indifferent citizens saw their ministers at work, they became ashamed and joined in. He visited Gettysburg and ministered to the wounded in the hospitals. In his address "Abraham Lincoln," given while Lincoln's body lay in state in Philadelphia, Brooks boldly indicted slavery as the true assassin: "Solemnly, in the sight of God, I charge this murder where it belongs, on slavery. . . . In the barbarism of slavery the foul act and its foul method had its birth."[8]

In 1869, Brooks became rector of historic Trinity Church in the heart of Boston's influential business district, a position he held until he became Bishop of Massachusetts in 1891. When he became a bishop, he said to a friend, "I resigned the rectorship of Trinity Church, and it seemed like dying!" But his ministry at Trinity for nearly a quarter of a century was a spiritual force that influenced not only the city and New England, but through his printed sermons, the whole English-speaking world.

He was only 57 years old when he died in Boston on January 23, 1893, having served as Bishop of Massachusetts for only 15 months. He caught a bad cold while ministering in East Boston, and the snow and subfreezing temperatures only made matters worse. In spite of his seeming endless supply of energy, Bishop Brooks was exhausted from his episcopal duties. He had made nearly 200 parish visits his first year in office, and his strong body was weakening under the load. It is also likely that diphtheria had set in to complicate his other afflictions.

The funeral was held at Trinity Church on Thursday, January 26. The church was filled and more than 10,000 people gathered outside where a second service was held. His body was buried near his parents in the family plot in Mt. Auburn Cemetery.

---

8. Brooks, Phillips, *Addresses* (Philadelphia: Henry Altemus; 1895), p. 158.

The Ministry

Phillips Brooks was at the height of his ministry and the peak of his abilities when he delivered the Lyman Beecher Lectures in 1877. The lectures were patterned after his usual sermonic form, but they reveal much more of the *person* of the preacher than ever would be found in his pulpit discourses. From the beginning, he admitted that he was sharing the principles of ministry by which he "had only half consciously been living and working for many years." In short, the lectures are strongly autobiographical.

It seems strange that Charles Smyth, in *The Art of Preaching*, describes Brooks' lectures as "essentially personal documents, and in that sense amateurish rather than professional. . . ."[9] Having tried to teach homiletics on the seminary level myself, I can assure Dean Smyth that most ministerial students and young preachers would rather hear an experienced preacher "open his heart" and share what had really worked in his life, than to listen to lectures on the science of sermon preparation. *That* is what textbooks are for!

Of course, both the practical and theoretical are necessary for a balanced education; and Phillips Brooks knew this. But the three previous lecturers—especially Henry Ward Beecher—had pretty much covered the "professional" aspects of the ministry. It was time somebody took a more personal approach. In spite of their seeming informality, there is nothing "amateurish" about Phillips Brooks' lectures. They may be informal, but they are not unprofessional. They adequately answer the two questions his listeners were asking: "What do you believe about preaching?" and "Why do you believe it?"

What were the times like in 1877? There were about 46 million people in the United States and 38 States in the Union. People were still feeling the impact of "the panic of 1873" and wealth was king. It was the age of the great fortunes; the men who were most admired were Andrew Mellon, J.P. Morgan, Jay Gould, Cornelius Vanderbilt, and John Jacob Astor. Horatio Alger had started publishing his rags-to-riches novels in 1867 and every young American dreamed of getting rich quick.

---

9. Smyth, Charles, *The Art of Preaching* (London: SPCK, 1940), p. 6. Interestingly enough, Smyth classified the lectures of R. W. Dale and J. Paterson Smyth the same way. However, his somewhat biased evaluation has hurt neither the reputation of Phillips Brooks nor the popularity of Brooks' lectures.

"Manifest Destiny" was still in the air. The completion of the transcontinental telegraph in 1861 and the railroad in 1869 only made "Manifest Destiny" that much more assured. Women's rights, the Indians, public education, trade unions, and "Reconstruction" were the most burning social issues of the day; and the churches could not easily avoid them. Darwin's *Origin of the Species* was published in England in 1859, and the theory of evolution soon crossed the ocean and joined the other new scientific theories that were attracting the popular mind and challenging the Christian faith. "Higher criticism of the Bible" had reached New England and was unsettling the faith of some.

The age had its share of political troubles: the impeachment trial of President Andrew Johnson in 1868; the investigation of Secretary of War William Belknap, accused of accepting bribes in selling trading posts; the "Whiskey Ring Scandal" involving key revenue officials; and the doings of the "carpetbaggers," who were engaged in various corrupt practices in the South. Eighteen seventy-six was the year of Custer's famous "last stand." It was also the year the Socialist Labor Party was founded in New York City.

But back to Phillips Brooks and his approach to preaching.

According to Bishop William Lawrence,[10] Brooks began each week pondering what he would preach the next Lord's Day. He often spent part of each Monday in relaxing fellowship with friends, but his mind was always on his sermon. On Tuesday, he would select the topic and text and begin to write ideas in his notebook. His sermons were true to his definition of preaching: The truth of the Word of God focused through his own thought, experience, and personality.

By Wednesday, the theme and development of the sermon were finalized; and on Thursday and Friday, Brooks wrote the message out in its first draft. He would then "sleep on it" and on Saturday morning put the sermon in its final form. This meant writing it out by hand and then stitching the pages together into a small booklet he could carry in his Bible.

Having completed his sermon, he would spend Saturday afternoon roaming the streets of Boston, looking in the shop

---

10. Lawrence, William, *The Life of Phillips Brooks* (New York: Harper, 1930), pp. 102-104. This is a sympathetic yet candid portrait of Brooks that would be appreciated by the average reader. Pastors and students of preaching will prefer the definitive biography by Allen and the more interpretive biography by Albright.

windows, visiting a friend or two, playing with the children, and trying to avoid anything that would quench the message that was burning in his heart. He needed this contact with humanity, but he wanted it to be contact without contamination. The sermon came first.

When he preached, Brooks spoke rapidly, averaging about 200 words a minute. Archdeacon Farrar compared Brooks' preaching to "an express train sweeping all minor obstacles out of its path in its headlong rush."[11] Professor Bruce of Glasgow described it this way: "Most preachers take to the pulpit a bucket full or half full of the Word of God and pump it out to the congregation; but this man is a great watermain, attached to the everlasting reservoir of truth, and a stream of life pours through him by heavenly gravitation to refresh weary souls."[12]

Truth and *life* are key words in Brooks' sermons, along with *sympathy*, *light*, and *principle*. The incarnation of Jesus Christ was the controlling doctrine of his ministry, and he was emphatically Trinitarian. Brooks said, "I should count any Sunday's work unfitly done in which the Trinity was not the burden of our preaching."[13]

His fellow Anglicans considered him a "broad churchman," which meant that he was too liberal for some and not liberal enough for others. His nomination for the office of Bishop was strenuously opposed by many who felt he was not truly orthodox. Brooks held to evangelical doctrine and faithfully taught it in his church Bible classes and lectures; but in his Sunday sermons, he seemed to deliberately avoid typical evangelical vocabulary and clichés. We wish he had emphasized the cross and the resurrection more, because he certainly believed in them.

Brooks was a great admirer of the British Anglican preacher Frederick W. Robertson. When Robertson died in 1853 at the age of 37, he left to the church several volumes of choice sermons that are still read and appreciated. Like Robertson

---

11. Howard, Harry C., *Princes of the Christian Pulpit and Pastorate* (Nashville: Cokesbury Press, 1927), p. 250. Quoted in *Twenty Centuries of Great Preaching*, edited by Clyde E. Fant, Jr., and William M. Pinson, Jr., vol. 6, p. 121 (Waco, TX: Word, 1971).

12. Quoted in *The Audacity of Preaching*, by Gene E. Bartlett (New York: Harper, 1962), p. 23.

13. Lawrence, *The Life of Phillips Brooks*, note 5, p. 16.

(from whom he may have learned it), Phillips Brooks taught truth *suggestively* rather than *exhaustively*. He felt that the "indirect path" was the best approach to truth because this was the approach our Lord took in His teaching. Jesus did not argue with people; rather, He told them parables and used rich imagery to arouse their interest and instruct their minds.[14]

This explains why you do not find precise doctrinal definitions or theological explanations in the sermons of Phillips Brooks. He admitted to his friend Dr. George A. Gordon, "When I am interesting, I am vague; when I am definite, I am dull."[15] In a sermon on John 1:8, Brooks said, "I believe in these larger conceptions of life which men call vague. . . . Much that seems petty and paltry in our ordinary life can only be exalted and made tolerable by being taken up and lost in some great idea of life. . . ."[16]

The late Ralph Turnbull, an able student of preaching, described Brooks' approach as follows: "He simply took a text and found its theme, then developed it as the flow of thought moved on, not with argument but with a persuasive spirit. He was poetic, using images freely and speaking in pictorial language. His gift of imagination was strong."[17]

Another specialist in the history of preaching, F. R. Webber, wrote, "Phillips Brooks had too lively an imagination for a good theologian. He would not have made a church historian of the first quality, because of his fondness for allegory

---

14. F. W. Robertson said, "There are two ways of reaching truth: by reasoning it out and by feeling it out. All the profoundest truths are felt out. The deep glances into truth are got by love. Love a man, that is the best way of understanding him. Feel a truth, that is the only way of comprehending it. Not that you can put your sense of such truths into words in the shape of accurate maxims or doctrines, but the truth is reached, notwithstanding." Robertson, F. W., *Sermons: Second Series* (London: Kegan Paul, Trench, Trubner & Co., 1900), p. 204. One of the finest studies of Robertson's life and preaching is James R. Blackwood's *The Soul of Frederick W. Robertson, The Brighton Preacher* (New York: Harper and Brothers, 1947).

15. Jones, *The Royalty of the Pulpit*, p. 20.

16. Brooks, Phillips, *Sermons for the Church Year* (New York: E. P. Dutton, 1895), p. 52.

17. Turnbull, Ralph G., *A History of Preaching*, vol. 3 (Grand Rapids: Baker Book House, 1974), p. 113. Dr. Turnbull completed the History of Preaching series begun by Edwin C. Dargan, a set that ought to be in the library of every minister who is serious about his calling as a preacher. I heartily recommend the other books written by Dr. Turnbull, especially *A Minister's Obstacles* (New York: Fleming H. Revell, 1946; reprint, Baker Book House, 1972), and *A Minister's Opportunities* (Grand Rapids: Baker Book House, 1979).

and analogy."[18] And Lewis O. Brastow wrote, "He knew more theology than appeared in his preaching."[19]

But Brooks was not hesitant to declare what he believed. "The saint is he in whom God dwells," he stated in a sermon on Revelation 7:9-10. "But God comes to dwell in men, by His Holy Spirit, in the great work of the personal regeneration."[20] "This is the gospel of reconciliation," he said in a sermon on Galatians 4:6. "Father, Son, and Holy Spirit have met in their divine omnipotence to rescue man."[21]

However, Brooks was not always definite in his proclamation of what Jesus did on the cross. In a Good Friday sermon, he said, "Now what relation this death of Jesus may have borne to the nature and the plans of God, I hold it the most futile and irreverent of all investigations to inquire. I do not know, and I do not believe that any theology is so much wiser than my ignorance as to know, the sacred mysteries that passed in the courts of the Divine Existence when the miracle of Calvary was perfect."[22] At times, he seemed to hold to a "moral influence" theory of the atonement, but later he would boldly affirm a more orthodox position.

Turnbull[23] has suggested that Brooks deliberately avoided the traditional orthodox vocabulary and approach because of the nature of his times. It was no longer the day of Whitefield and Edwards; people were not responding to "the old-time religion." Unitarianism and Emerson's "transcendentalism" were still popular, and even that new religion, "Christian Science," was making headway in New England. By presenting Jesus as "the Ideal Man," Brooks hoped to attract his listeners' interest and then lead them to faith in Christ.

Perhaps accommodating his message to the times was the right approach for Brooks, and we must confess that he did influence many people. However, D. L. Moody was having a great ministry preaching "the old-time gospel" in the traditional way, and thousands were coming to Christ. We

18. Webber, F. R., *A History of Preaching in Britain and America* (Milwaukee: Northwestern Publishing House, 1957), vol. 3, p. 422. It is unfortunate that this valuable set is now out of print.

19. Brastow, *Representative Modern Preachers*, p. 219. Brastow felt that the deliberate "vagueness" of Brooks' preaching enabled him to be an "interpreter" rather than a "defender" of the great truths of the Christian faith.

20. Brooks, Phillips, *Sermons* (London: Richard Dickinson, 1879), p. 134.

21. Brooks, Phillips, *Sermons for the Church Year* (New York: E. P. Dutton, 1895), p. 104.

22. Brooks, ibid., p. 257.

23. Turnbull, *A History of Preaching*, vol. 3 , p. 115.

must be careful not to judge. "Now there are diversities of gifts, but the same Spirit" (1 Cor. 12:4).

Any evaluation of Brooks' preaching must take into consideration *the reason he preached.* He believed that the preacher's task was to transform lives by building character through truth. "To declare true ideas, to speak the truth to men, is the noblest work that any man can covet or try to do. To attempt to gain power over men which shall not be really the power of an idea is poor, ignoble work."[24] He did not equate ecclesiastical doctrinal formulations with "truth," and he did not feel it necessary to "defend the truth" as either an apologist or a crusader.

"The chief function of the minister," he wrote in one of his many notebooks, "is to translate speculative truth into personal character and to relate it clearly and practically to daily life."[25] When addressing the Phi Beta Kappa Society at Brown University, Providence, R. I., he asserted, "All scholarship must minister immediately to life."[26] He believed that truth, rightly presented, not only enlightened the mind but also stirred the heart and captured the will.

The preacher, then, must be "a man of the truth." In one of his lectures in *The Influence of Jesus,* Brooks said:

> A "man of the truth" is something more than a man who knows the truth, whose intellect has seized it. That, we are sure, would be the very tamest paraphrase of the suggestive words. It would take the whole life and depth out of them. A "man of the truth" is a man into whose life the truth has been pressed till he is full of it, till he has been given to it, and till it has been given to him. He remains the complete being whose unity is in that total of moral, intellectual, and spiritual life that creates what we call character.[27]

---

24. Brooks, Phillips, *Seeking Life and Other Sermons* (London: Macmillan and Co., 1904), p. 250.

25. Albright, *Focus on Infinity: A Life of Phillips Brooks,* p. 162.

26. Brooks, Phillips, *Essays and Addresses, Religious, Literary and Social,* edited by John Cotton Brooks (New York: E. P. Dutton, 1894), p. 250. It is in this volume that you find the "forgotten" lecture on preaching that we have included in this new edition. Phillips Brooks gave this lecture at Yale University on February 28, 1878, a year after his 1877 series. In fact, in this volume there are several essays and addresses that enlarge our understanding of this famous preacher's approach to truth and life.

27. Brooks, Phillips, *The Influence of Jesus* (London: H. R. Allenson, Ltd., n.d.), p. 218. These were "The Bolen Lectures," and Brooks delivered them in February, 1879 at his former charge, the Church of the Holy Trinity, Philadelphia. The series, founded by John Bolen, a wealthy Philadelphia philanthropist, followed the pattern set by the famous "Bampton Lectures" in England. Prepared especially for the students of the Philadelphia Divinity School, these four lectures are some of Brooks'

If we must put a label on Phillips Brooks, something he himself would have resisted doing to others, it would probably be that of a Christian humanist, with the emphasis on Christian. He believed that all men were children of God, but they did not know it. Our task is to tell them what they can be in Jesus Christ. All men were "naturally religious" and only needed the grace of God to help them get started and grow in the Christian life. In these beliefs, Brooks was certainly influenced by Horace Bushnell's *Christian Nurture*, published in 1847.

In 1877, Brooks preached for D. L. Moody at the great Boston Crusade and used Acts 26:19 as his text, "I was not disobedient unto the heavenly vision." In the sermon, he described four steps in the experience of conversion: seeing the vision, obeying it, having a sense of sin, and experiencing the assurance of forgiveness. Alexander V. G. Allen, Brooks' biographer, wrote: "He assumed throughout that religion was natural to man, because all men were by creation and by redemption the children of God. They had wandered, they had forgotten or neglected or were ignorant of their birthright; but when the vision came, it appealed to something in every man's constitution, rousing within him the dormant faculties of a divine relationship."[28]

In an address to the students of Johns Hopkins University, Brooks said, "These two facts—we are the children of God, and God is our Father—make us look very differently at ourselves, very differently at our neighbors, very differently at God."[29]

When you read his closing lecture on "The Value of the Human Soul," you discover that Brooks has the heart of an evangelist even though he might not have the mind of a systematic theologian. The controlling force behind all of his ministry was the salvation of sinners.

And his was a joyful ministry, a ministry that brought encouragement to others. The common people heard him gladly and went away determined to be better men and

---

finest work, although he considered the task "a fearful invasion of the legitimate and regular work of the ministry. . . ." (See Albright, *Focus on Infinity: A Life of Phillips Brooks* , p. 202).

28. Allen, Alexander V. G., *Phillips Brooks* (New York: E. P. Dutton, 1907), p. 326. We wonder what Mr. Moody thought of the sermon.

29. This quotation is found in the memorial address given by Bishop Henry C. Potter and included in volume 8 of *The World's Great Sermons*, compiled by Grenville Kleiser (New York: Funk and Wagnalls, 1909), p. 48.

women. Brooks truly meant it when he said to the ministerial students in his first lecture: "I cannot help bearing witness to the joy of the life which you anticipate. . . . Let us rejoice with one another that in a world where there are a great many good and happy things for men to do, God has given us the best and happiest, and made us preachers of His Truth."

1

THE TWO ELEMENTS IN PREACHING

Since I received, some months ago, the invitation to deliver these lectures which I begin today, I have been led to ponder much upon the principles by which I have only half consciously been living and working for many years. This is part of the debt which I owe to those who have honored me with their invitation. It is interesting to one's self to examine and recognize and arrange the ideas which have been slowly taking shape within him during the busy years of work. I shall be very glad if you too are interested, as I try to recount them to you, and very thankful if you find in them any help or inspiration.

The personal character of this lectureship is very evident. It is always to be filled by preachers in active work, who are to come and speak to you of preaching. It is not a homiletical professorship. It is each man's own life in the ministry of which he is to tell.

But certainly you do not expect from your successive lecturers a series of anecdotes of what has happened to them in their ministry, nor a mere recital of their ways of working. It cannot be intended that this lectureship should exalt the interviewer into an organized and permanent institution. The hope must rather be that as each preacher speaks of our common work in his own way, whatever there may be of value in his personal experience may come, not directly but indirectly, into what he says, and make the privilege of preaching shine for the moment in your eyes with the same kind of light which it has won in his.

I feel as I begin something of the fear which I have often felt in commencing a new sermon. It has often seemed to me as if the vast amount of preaching which people hear must have one bad effect in leaving on their minds a vague impression that this Christian life to which they are so continually urged must be a very difficult and complicated thing that it should take such a multitude of definitions to make it clear. And so there is some danger lest these multiplied lectures upon preaching should give to those who are preparing to preach an uncomfortable feeling that the work of preaching is a thing of many rules, hard to understand, and needing a great deal of commentary. For my part, I am startled when I think how few and simple are the things which I have to say to you. The principles which one can recognize in his ministry are very broad and plain. The applications of those principles are endless; but I should be very sorry indeed if anything that I shall say should lead any of you to confound the few plain principles with their many varied applications, and so make you think that work complicated and difficult which to him who is equipped for it, and loves it, is the easiest and simplest work in life.

Let me say one word more in introduction. He who is called upon to give these lectures cannot but remember that they are given every year, and that he has had very able and faithful predecessors. There are certainly, therefore, some things which he may venture to omit without being supposed to be either ignorant or careless of them. There are certain first principles, of primary importance, which he may take for granted in all that he says. They are so fundamental, that they must be always present, and their power must pervade every treatment of the work which is built upon them. But they need not be deliberately stated anew each year. It would make these courses of lectures very monotonous; and one may venture to assume that there are some elementary principles upon whose truth all students of theology are agreed, and whose importance they all feel.

I cannot begin, then, to speak to you who are preparing for the work of preaching, without congratulating you most earnestly upon the prospect that lies before you. I cannot help bearing witness to the joy of the life which you anticipate.

There is no career that can compare with it for a moment in the rich and satisfying relations into which it brings a man with his fellow man, in the deep and interesting insight which it gives him into human nature, and in the chance of the best culture for his own character. Its delight never grows old, its interest never wanes, its stimulus is never exhausted. It is different to a man at each period of his life; but if he is the minister he ought to be, there is no age, from the earliest years when he is his people's brother to the late days when he is like a father to the children on whom he looks down from the pulpit, in which the ministry has not some fresh charm and chance of usefulness to offer to the man whose heart is in it. Let us never think of it in any other way than this. Let us rejoice with one another that in a world where there are a great many good and happy things for men to do, God has given us the best and happiest, and made us preachers of His truth.

I propose in this introductory lecture to lay before you some thoughts which cover the whole field which we shall have to traverse; and the lectures which follow will be mainly applications and illustrations of the principles which I lay down today. It may make my first lecture seem a little too general, but perhaps it will help us to understand each other better as we go on.

A Definition of Preaching

What, then, is preaching of which we are to speak? It is not hard to find a definition. *Preaching is the communication of truth by man to men.* It has in it two essential elements, truth and personality. Neither of those can it spare and still be preaching. The truest truth, the most authoritative statement of God's will, communicated in any other way than through the personality of brother man to men is not preached truth. Suppose it written on the sky, suppose it embodied in a book which has been so long held in reverence as the direct utterance of God that the vivid personality of the men who wrote its pages has well nigh faded out of it; in neither of these cases is there any preaching. And on the other hand, if men speak to other men that which they do not claim for truth, if they use their powers of persuasion or of entertainment to make other men listen to their speculations, or do their will, or applaud their cleverness, that is not preaching either. The first lacks personality. The second lacks truth.

And preaching is the bringing of truth through personality. It must have both elements. It is in the different proportion in which the two are mingled that the difference between two great classes of sermons and preaching lies. It is in the defect of one or the other element that every sermon and preacher falls short of the perfect standard. It is in the absence of one or the other element that a discourse ceases to be a sermon, and a man ceases to be a preacher altogether.

If we go back to the beginning of the Christian ministry we can see how distinctly and deliberately Jesus chose this method of extending the knowledge of Himself throughout the world. Other methods no doubt were open to Him, but He deliberately selected this. He taught His truth to a few men and then He said, "Now go and tell that truth to other men."

Both elements were there, in John the Baptist who prepared the way for Him, in the seventy whom He sent out before His face, and in the little company who started from the chamber of the Pentecost to proclaim the new salvation to the world. If He gave them the power of working miracles, the miracles themselves were not the final purpose for which He gave it. The power of miracle was, as it were, a divine fire pervading the Apostle's being and opening his individuality on either side; making it more open God-wards by the sense of awful privilege, making it more open man-wards by the impressiveness and the helpfulness with which it was clothed. Everything that was peculiar in Christ's treatment of those men was merely part of the process by which the Master prepared their personality to be a fit medium for the communication of His Word. When His treatment of them was complete, they stood fused like glass, and able to take God's truth in perfectly on one side and send it out perfectly on the other side of their transparent natures.

This was the method by which Christ chose that His Gospel should be spread through the world. It was a method that might have been applied to the dissemination of any truth, but we can see why it was especially adapted to the truth of Christianity. For that truth is preeminently personal. However, the Gospel may be capable of statement in dogmatic form, its truest statement we know is not in dogma but in personal life. Christianity is Christ; and we can easily understand how a truth which is of such peculiar character that a person can stand forth and say of it, "I am the Truth," must always be best conveyed through, must indeed be almost incapable of being perfectly conveyed except through personality. And so some form of preaching must be essential to the prevalence and spread of the knowledge of Christ among men. There seems to be some such meaning as this in the words of Jesus when He said to His disciples, "As My Father has sent Me into the world, even so have I sent you into the world." It was the continuation, out to the minutest ramifications of the new system of influence, of that personal method which the Incarnation itself had involved.

Truth Through Personality

If this be true, then, it establishes the first of all principles concerning the ministry and preparation for the ministry. Truth through Personality is our description of real preaching. The truth must come really through the person, not merely over his lips, not merely into his understanding and out through his pen. It must come through his character, his affections, his whole intellectual and moral being. It must come genuinely through him. I think that, granting equal intelligence and study, here is the great difference which we feel between two preachers of the Word. The Gospel has come *over* one of them and reaches us tinged and flavored with his superficial characteristics, belittled with his littleness. The Gospel has come *through* the other, and we receive it impressed and winged with all the earnestness and strength that there is in him. In the first case, the man has been but a printing machine or a trumpet. In the other case, he has been a true man and a real messenger of God. We know how the views which theologians have taken of the agency of the Bible writers in their work differ just here. There have been those who would make them mere passive instruments. The thought of our own time has more and more tended to consider them the active messengers of the Word of God. This is the higher thought of inspiration. And this is the only true thought of the Christian preachership. I think that one of the most perplexing points in a man's ministry is in a certain variation of this power of transmission. Sometimes you are all open on both sides, open to God and to fellow man. At other times something clogs and clouds your transparency. You will know the differences of the sermons which you preach in those two conditions, and, however little they describe it to themselves or know its causes, your congregation will feel the difference as well.

But this, as I began to say, decrees for us in general what the preparation for the ministry is. It must be nothing less than the making of a man. It cannot be the mere training to certain tricks. It cannot be even the furnishing with abundant knowledge. It must be nothing less than the kneading and tempering of a man's whole nature till it becomes of such a consistency and quality as to be capable of transmission. This is the largeness of the preacher's culture. It is not for me, standing here or anywhere, to depreciate the work which our theological schools do. It certainly is not my place to undervalue the usefulness of lectures on preaching, or books on clerical manners. But none of these things make the preacher. You are surprised, when you read the biographies of the most successful ministers, to see how small a part of their culture came from their professional schools. It is a real part, but it is a small part. Everything that opens their lives towards God and towards man makes part of their education. The professional schools furnish them. The whole world is the school that makes them. This is the value of the biographies of the great preachers if we can only read them largely enough, if we can read them not in a small desire to copy their details of living, but in a large sympathetic wish to know what their life was, to see how the men became the men they were.

This is the value of Baxter's story of himself, so unsuspiciously confident of the reader's interest in everything that concerns him, or of Robertson's painful but precious history, or of the strong, manly, constantly advancing life of Norman Macleod. I think that either of these books might be the ruin of a young minister who read it for the methods of his work, as either of them might be the making of him if he read it for the spirit and the spiritual history of the man of whom it told the story. In a time which abounds in biographies as ours does, especially in the biographies of preachers, it is worth while, I am sure, to remember that another man's life may be the noblest inspiration or the heaviest burden, according as we take its spirit into our spirit, or only bind its methods like a fagot of dry sticks upon our back.

One other consequence of the fundamental character of preaching which I have stated must be the perpetual function of the pulpit.

Books of Sermons

Every now and then we hear some speculations about the prospects of preaching. Will men continue to preach and will other men continue to go and hear them? Books are multiplying enormously. Any man may feel reasonably sure on any Sunday morning that in a book which he can choose from his shelf he can read something more wisely thought and more perfectly expressed than he will hear from the pulpit if he goes to church.

Why should he go? One answer to the question certainly would be in the assertion that preaching is only one of the functions of the Christian church and that, even if preaching should grow obsolete, there would still remain reason enough why Christians should meet together for worship and for brotherhood. But even if we look at preaching only, it must still be true that nothing can ever take its place because of the personal element that is in it.

No multiplication of books can ever supersede the human voice. No newly opened channel of approach to man's mind and heart can ever do away with man's readiness to receive impressions through his fellow-man. There is no evidence, I think, in all the absorption in books which characterizes our much reading age, of any real decline of the interest in preaching.

Let a man be a true preacher, really uttering the truth through his own personality, and it is strange how men will gather to listen to him. We hear that the day of the pulpit is past, and then some morning the voice of a true preacher is heard in the land and all the streets are full of men crowding to hear him, just exactly as were the streets of Constantinople when Chrysostom was going to preach at the Church of the Apostles, or the streets of London when Latimer was bravely telling his truth at St. Paul's.

The same is true of reading sermons. I think, as I shall have occasion to say more fully in some other lecture, that a sermon that has the true sermon quality in it, when it is made, preserves that quality even under the constraints of manuscript or print. And books of sermons which really bring the truth through personality to men, were never bought and read more largely than they are today.

No, the truth about this matter of the competition of the printed book with the preached sermon, seems to be what is true of every competition. It has led to more discrimination.

There were things which people went to hear once but which they will not go to hear today. They can read better things of the same sort at home. But those things are not sermons. They never were sermons. The competition of print has interfered very much, is destined to interfere much more— we may hope will not cease to interfere until it has caused it to disappear—with the "pulpit droning of old saws" with the monotonous reiterations of commonplaces and abstractions; but the true sermon, the utterance of living truth by living men, was never more powerful than it is today. People never came to it with more earnestness, or carried away from it more good results.

No Excuses

I cannot help begging you, in the ministry which is before you, to beware of excusing your own failures by foolish talk about the obstinate aversion which the age has to the preaching of the Gospel. It is the meanest and shallowest kind of excuse. The age has no aversion to preaching as such. It may not listen to your preaching. If that proves to be the case, look for the fault first in your preaching, and not in the age.

I wonder at the eagerness and patience of congregations. I think that there are two things which we ministers have to guard against in this matter: one, the tendency of which I have just spoken, to blame the impatience which men feel with false pretences of preaching, for the lack of success which our preaching brings; the other, an exactly opposite tendency, to trust so confidently to the much tried patience of the people, that we shall do our work carelessly from feeling too secure about our power.

He who escapes both of these dangers, he who feels the magnitude and privilege of his work, he who both respects and trusts his people, neither assuming their indifference, so that he is paralysed, nor assuming their interest, so that he grows careless,—that man, I think, need envy no one of the preachers of the ages that are past the pulpit in which he stood, or the congregation to which he preached.

Suggestions About Truth and Personality

Let us look now for a few moments at these two elements of preaching—truth and personality; the one universal and invariable, the other special and always different. There are a few suggestions that I should like to make to you about each. And first with regard to the truth. It is strange how impossible it is to separate it and consider it wholly by itself. The personalness will cling to it. There are two aspects of the minister's work, which we are constantly meeting in the New Testament. They are really embodied in two words: one of which is "message," and the other is "witness." "This is the message which we have heard of Him and declare unto you," says St. John in his first Epistle. "We are His witnesses of these things," says St. Peter before the Council at Jerusalem. In these two works together, I think, we have the fundamental conception of the matter of all Christian preaching. It is to be a message given to us for transmission, but yet a message which we cannot transmit until it has entered into our own experience, and we can give our own testimony of its spiritual power. The minister who keeps the word "message" always written before him, as he prepares his sermon in his study, or utters it from his pulpit, is saved from the tendency to wanton and wild speculation, and from the mere passion of originality. He who never forgets that word "witness," is saved from the unreality of repeating by rote mere forms of statement which he has learned as orthodox, but never realized as true. If you and I can always carry this double consciousness, that we are messengers, and that we are witnesses, we shall have in our preaching all the authority and independence of assured truth, and yet all the appeal and convincingness of personal belief. It will not be we that speak, but the spirit of our Father that speaketh in us, and yet our sonship shall give the Father's voice its utterance and interpretation to His other children.

I think that nothing is more needed to correct the peculiar vices of preaching which belong to our time, than a new prevalence among preachers of this first conception of the truth which they have to tell as a message. I am sure that one great source of the weakness of the pulpit is the feeling among the people that these men who stand up before them every Sunday have been making up trains of thought, and thinking how they should "treat their subject," as the phrase runs. There is the first ground of the vicious habit that our congregations have of talking about the preacher more than they think about the truth. The minstrel who sings before you to show his skill, will be praised for his wit, and rhymes, and voice. But the courier who hurries in, breathless, to bring you a message, will be forgotten in the message that he brings.

Among the many sermons I have heard, I always remember one, for the wonderful way in which it was pervaded by this quality. It was a sermon by Mr. George Macdonald, the English author, who was in this country a few years ago; and it had many of the good and bad characteristics of his interesting style. It had his brave and manly honesty, and his tendency to sentimentality. But over and through it all it had this quality; it was a message from God to these people by him. The man struggled with language as a child struggles with his imperfectly mastered tongue, that will not tell the errand as he received it, and has it in his mind. As I listened, I seemed to see how weak in contrast was the way in which other preachers had amused me and challenged my admiration for the working of their minds. Here was a gospel. Here were real tidings. And you listened and forgot the preacher.

What It Means to Be a Messenger

Whatever else you count yourself in the ministry, never lose this fundamental idea of yourself as a messenger. As to the way in which one shall best keep that idea, it would not be hard to state; but it would involve the whole story of the Christian life. Here is the primary necessity that the Christian preacher should be a Christian first, that he should be deeply cognizant of God's authority, and of the absoluteness of Christ's truth. That was one of the first principles which I ventured to assume as I began my lecture.

The Quality of Breadth

But without entering so wide a field, let me say one thing about this conception of preaching as the telling of a message which constantly impresses me. I think that it would give to our preaching just the quality which it appears to me to most lack now. That quality is breadth. I do not mean liberality of thought, nor tolerance of opinion, nor anything of that kind. I mean largeness of movement, the great utterance of great truths, the great enforcement of great duties, as distinct from the minute, and subtle, and ingenious treatment of little topics, side issues of the soul's life, bits of anatomy, the bric-a-brac of theology.

Take up, some Saturday, the list of subjects on which the ministers of a great city are to preach the next day. See how many of them seem to have searched in strange corners of the Bible for their topics, how small and fantastic is the bit of truth which their hearers are to have set before them. Then turn to Barrow, or Tillotson, or Bushnell—"Of being imitators of Christ;" "That God is the only happiness of man;" "Every man's life a plan of God."   There is a painting of ivory miniatures, and there is a painting of great frescoes. One kind of art is suited to one kind of subject, and another to another.

I suppose that all preachers pass through some fantastic period when a strange text fascinates them; when they like to find what can be said for an hour on some little topic on which most men could only talk two minutes; when they are eager for subtlety more than force, and for originality more than truth. But as a preacher grows more full of the conception of the sermon as a message, he gets clear of those brambles. He comes out on to open ground. His work grows freer, and bolder, and broader. He loves the simplest texts, and the great truths which run like rivers through all life. God's sovereignty, Christ's redemption, man's hope in the Spirit, the privilege of duty, the love of man in the Savior, make the strong music which his soul tries to catch.

The Quality of Historicity

And then another result of this conception of preaching as the telling of a message is that it puts us into right relations with all historic Christianity. The message never can be told as if we were the first to tell it. It is the same message which the church has told in all the ages. He who tells it today is backed by all the multitude who have told it in the past. He is companied by all those who are telling it now. The message is his witness; but a part of the assurance with which he has received it, comes from the fact of its being the identical message which has come down from the beginning.

Men find on both sides how difficult it is to preserve the true poise and proportion between the corporate and the individual conceptions of the Christian life. But all will own today the need of both. The identity of the church in all times consists in the identity of the message which she has always had to carry from her Lord to men. All outward utterances of the perpetual identity of the church are valuable only as they assert this real identity. There is the real meaning of the perpetuation of old ceremonies, the use of ancient liturgies, and the clinging to what seem to be apostolic types of government.

The heretic in all times has been not the errorist as such, but the self-willed man, whether his judgments were right or wrong. "A man may be a heretic in the truth," says Milton. He is the man who, taking his ideas not as a message from God, but as his own discoveries, has cut himself off from the message-bearing church of all the ages. I am sure that the more fully you come to count your preaching the telling of a message, the more valuable and real the church will become to you, the more true will seem to you your brotherhood with all messengers of that same message in all strange dresses and in all strange tongues.

Two Tendencies of Teaching Truth

I should like to mention, with reference to the truth which the preacher has to preach, two tendencies which I am sure that you will recognize as very characteristic of our time. One is the tendency of criticism, and the other is the tendency of mechanism. Both tendencies are bad. By the tendency of criticism I mean the disposition that prevails everywhere to deal with things from outside, discussing their relations, examining their nature, and not putting ourselves into their power.

Criticism

Preaching in every age follows, to a certain extent, the changes which come to all literature and life. The age in which we live is strangely fond of criticism. It takes all things apart for the mere pleasure of examining their nature. It studies forces, not in order to obey them, but in order to understand them. It talks about things for the pure pleasure of discussion. Much of the poetry and prose about nature and her wonders, much of the investigation of the country's genius and institutions, much of the subtle analysis of human nature is of this sort. It is all good; but it is something distinct from the cordial sympathy by which one becomes a willing servant of any of these powers, a real lover of nature, or a faithful citizen, or a true friend.

Now it would be strange if this critical tendency did not take possession of the preaching of the day. And it does. The disposition to watch ideas in their working, and to talk about their relations and their influence on one another, simply as problems, in which the mind may find pleasure without any real entrance of the soul into the ideas themselves, this, which is the critical tendency, invades the pulpit, and the result is an immense amount of preaching which must be called preaching about Christ as distinct from preaching Christ. There are many preachers who seem to do nothing else, always discussing Christianity as a problem instead of announcing Christianity as a message, and proclaiming Christ as a Savior.

I do not undervalue their discussions. But I think we ought always to feel that such discussions are not the type or ideal of preaching. They may be necessities of the time, but they are not the work which the great Apostolic preachers did, or which the true preacher will always most desire. Definers and defenders of the faith are always needed, but it is bad for a church when its ministers count it their true work to define and defend the faith rather than to preach the Gospel.

Beware of the tendency to preach about Christianity, and try to preach Christ. To discuss the relations of Christianity and science, Christianity and society, Christianity and politics, is good. To set Christ forth to men so that they shall know Him, and in gratitude and love become His, that is far better. It is good to be a Herschel who describes the sun; but it is better to be a Prometheus who brings the sun's fire to the earth.

Mechanism

I called the other tendency the tendency of mechanism. It is the disposition of the preacher to forget that the Gospel of Christ is primarily addressed to individuals and that its ultimate purpose is the salvation of multitudes of men. Between the time when it first speaks to a man's soul, and the time when that man's soul is gathered into heaven, with the whole host of the redeemed, the Gospel uses a great many machineries which are more or less impersonal.

The church, with all its instrumentalities, comes in. The preacher works by them. But if the preacher ever for a moment counts them the purpose of his working, if he takes his eye off the single soul as the prize he is to win, he falls from his highest function and loses his best power. All successful preaching, I more and more believe, talks to individuals. The church is for the soul.

I am not thinking of the fault or danger of any one body of Christians alone when I say this, not of my own or any other. The tendency to work for the means instead of for the end is everywhere. And, my friends, learn this at the beginning of your ministry, that just as surely as you think that any kind of fault or danger belongs wholly to another system than your own, and that you are not exposed to it, just so surely you will reproduce that fault or danger in some form in your own life. This surely is a good rule: whenever you see a fault in any other man, or any other church, look for it in yourself and in your own church.

Where is the church which is not liable to value its machineries above its purposes, whose ministers are not tempted to preach for the denomination and its precious peculiarities, instead of for men and for their precious souls? Let your preaching be to individuals, and to the church always as living for and made up of individuals.

Personality: Some Fundamentals

Of the second element in preaching, namely, the preacher's personality, there will be a great deal to say, especially in the next lecture. But there are two or three fundamental things which I wish to say today.

Preserve Individuality

The first is this, that the principle of personality once admitted involves the individuality of every preacher. The same considerations which make it good that the Gospel should not be written on the sky, or committed merely to an almost impersonal book, make it also most desirable that every preacher should utter the truth in his own way, and according to his own nature. It must come not only through man but through men. If you monotonize men you lose their human power to a large degree. If you could make all men think alike it would be very much as if no man thought at all, as when the whole earth moves together with all that is upon it, everything seems still.

Now the deep sense of the solemnity of the minister's work has often a tendency to repress the free individuality of the preacher and his tolerance of other preachers' individualities. His own way of doing his work is with him a matter of conscience, not of taste, and the conscience when it is thoroughly awake is more intolerant than the taste is. Or, working just the other way, his conscience tells him that it is not for him to let his personal peculiarities intrude in such a solemn work, and so he tries to bind himself to the ways of working which the most successful preachers of the Word have followed. I have seen both these kinds of ministers: those whose consciences made them obstinate, and those whose consciences made them pliable, those whose consciences hardened them to steel or softened them to wax.

However, it comes about, there is an unmistakable tendency to the repression of the individuality of the preacher. It is seen in little things: in the uniform which preachers wear and the disposition to a uniformity of language. It is seen in great things: in the disposition which all ages have witnessed to draw a line of orthodoxy inside the lines of truth. Wisely and soberly let us set ourselves against this influence. The God who sent men to preach the Gospel of His Son in their humanity, sent each man distinctively to preach it in his humanity.

Be yourself by all means, but let that good result come not by cultivating merely superficial peculiarities and oddities. Let it be by winning a true self full of your own faith and your own love. The deep originality is noble, but the surface originality is miserable. It is so easy to be a John the Baptist, as far as the desert and camel's hair and locusts and wild honey go. But the devoted heart to speak from, and the fiery words to speak, are other things.

Again, we never can forget in thinking of the preacher's personality that he is one who lives in constant familiarity with thoughts and words which to other men are occasional and rare, and which preserve their sacredness mainly by their rarity. That fact must always come in when we try to estimate the influences of a preacher's life. What will the power of that fact be? I am sure that often it weakens the minister.

I am sure that many men who, if they came to preach once in a great while in the midst of other occupations, would preach with reality and fire, are deadened to their sacred work by their constant intercourse with sacred things. Their constant dealing with the truth makes them less powerful to bear the truth to others, as a pipe through which the water always flows collects its sediment, and is less fit to let more water through.

And besides this, it ministers to self-deception and to an exaggeration or distortion of our own history. The man who constantly talks of certain experiences, and urges other men to enter into them, must come in time, by very force of describing those experiences to think that he has undergone them. You beg men to repent, and you grow so familiar with the whole theory of repentance that it is hard for you to know that you yourself have not repented. You exhort to patience till you have no eyes or ears for your own impatience.

It is the way in which the man who starts the trains at the railroad station must come in time to feel as if he himself had been to all the towns along the road whose names he has always been shouting in the passenger's ears, and to which he has for years sold them their tickets, when perhaps he has not left his own little way-station all the time.

I know that all this is so, and yet certainly the fault is in the man, not in the truth. The remedy certainly is not to make the truth less familiar. There is a truer relation to preaching, in which the constancy of it shall help instead of harming the reality and earnestness with which you do it. The more that you urge other people to holiness the more intense may be the hungering and thirsting after holiness, in your own heart. Familiarity does not breed contempt except of contemptible things or in contemptible people. The adage, that no man is a hero to his *valet de chambre* is sufficiently answered by saying that it is only to a *valet de chambre* that a truly great man is unheroic. You must get the impulse, the delight, and the growing sacredness of your life out of your familiar work. You are lost as a preacher if its familiarity deadens and encrusts, instead of vitalizing and opening your powers. And it will all depend upon whether you do your work for your Master and His people or for yourself. The last kind of labor slowly kills, the first gives life more and more.

Preparing the Personality

The real preparation of the preacher's personality for its transmissive work comes by the opening of his life on both sides, towards the truth of God and towards the needs of man. To apprehend in all their intensity the wants and woes of men, to see the problems and dangers of this life, then to know all through us that nothing but Christ and His Redemption can thoroughly satisfy these wants, that is what makes a man a preacher.

Alas for him who is only open on the man-ward side, who only knows how miserable and wicked man is, but has no power of God to bring to him! He lays a kind but helpless hand upon the wound. He tries to relieve it with his sympathy and his philosophy. He is the source of all he says. There is no God behind him. He is no preacher. The preacher's instinct is that which feels instantly how Christ and human need belong together, neither thinks Christ too far off for the need, nor the need too insignificant for Christ.

Never be afraid to bring the transcendent mysteries of our faith, Christ's life and death and resurrection, to the help of the humblest and commonest of human wants. There is a sort of preaching which keeps them for the great emergencies, and soothes the common sorrows and rebukes the common sins with lower considerations of economy. Such preaching fails. It neither appeals to the lower nor to the higher perceptions of mankind. It is useful neither as a law nor as a gospel. It is like a river that is frozen too hard to be navigable but not hard enough to bear. Never fear, as you preach, to bring the sublimest motive to the smallest duty, and the most infinite comfort to the smallest trouble. They will prove that they belong there if only the duty and trouble are real and you have read them thoroughly aright.

Retaining Both Truth and Personality

These are the elements of preaching, then—truth and personality. The truth is in itself a fixed and stable element; the personality is a varying and growing element. In the union of the two we have the provision for the combination of identity with variety, of stability with growth, in the preaching of the Gospel.

The truth which you are preaching is the same which your brother is preaching in the next pulpit, or in some missionary station on the other side of the globe. If it were not, you would get no strength from one another. You would not stand back to back against the enemy, sustaining one another, as you do now. But the way in which you preach the truth is different, and each of you reaches some ears that would be deaf to the most persuasive tones of the other. The Gospel you are preaching now is the same Gospel that you preached when you were first ordained, in that first sermon which it was at once such a terror and such a joy to preach, but if you have been a live man all the time, you are not preaching it now as you did then. If the truth had changed, your life would have lost its unity. The truth has not changed, but you have grown to fuller understanding of it, to a larger capacity of receiving and transmitting it. There is no pleasure in the minister's life stronger than this,—the perception of identity and progress in his preaching of the truth as he grows older. It is like a man's pleasure in watching the growth of his own body or his own mind, or of a tree which he has planted. Always the same it is, yet always larger.

It is a common experience of ministers, I suppose, to find that sentences in their old sermons which were written years ago contain meanings and views of truth which they hold now but which they never had thought of in those early days. The truth was there, but the man had not appropriated it. The truth has not changed, but the man is more sufficient for it.

Here is the power by which the truth becomes related to each special age. It is brought to it through the men of the age. If a preacher is not a man of his age, in sympathy with its spirit, his preaching fails. He wonders that the truth has failed. It is the other element, the person. That is the reason why sometimes the old preacher finds his well-known power gone, and he complains that while he is still in his vigor people are looking to younger men for the work which they once delighted to demand of him. There are noble examples on the other side: old men with a personality as vitally sympathetic with the changing age as the truth which they preach is true to the Word of God. They have a power which no young man can begin to wield, and the world owns it willingly. People would rather see old men than young men in their pulpits, if only the old men bring them both elements of preaching, a faith that is eternally true, and a person that is in quick and ready sympathy with their present life. If they can have but one, they are apt to choose the latter; but what they really want is both, and the noblest ministries in the church are those of old men who have kept the freshness of their youth.

It is in the poise and proportion of these two elements of preaching that we secure the true relation between independence and adaptation in the preacher's character. The desire to meet the needs of the people to whom we preach may easily become servility. Many a man has lost his manliness and won people's contempt in a truly earnest desire to win their hearts for his great message. Here is where the stable and unchanging element of our work comes in.

There is something that you owe to the truth and to yourself as its preacher. There is a line beyond which adaptation becomes feebleness. There are some things which St. Paul will not become to any man. Nothing but this sense of the unchanging demands of the truth which we are sent to preach can keep us from giving our people what they want, instead of what they need.

Keep a clear sense of what your truth requires of you. Count it unworthy of yourself as a minister of the Gospel to comfort any sorrow with less than the Gospel's whole comfortableness, or to bid any soul be perfectly happy in anything less than the highest spiritual joy. The saddest moments in every preacher's life, I think, are those in which he goes away from his pulpit conscious that he has given the people, not the highest that he knew how to give, but only the highest that they know how to ask. He has satisfied them, and he is thoroughly discontented with himself. When a friend of Alexander the Great had asked of him ten talents, he tendered to him fifty, and when reply was made that ten were sufficient, "True," said he, "ten are sufficient for you to take, but not for me to give."

If it is the decay of the personal element that weakens the ministry of some old men, I think it is the slighting of the element of absolute truth that degrades the work of preaching in many young men's eyes, and keeps such numbers of them, who ought to be there, from its sacred duties. The prevalence of doubt about all truth, and to some extent also the general eagerness of preachers to find out and meet the people's desires and demands—these two causes together have created the impression that the ministry had no certain purposes or definite message, that the preacher was a promiscuous caterer for men's whims, wishing them well, and inspired by a certain general benevolence, but in no sense a prophet uttering positive truth to them which they did not know before, uttering it whether they liked it or hated it.

Is not that the impression which many young men have of the ministry? Is it not natural that with that impression they should seek some other way to help their fellow men? And is there not very much indeed in the way in which preachers do their work to give such an impression? Everywhere, for the strengthening of the weak preacher, the enlivening of the dull preacher, the sobering of the flippant preacher, the freshening of the old preacher, the maturing of the young preacher, what we need is the just poise and proportion of these two elements of the preacher's work, the truth he has to tell and the personality through which he has to tell it.

Discovering a Purpose

The purpose of preaching must always be the first condition that decrees its character. The final cause is that which really shapes everything's life. And what is preaching for? The answer comes without hesitation. It is for men's salvation. But the idea of what salvation is has never been entirely uniform or certain, and all through the history of preaching we can see that the character of preaching varied continually, rose or fell, enlarged or narrowed, with the constant variation of men's ideas as to what it was to be saved.

If salvation was something here and now, preaching became a direct appeal to man's present life.

If salvation was something future and far away, preaching died into remote whispers and only made itself graphic and forcible by the vivid pictures of torture addressed to the senses whose pain men most easily understand.

If to be saved was to be saved from sin, preaching became spiritual.

If to be saved was to be saved from punishment, preaching became forensic and economical.

If salvation was the elevation of society, preaching became a lecture upon social science.

The first thing for you to do is to see clearly what you are going to preach for, what you mean to try to save men from. By your conviction about that, the whole quality of your ministry will be decided. To the absence of any clear answer to that question, to the entire vagueness as to what men's danger is, we owe the vagueness as to what men's danger is, we owe the vagueness with which so many of our preachers preach.

The Best Is Yet to Come

The world has not heard its best preaching yet. If there is more of God's truth for men to know, and if it is possible for the men who utter it to become more pure and godly, then, with both of its elements more complete than they have ever been before, preaching must some day be a completer power. But that better preaching will not come by any sudden leap of inspiration. As the preaching of the present came from the preaching of the past, so the preaching that is to be will come from the preaching that is now. If we preach as honestly, as intelligently, and as spiritually as we can, we shall not merely do good in our own day, but help in some real though unrecorded way the future triumphs of the work we love.

2

THE PREACHER HIMSELF

My last lecture indicated very clearly the importance which I think belongs to the preacher's person in the work to which he is ordained. In my second and third lectures I want to dwell upon this subject and consider distinctively the preacher. After that we will look at the sermon.

And in considering the preacher, we may think of him first in himself and then in relation to his work. It is not a distinction that can be accurately and constantly maintained. The two views run together. But it will help me in making an arrangement of what I have to say; and if we do not insist on it too strongly, it will aid our thoughts. Today I take the first of these two topics, and shall speak of the preacher's personal character, the preacher in himself.

Who Can Be a Minister?

Let us ask, then, first, What sort of man may be a minister? It would be good for the church if it were a more common question. Partly because the motives which lead a young man to the ministry are so personal and spiritual, partly because of our sense of the magnitude and privilege of the work, which makes us fear to be the means of excluding any worthy man from it, partly it is because, at present, while the harvest is so plenteous the laborers are so very few—for these and other reasons. There is far too little discrimination in the selection of men who are to preach, and many men find their way into the preacher's office who discover only too late that it is not their place.

When our Lord selected those to whom He was to commit His gospel, we are impressed with the deliberation and solemnity of the act: "And it came to pass in those days that He went out into a mountain to pray, and continued all night in prayer to God. And when it was day, He called unto Him His disciples, and of them He chose twelve, whom also He named apostles" (Luke 6:12-13).

There has certainly grown up in the church a strong misgiving as to the whole policy of charitable people and benevolent societies who, with their lavish offers of help, gather into the ministry, along with many noble, faithful men, a multitude who, amiable and pious as they may be, are of the kind who make no place in life for themselves, but wait till some one kindly makes one for them and drops them into it. I am convinced that the ministry can never have its true dignity or power till it is cut aloof from this sort of mendicancy—till young men whose hearts are set on preaching make their way to the pulpit by the same energy and through the same difficulties which meet countless young men on their way to business and the bar. We believe the influence which brings men to the pulpit to be a far holier one. It ought, then, to be a far stronger one; and yet we trust less to its power than we do to the power of ambition and self-interest. It is a part of the whole unmanly way of treating ministers, of which there will be more to say.

The Qualities of a Preacher

It is not easy to describe, with our large views of personal liberty and personal rights, what methods of inspection and authentication it may be well to use on the admission of preachers to their sacred work, but what we most of all need is a clearer understanding and a fuller statement of what are the true conditions of a minister's success, and so what qualities we have a right to ask of ourselves and of one another before we can feel that the true call to the ministry has been established.

We must not draw the line too narrowly. There is nothing more striking about the ministry than the way in which very opposite men do equally effective work. You look at some great preacher, and you say, "There is the type. He who is like that can preach," and just as your snug conclusion is all made, some other voice rings out from a neighboring pulpit, and the same power of God reaches the hearts of men in a totally new way, and your neat conclusion cracks and breaks. Spurgeon preaches at his Surrey Tabernacle, and Liddon preaches at St. Paul's, and both are great preachers, and yet no two men could be more entirely unlike. It must be so. If the preacher is after all only the representative man, the representative Christian doing in special ways and with a special ordination that which all men ought to be doing for Christ and fellowman, then there ought to be as many kinds of preachers as there are kinds of Christians; and there are as many kinds of Christians as there are kinds of men.

It is evident, then, that only in the largest way can the necessary qualities of the preacher be enumerated. With this provision such an enumeration may be attempted.

Quality 1: *Personal Piety*

I must not dwell upon the first of all the necessary qualities, and yet there is not a moment's doubt that it does stand first of all. It is personal piety, a deep possession in one's own soul of the faith and hope and resolution which he is to offer to his fellowmen for their new life. Nothing but fire kindles fire. To know in one's whole nature what it is to live by Christ; to be His, not our own; to be so occupied with gratitude for what He did for us and for what He continually is to us that His will and His glory shall be the sole desires of our life, I wish that I could put in some words of new and overwhelming force the old accepted certainty that that is the first necessity of the preacher, that to preach without that is weary and unsatisfying and unprofitable work, to preach with that is a perpetual privilege and joy.

Quality 2: *Unselfishness*

And next to this I mention what we may call mental and spiritual unselfishness. I do not speak so much of a moral as of an intellectual quality. I mean that kind of mind which always conceives of truth with reference to its communication and receives any spiritual blessing as a trust for others. Both of these are capable of being cultivated, but I hold that there is a natural difference between men in this respect. Some men by nature receive truth abstractly. They follow it into its developments. They fathom its depths. But they never think of sending it abroad. They are so enwrapt in seeing what it is that they never care to test what it can do. Other men necessarily think in relation to other men, and their first impulse with every new truth is to give it its full range of power. Their love for truth is always complemented by a love for man. They are two clearly different temperaments. One of them does not and the other does make the preacher.

Quality 3: Hopefulness

Again, hopefulness is a necessary quality of the true preacher's nature. You know how out of every complicated condition of affairs one man naturally appropriates all the elements of hope, while another invariably gathers up all that tends to despair. The latter kind of man may have his uses. There are tasks and times for which no prophet but Cassandra is appropriate. There were duties laid on some of the old Hebrew prophets which perhaps they might have done with hearts wholly destitute of any ray of light. But such a temper is entirely out of keeping with the Christian Gospel. The preacher may sometimes denounce, rebuke, and terrify. When he does that, he is not distinctively the preacher of Christianity. If his nature is such that he must dread and fear continually, he was not made to preach the Gospel.

Quality 4: Good Health

If I go on and mention a certain physical condition as essential to the preacher, I do so on very serious grounds. I am impressed with what seems to me the frivolous and insufficient way in which the health of the preacher is often treated. It is not simply that the sick minister is always hampered and restrained. It is not merely that the truth he has within him finds imperfect utterance. It is that the preacher's work is the most largely human of all occupations. It brings a man into more multiplied relations with his fellow-man than any other work.

It is not the doing of certain specified duties. You will be sadly mistaken if you think it is, and try to set down in your contract with your parish just what you are to do, and where your duties are to stop. It is the man offered as a medium through whom God's influence may reach his fellow-man. Such an offering involves the whole man, and the whole man is body and soul together. Therefore the ideal preacher brings the perfectly healthy body with the perfectly sound soul.

Remember that the care for your health, the avoidance of nervous waste, the training of your voice, and everything else that you do for your body is not merely an economy of your organs that they may be fit for certain works; it is part of that total self-consecration which cannot be divided, and which all together makes you the medium through which God may reach His children's lives. I cannot but think that so high a view of the consecration of the body would convict many of the reputable sins against health in which ministers are apt to live, and do the fundamental good which the tinkering of the body by specifics for special occasions so completely fails to do.

Quality 5: An Intangible

I speak of only one thing more. I do not know how to give it a name, but I do think that in every man who preaches there should be something of that quality which we recognize in a high degree in some man of whom we say, when we see him in the pulpit, that he is a "born preacher." Call it enthusiasm; call it eloquence; call it magnetism; call it the gift for preaching. It is the quality that kindles at the sight of men, that feels a keen joy at the meeting of truth and the human mind, and recognizes how God made them for each other. It is the power by which a man loses himself and becomes but the sympathetic atmosphere between the truth on one side of him and the man on the other side of him. It is the inspiration, the posession—what I have heard called the "demon" of preaching. Something of this quality there must be in every man who really preaches. He who wholly lacks it cannot be a preacher.

All of these qualities which I have thus enumerated exist in degrees. All of them are capable of culture if they exist at all. All of them are difficult to test except by the actual work of preaching. I grant, therefore, fully, that it is difficult to draw out of them a set of tests which the secretary of an education society can apply to candidates—as a recruiting sergeant measures volunteers around the chest—and mark them as fit or unfit for the ministry. But from their enumeration I think still that there does rise up before us a clear picture of the man who ought to be a preacher. Full of the love of Christ, taking all truth and blessing as a trust, in the best sense *didactic*, hopeful, healthy, and counting health, as far as it is in his power, a part of his self-consecration;

willing, not simply as so many men are, to bear sickness for God's work, but willing to preserve health for God's work; and going to his preaching with the enthusiasm that shows it is what God made him for. The nearer you can come to him, my friends, the better preachers you will be, the surer you may be that you have a right to be preachers at all.

And the next question will be, When you have the right kind of man to make a preacher of, what are the changes you will want him to undergo that he may become a preacher? The formal ordination which he will meet by and by will be nothing, of course, unless it signifies some real experiences which have filled these years since his soul heard what it recognized as God's call to the ministry. We may set him apart from other men with what solemn ceremonies we may please, but he will be just like other men still, unless the power of the work to which he looks forward has entered into him during his careful preparation and made him different.

What does this difference consist in? What is the true preparation? First, and most evident, there are his special studies which have been filling him with their spirit. Most men begin really to study when they enter on the preparation for their professions. Men whose college life, with its general culture, has been very idle, begin to work when at the door of the professional school the work of their life comes into sight before them. It is the way in which a bird who has been wheeling vaguely hither and thither sees at last its home in the distance and flies towards it like an arrow. But shall I say to you how often I have thought that the very transcendent motives of the young minister's study have a certain tendency to bewilder him and make his study less faithful than that of men seeking other professions from lower motives? The highest motive often dazzles before it illuminates. It is one of the ways in which the light within us becomes darkness.

I never shall forget my first experience of a divinity school. I had come from a college where men studied hard but said nothing about faith. I had never been at a prayer meeting in my life. The first place I was taken to at the seminary was the prayer meeting; and never shall I lose the impression of the devoutness with which those men prayed and exhorted one another. Their whole souls seemed exalted and their natures were on fire. I sat bewildered and ashamed, and went away depressed.

On the next day I met some of those same men at a Greek recitation. It would be little to say of some of the devoutest of them that they had not learned their lessons. Their whole way showed that they never learned their lessons; that they had not got hold of the first principles of hard, faithful, conscientious study. The boiler had no connection with the engine. The devotion did not touch the work which then and there was the work and the only work for them to do. By and by I found something of where the steam did escape to. A sort of amateur, premature preaching was much in vogue among us. We were in haste to be at what we called "our work." A feeble twilight of the coming ministry we lived in. The people in the neighborhood dubbed us "parsonnettes."

Oh, my fellow students, the special study of theology and all that appertains to it, that is what the preacher must be doing always; but he never can do it afterwards as he can in the blessed days of quiet in Arabia, after Christ has called him, and before the apostles lay their hands upon him. In many respects an ignorant clergy, however pious he may be, is worse than none at all. The more the empty head glows and burns, the more hollow and thin and dry it grows. "The knowledge of the priest," said St. Francis de Sales, "is the eighth sacrament of the church."

Applying the Truth

But again, the minister's preparation of character for his work involves something more intimate than the accumulation of knowledge. The knowledge which comes into him meets in him the intention of preaching, and, touched by that, undergoes a transformation. It is changed into doctrine. Doctrine means this: truth considered with reference to its being taught. The reason why many men dislike the word "doctrine" is from their dislike of the whole notion of docility which is attached to it. Just as a citizen who is preparing himself for public office considers the law and character of the State not abstractly, but with reference to their application to the people whom he aspires to govern; just as the student in a normal school learns everything with an under consciousness that he is going to teach that same thing some day, influencing all the methods of his learning; so the student preparing to be a preacher cannot learn truth as the mere student of theology for its own sake might do. He always feels it reaching out through him to the people to whom he is some day to carry it.

He cannot get rid of this consciousness. It influences all his understanding. We can see that it must have its dangers. It will threaten the impartiality with which he will seek truth. It will tempt him to prefer those forms of truth which most easily lend themselves to didactic uses, rather than those which bring evidence of being most simply and purely true. That is the danger of all preachers. Against that danger the men meaning to be a preacher must be on his guard, but he cannot avoid the danger by sacrificing the habit out of which the danger springs.

He must receive truth as one who is to teach it. He cannot, he must not study as if the truth he sought were purely for his own culture or enrichment. And the result of such a habit, followed with due guard against its dangerous tendencies, will be threefold. It will bring, first, a deeper and more solemn sense of responsibility in the search of truth; second, a desire to find the human side of every truth, the point at which every speculation touches humanity; and third, a breadth which comes from the constant presence in the mind of the fact that truth has various aspects and presents itself in many ways to different people, according to their needs and characters.

Seeing the Divine Side of Life

Along with this preparation for preaching goes another. I said the man who studied with the intention of teaching learned to see and seize the human side of all divinity. It is true, also, that he learns to seize the divine side of all humanity. The sources from which his preaching is to be fed open on every side of him.

I can remember how, as I looked forward to preaching, every book I read and every man I talked with seemed to teem with sermons. They all suggested something which it seemed as if the preacher of the Gospel ought to say to men. I have not found the sermons in them all as I went on; not, I believe, because I was mistaken in thinking they were there, but because I have grown less eager or keen in finding them.

I think there is no point in which ministers differ from one another, and in which we all differ from ourselves, more than in this—this open mindedness and power of appropriating out of everything the elements of true instruction. I find two classes of ministers of different habits in this respect. One of them abjures everything outside the narrowest lines of technically religious reading; he has no knowledge of literature or art or science. The other minister cultivates them all, but his life in them is wholly outside of his life as a preacher. He changes his nature when he turns away from his sermon and takes a volume from his shelves. And his shelves themselves are divided. His secular and his religious books are ranged on opposite sides of his study.

There is something better than either—a true devotion to our work which will not let us leave it for a moment when we are once ordained; preachers once and preachers always; but a conception of our work so large that everything which a true man has any right to do or know may have some help to render it. And this is what you ought to be laying the foundation of in these preparatory days.

The Importance of Preparation

You will see that I place very great value on this preparation, in which a man who is devout and earnest comes to that fitness for his work which St. Paul describes in a word that he uses twice to Timothy, "apt to teach"—διδακτικός— the didactic man. It is not something to which one comes by accident or by any sudden burst of fiery zeal. No doubt there is a power in the untutored utterance of the new convert that the ripe utterances of the educated preacher often lack; but it is not so much a praise to the new convert that he has that power as it is a shame to the educated preacher that he does not have it all the more richly in proportion to his education.

And whatever else he has, the man who has leaped directly from his own experience into the pulpit will almost certainly be wanting in that breadth of sympathy and understanding which comes in the studies of the waiting years. He will know that other men are not made just like himself, but he will realize only himself, and preach to them as if they were. He will be like the man whom Archbishop Whately tells of, who was born blind and afterwards brought to sight. "The room he was in", he said, "he knew must be part of the house, yet he could not conceive that the whole house could look bigger than that one room." So our new Christian experience only slowly realizes that it is but one part of the universal Christian life. Only as our study carries us from room to room does the whole house grow real to us.

Elements of Personal Power

Suppose our minister now is actually preaching, and next let us ask, What are the elements of personal power which will make him successful? Remember success in preaching is no identical, invariable thing. It differs in all whom we call successful men, and so only the broadest and most general description can be given of the qualities that will secure it. Special successes will require special fitness. But he who has these qualities that I enumerate is sure to succeed somewhere and somehow.

Element 1: Character

And first among the elements of power which made success I must put the supreme importance of character, of personal uprightness and purity impressing themselves upon the men who witness them. There is a very striking remark in Lord Nugent's *Memorials of John Hampden*, where, speaking of the English Reformation, he is led to make this general observation: "Indeed, no hierarchy and no creed has ever been overthrown by the people on account only of its theoretical dogmas, so long as the practice of the clergy was uncorrupt and conformable with their professions."

I believe that that is strictly true. And it is always wonderful to see how much stronger are the antipathies and sympathies which belong to men's moral nature than those which are purely intellectual. Baxter tells us in an interesting passage how in the civil wars "an abundance of the ignorant sort of the common people which were civil did flock in to the Parliament and filled up their armies merely because they heard men swear for the Common Prayer and bishops, and heard men pray that were against them. And all the sober men that I was acquainted with who were against the Parliament were wont to say, 'The king hath the better cause, but the Parliament the better men.'" The better men will always conquer the better cause. I suppose no cause could be so good that, sustained by bad men and opposed by any error whose champions were men of spotless lives, it would not fall. The truth must conquer, but it must first embody itself in goodness.

And in the ministry it is not merely by superficial prejudice, but by the soundest reason, that intellect and spirituality come to be tested, not by the views men hold so much as by the way in which they hold them, and the sort of men which their views seem to make of them. Whatever strange and scandalous eccentricities the ministry has sometimes witnessed, this is certainly true, and is always encouraging, that no man permanently succeeds in it who cannot make men believe that he is pure and devoted, and the only sure and lasting way to make men believe in one's devotion and purity is to be what one wishes to be believed to be.

Element 2: Freedom From Selfconsciousness

I put next to this fundamental necessity of character as an element of the preacher's power, the freedom from self-consciousness. My mind goes back to a young man whom I knew in the ministry, who did an amount of work at which men wondered, and who, dying early, left a power behind him whose influence will go on long after his name is forgotten; and the great feature of his character was his forgetfulness of self. He had not two questions to ask about every piece of work he did: first, "How shall I do it most effectively for others?" and second, "How shall I do it most creditably to myself?" Only the first question ever seemed to come to him; and when a task was done so that it should most perfectly accomplish its designed result, he left it and went on to some new task. There is wonderful clearness and economy of force in such simplicity.

No man ever yet thought whether he was preaching well without weakening his sermon. I think there are few higher or more delightful moments in a preacher's life than that which comes sometimes when, standing before a congregation and haunted by questionings about the merit of your preaching, which you hate but cannot drive away, at last, suddenly or gradually, you find yourself taken into the power of your truth, absorbed in one sole desire to send it into the men whom you are preaching to; and then every sail is set, and your sermon goes bravely out to sea, leaving yourself high and dry upon the beach, where it has been holding your sermon stranded. The second question disappears out of your work, just in proportion as the first question grows intense. No man is perfectly strong until the second question has disappeared entirely. Devotion is like the candle which, as Vasari tells us, Michaelangelo used to carry stuck on his forehead in a pasteboard cap, and which kept his own shadow from being cast upon his work while he was hewing out his statues.

Element 3: Respect for the People

The next element of a preacher's power is genuine respect for the people whom he preaches to. I should not like to say how rare I think this power, or how plentiful a source of weakness I think its absence is. There is a great deal of the genuine sympathy of sentiment. There is a great deal of liking for certain people in our congregations who are interesting in themselves and who are interested in what interests us. There is a great deal of the feeling that the clergy need the cooperation of the laity, and so must cultivate their intimacy. But of a real profound respect for the men and women whom we preach to, simply as men and women, of a deep value for the capacity that is in them, a sense that we are theirs and not they ours, I think that there is far too little.

But without this there can be no real strength in the preacher. We patronize the laity now that our power of domineering over them has been mercifully taken away. Many a time the tone of a clergyman who has talked of the relations of the preacher and the people, setting forth, with the best will in the world, their mutual functions, reminds one of the sermon of the mediaeval preacher, who, discoursing on the same subject, on the necessary cooperation of the clergy and the laity, took his text out of Job 1:14: "The oxen were ploughing and the asses feeding beside them." There is no good preaching in the supercilious preacher. No man preaches well who has not a strong and deep appreciation of humanity. The minister is often called upon to give up the society of the cultivated and learned to whom he would most be drawn, but he finds his compensation and strength in knowing man, simply as man, and learning his inestimable worth.

Element 4: Enjoying His Work

I think, again, that it is essential to the preacher's success that he should thoroughly enjoy his work. I mean in the actual doing of it, and not only in its idea. No man to whom the details of his task are repulsive can do his task well constantly, however full he may be of its spirit. He may make one bold dash at it and carry it over all his disgusts, but he cannot work on at it year after year, day after day. Therefore, count it not merely a perfectly legitimate pleasure, count it an essential element of your power, if you can feel a simple delight in what you have to do as a minister, in the fervor of writing, in the glow of speaking, in standing before men and moving them, in contact with the young. The more thoroughly you enjoy it, the better you will do it all.

Element 5: Gravity

I almost hesitate as I speak of the next element of the preacher's power. I almost doubt by what name I shall call it to give the impression of the thing I mean. Perhaps there is no better name than "gravity." I mean simply that grave and serious way of looking at life which, while it never repels the true lightheartedness of pure and trustful hearts, welcomes into a manifest sympathy the souls of men who are oppressed and burdened, anxious and full of questions which for the time at least have banished all laughter from their faces.

I know, indeed, the miserableness of all mock gravity. I think I am as much disgusted at it as anybody. The abuse and satire that have been heaped upon it are legitimate enough, though somewhat cheap. The gravity that is assumed, that merely hides with solemn front the lack of thought and feeling, that is put on as the uniform of a profession, that consists in certain forms, and is shocked at any serious thought of life more truly grave than it is, but which happens to show itself under other forms which it chooses to call frivolous, this is worthy of all satire and contempt. The merely solemn ministers are very empty and deserve all that has been heaped upon them of contempt through all the ages. They are cheats and shams. As they stand with their little knobs of prejudice down their straight coats of precision, they are like nothing so much as the chest of drawers which Mr. Bob Sawyer showed to Mr. Winkle in his little surgery: "Dummies, my dear boy," said he to his impressed, astonished visitor; "half the drawers have nothing in them, and the other half don't open." I know there are men who deserve it. But I cannot help thinking that we have about come to the time when all of that abuse is of the safe and feeble character which belongs to all satire of unpopular foibles and abuses which are in decay.

I think that at least there is another creature who ought to share with the clerical prig the contempt of Christian people. I mean the clerical jester in all the varieties of his unpleasant existence. He appears in and out of the pulpit. He lays his hands on the most sacred things, and leaves defilement upon all he touches. He is full of Bible jokes. He talks about the church's sacred symbols in the language of stale jests that have come down from generations of feeble clerical jesters before him. The doctrines which, if they mean anything, mean life or death to souls, he turns into material for chaff that flies back and forth, like the traditional banter of the Thames, between the clerical watermen who ply their boats on this side or that side of the river of Theology. There are passages in the Bible which are soiled for ever by the touches which the hands of ministers who delight in cheap and easy jokes have left upon them.

I think there is nothing that stirs one's indignation more than this, in all he sees of ministers. It is a purely wanton fault. What is simply stupid everywhere else becomes terrible here. The buffoonery which merely tries me when I hear it from a gang of laborers digging a ditch beside my door angers and frightens me when it comes from the lips of the captain who holds the helm or the surgeon on whose skill my life depends.

You will not misunderstand me, I am sure. The gravity of which I speak is not inconsistent with the keenest perception of the ludicrous side of things. It is more than consistent with—it is even necessary to—humor. Humor involves the perception of the true proportions of life. It is one of the most helpful qualities that the preacher can possess. There is no extravagance which deforms the pulpit which would not be modified and repressed, often entirely obliterated, if the minister had a true sense of humor. It has softened the bitterness of controversy a thousand times. You cannot encourage it too much. You cannot grow too familiar with the books of all ages which have in them the truest humor, for the truest humor is the bloom of the highest life. Read George Eliot and Thackeray, and, above all, Shakespeare. They will help you to keep from extravagances without fading into insipidity. They will preserve your gravity while they save you from pompous solemnity.

But humor is something very different from frivolity. People sometimes ask whether it is right to make people laugh in church by something that you say from the pulpit—as if laughter were always one invariable thing; as if there were not a smile which swept across a great congregation like the breath of a May morning, making it fruitful for whatever good thing might be sowed in it, and another laughter that was like the crackling of thorns under a pot. The smile that is stirred by true humor and the smile that comes from the mere tickling of the fancy are as different from one another as the tears that sorrow forces from the soul are from the tears that you compel a man to shed by pinching him.

And there is no delusion greater than to think that you commend your work and gain an influence over people by becoming the clerical humorist. It builds a wall between your fellowmen and you. It makes them less inclined to seek you in their spiritual need. I think that many of us feel this, and have a sort of dread when we see laymen growing familiar with clergymen's society. That society is on the whole lofty and inspiring, but there are some things in it of which you who are soon to become clergymen must beware.

Keep the sacredness of your profession clear and bright even in little things. Refrain from all joking about congregations, flocks, parish visits, sermons, the mishaps of the pulpit, or the makeshifts of the study. Such joking is always bad, and almost always stupid; but it is very common, and it takes the bloom off a young minister's life. This is the reason why so many people shrink, I believe, from personally knowing the preachers to whom they listen with respect and gratitude. They fear what they so often find.

But really the minister's life may be a help and enforcement of all his preaching. The quality which makes it so is this which I call gravity. It has a delicate power of discrimination. It attracts all that it can help and it repels all that could harm it or be harmed by it. It admits the earnest and simple with a cordial welcome. It shuts out the impertinent and insincere inexorably. Pure gravity is like the hinges of the wonderful gates of the ancient labyrinth, so strong that no battery could break them down, but so delicately hung that a child's light touch could make them swing back and let him in.

Element 6: Courage

There is another source of power which I can hardly think of as a separate quality, but rather as the sum and result of all the qualities which I have been naming. I mean "courage." It is the indispensable requisite of any true ministry. The timid minister is as bad as the timid surgeon. Courage is good everywhere, but it is necessary here. If you are afraid of men and a slave to their opinion, go and do something else. Go and make shoes to fit them. Go even and paint pictures which you know are bad but which suit their bad taste. But do not keep on all your life preaching sermons which shall say not what God sent you to declare, but what they hire you to say. Be courageous. Be independent. Only remember where the true courage and independence comes from.

Courage in the ministry is, I think, one of those qualities which cannot be healthily acquired if it is sought for directly. It must come as health comes in the body, as the result of the seeking for other things. It must be from a sincere respect for men's higher nature that you must grow bold to resist their whims. He who begins by despising men will often end by being their slave. A passionate desire to do men good is always the surest safeguard that they shall not do us harm. Jesus Himself was bold before men out of the infinite love which He felt for them. That was the way in which He ruled them from His cross, and was their Master because He was their servant even unto death.

Warning: Danger

There is one other topic upon which I wished to dwell in this lecture, but on this I must speak very briefly. I wanted to try to estimate with you some of the dangers to a man's own character which come from his being a preacher.

Danger 1: Self-conceit

The first of these dangers, beyond all doubt, is self-conceit. In a certain sense every young minister is conceited. He begins his ministry in a conceited condition. At least every man begins with extravagant expectations of what his ministry is to result in. We come out from it by and by. A man's first wonder when he begins to preach is that people do not come to hear him. After a while, if he is good for anything, he begins to wonder that they do. He finds out that old Adam is too strong for young Melanchthon. It is not strange that it should be so. It is not to the young minister's discredit that it should be so.

The student for the ministry has to a large extent comprehended the force by which he is to work, but he has not measured the resistance that he is to meet. He knows the power of the truth of which he is all full, but he has not estimated the sin of which the world is all full. The more earnest and intense and full of love for God and man he is, the more impossible does it seem that he should not do great things for his Master. And then the character of men's ministries, it seems to me, depends very largely upon the ways in which they pass out of that first self-confidence and upon what condition comes afterwards when it is gone.

Self-conceit and Success

The first way in which life affects this self-confidence and lifts men out of their conceits is by success, by letting us see the work which we are undertaking actually going on under our hands. It is only in poor men and in the lower things that success increases self-conceit. In every high work and in men worthy of it, success is always sure to bring humility. "Recognition," said Hawthorne once, "makes a man very modest." The knowledge that you are really accomplishing results, and the reassurance of that knowledge by the judgment of your fellowmen, opens to you the deeper meaning of your work, shows you how great it is, makes you ashamed of all the praise men give you, as you see gradually how much better your work might have been done. I think that some of the noblest and richest characters among ministers in all times are those who have been humiliated by men's praises and enlightened by success.

Self-conceit and Failure

But there is another way by which men go out of their first satisfaction, by a door directly opposite to this—by failure. Failure and success to really working ministers are only relative. Remember that no true man wholly succeeds or wholly fails. But the main difference in effect between what we call success and what we call failure in the ministry is here: Success makes a man dwell upon and be thankful for how much a preacher can do; failure makes a man think how much there is which no preacher can do, and is apt to weigh him down into depression. It confronts him with the magnitude of the task of the Christian ministry, not as a great temptation, but as a great burden. He is paralyzed as Hamlet was.

> The time is out of joint: O cursed spite,
> That ever I was born to set it right!

Such an end of a young man's first high hopes is terrible to see. The very power that once made him strong now weakens him. The weight that was his ballast and helped his speed sinks him when once the leak has come. There is no help except in a profounder retreat of the whole nature upon God—such a perception of Him and of His dearness that will take off our heavy responsibility and make us ready to fail for Him with joy as well as to succeed for Him, if such shall be His choice, and ready to work as hard for Him in failure as in success, because we work not for success but for Him. The drawing of the man back into God by failure is always a noble sight, and no region of life has such noble specimens of it to show as the Christian ministry.

Self-conceit and Littleness

There is another refuge when the young preacher's first self-conceit is shaken. It is into another self-conceit which is smaller than the first. The beleaguered householder refuses to surrender, and retreats from his strong outer ramparts, defending one line after another till at last he dwells only in his most mean and worthless chamber.

A man makes up his mind that he is not going to convert the world. The strongholds of the Prince of Evil evidently will not fall before him. He is to leave the unbuilt kingdom of God very much as he found it when he came into the ministry. But then he falls back upon some petty pride. "My church is full;" "My name is prominent in the movements of my denomination;" "My sermons win the compliments of people;" or simply this, "I am a minister. I bear a dignity that these laymen cannot boast. I have an ordination which separates me into an indefinable, mysterious privilege." Here is the beginning of many of the fantastic and exaggerated theories about the ministry. The little preacher magnifies his office in a most unpauline way. And you hear a man to whom no one cares to listen quoting the solemn words of God about "whether men will hear or whether they will forbear," as if they had been spoken to him as much as to Ezekiel.

What shall we say then? What is the true escape which many a preacher has found and gradually passed into. It is the growing devotion of his life to God, the more and more complete absorption of his being in the seeking of God's glory. As he goes on, the work unfolds itself. It outgoes all his powers. But as he looks over its increasing vastness he sees it on every side touching the omnipotence of God. As he sees more and more clearly that he will never do what he once hoped to do, it becomes clear to him at the same time that

God will do it in His own time and way. His own disappointment is swallowed up and drowned in the promise of his Lord's success. He becomes a true John Baptist. He is happy with a higher joy, and works with an energy that he never knew before. This is the true refuge of the minister in the disenchantment of his earliest dreams.

Danger 2: Self-indulgence

Another of the dangers of the clergyman's life is self-indulgence. The ways and methods of the minister's work are almost wholly at his own control. It is impossible for him to reduce his life to a routine. There are but few tests which he must meet at special times, as a businessman must meet his notes when they are due. And a great deal of his work is of that sort which requires spontaneity for its best execution. The result of all these causes working together is to create in many a minister a certain feeling that his faithfulness in his work is not to be judged as other men's faithfulness in their work is. Indeed, I think, the very consciousness of laboring under a loftier motive has often a tendency to weaken the conscientiousness with which each minute detail of work is met.

There is a lurking Antinomianism in many a most Arminian study. We are apt to become men of moods, thinking we cannot work unless we feel like it. There is just enough of the artistic element in what we have to do, to let us fall into the artist's ways and leave our brushes idle when the sky frowns or the head aches. But the artistic element is, after all, the smallest element in the true sermon. Its best qualities depend on those moral and spiritual conditions which may be always present in the devoted servant of God.

And so the first business of the preacher is to conquer the tyranny of his moods, and to be always ready for his work. It can be done. The man who has not learned to do it has not really reached the secret of Jesus, which was such utter love for His Father and man, between whom He stood, as obliterated all thought of Himself save as a medium, through which the divine might come down to the human. We read of Jesus that He again and again grew heavy in spirit. In utter weariness, sometimes, when His work was done, He would withdraw into a mountain, or put out in a boat upon the lake. We can feel the fluctuations of that humanity of His, and, interpreting it by our own, we can seem to see how one bright morning by the seaside He was exuberant and joyous, and on another morning He would be sad and burdened. We can trace the differences in the kind of preaching of the two different days. But through it all there is nothing in the least like self-indulgence. We are sure that no day ever went without its preaching, because it found Him moody and depressed. He did no mighty works in Nazareth; but it was because of the people's unbelief, not because of His own reluctance.

So it may be with us. It is part of the privilege of our humanity, it is part of the advantage of our people in having men and not machines for ministers, that we preach the truth in various lights, or shades, according as God brightens or darkens our own experience; but any mood which makes us unfit to preach at all, or really weakens our will to preach, is bad, and can be broken through. Then is the time for the conscience to bestir itself and for the man to be a man.

I wish that it were possible for one to speak to the laity of our churches frankly and freely about their treatment of the clergy. The clergy are largely what the laity make them. And though one may look wholly without regret upon the departure of that reverence which seems to have clothed the preacher's office in our fathers' days, I think he must have many misgivings about the weaker substitute for it, which in many instances has taken its place. It was not good that the minister should be worshiped and made an oracle. It is still worse that he should be flattered and made a pet. And there is such a tendency in these days among our weaker people.

I have already spoken of the way in which many men are petted into the ministry. It is possible for such a man, if he has popular gifts, to be petted all through his ministry, never once to come into strong contact with other men, or to receive one good hard knock of the sort that brings out manliness and character. The people who gather closest around a minister's life, believing his beliefs, and accepting his standards, make a sort of cushion between him and the unbelief and wickedness which smite other men in the face and wound them mercilessly at every turn. It is not wholly unnatural.

The minister stands in a unique position to the community. In no other man's private affairs, his health, his comfort, his freedom from financial care, are so many people so directly interested. It is not strange that that interest in him and care for him, which ought simply to put him where, without personal fear or personal indebtedness, he may bravely and independently be himself and speak out his own soul, should often be corrupted into a poison of his manhood, and a temptation to his self-indulgence. It is beyond all doubt the weak point of our American voluntary system, which brings the minister into those close personal relations to his people which on the whole are good and healthy, but which have this one defect and danger.

If you have read the life of Frederick Robertson, you know how hateful many of the incidents of the life of a popular minister were to him. So they must be to every true man. If a man is not wholly true they find out his weak point and fix upon it. He begins to expect different treatment from other men. His personal woes and pains seem to him things of public interest. He grows first inhuman in the separation from the ordinary standard of his race, and that makes him inhuman, unsympathetic. The weak is always cruel.

Mr. Galton, in his work on *Hereditary Genius*, summing up the result of his reading in clerical biographies, declares that "a gently complaining and fatigued spirit is that in which Evangelical Divines are very apt to pass their days." These words tell perfectly a story that we all know who have been intimate with many ministers. That which ought to be the manliest of all professions has a tendency, practically, to make men unmanly. Men make appeals for sympathy that no true man should make. They take to themselves St. Paul's pathos without St. Paul's strength.

Against that tendency, my friends, set your whole force. Fear its insidiousness. "I feel no intoxicating effect," wrote Macaulay when the first flush of his success was on him, "but a man may be drunk without knowing it." Insist on applying to yourself tests which others refuse to apply to you. Resent indulgences which are not given to men of other professions. Learn to enjoy and be sober; learn to suffer and be strong. Never appeal for sympathy. Let it find you out if it will. Count your manliness the soul of your ministry and resist all attacks upon it however sweetly they may come.

Danger 3: Narrowness

I had hoped to say some words today, about one other danger of the preacher's life, I mean the danger of narrowness. We all live within the rings of concentric circles. They extend one beyond another till they come to that outmost circle of all, the horizon where humanity touches divinity, as the earth meets the sky. Now I hold that all that is by God's appointment, and is intended for our best good. The narrowness is for the sake of breadth. I hold that every smaller circle is meant to carry the eye out to the next larger than itself, and so, at last, to the largest of all. You stand firm on your one little spot, and thence you look out and find yourself, like Tennyson's eagle, "ringed with the azure world." So every smaller circle of your moral life is meant to carry you out, and make you realize the larger circles. You may be a better minister because you are clear in your denominational position as a Congregationalist or Episcopalian; and because you are a minister you may be a better man. The danger is lest the smaller circle, instead of tempting the sight onward, jealously confines it to itself.

Narrowness is to be escaped, not by deserting our special function, but by compelling it to open to us the things beyond itself. You will not be a better man by pretending that you are not a Christian, nor a better Christian by pretending to have no dogmatic faith. The true breadth comes by the strength of your own belief making you tolerant of other believers; and by the earnestness of your Christianity teaching you your brotherhood even to the most unchristian men.

I must stop here. I have spoken very freely of these dangers and hindrances with which the preacher's occupations beset his character. Yet you must not misunderstand me. There is no occupation in which it is so possible, nay so easy to live a noble life. These tares grow rank only because the soil is rich. The wheat grows rich beside them. The Christian ministry is the largest field for the growth of a human soul that this world offers. In it he who is faithful must go on learning more and more for ever. His growth in learning is all bound up with his growth in character. Nowhere else do the moral and intellectual so sympathize, and lose or gain together. The minister must grow. His true growth is not necessarily a change of views. It is a change of view. It is not revolution. It is progress. It is a continual climbing which opens continually wider prospects. It repeats the experience of Christ's disciples, of whom their Lord was always making larger men and then giving them the larger truth of which their enlarged natures had become capable. Once more, I rejoice for you that this is the ministry in which you are to spend your lives.

3

THE PREACHER IN HIS WORK

When I was just about to begin the writing of this lecture, I chanced to be thrown for a day or two into the company of a young man who had been engaged in the work of the ministry only a few months. He was in the first flush and fervor of his new experience, and in listening to him I recalled much of the spirit with which I myself began many years ago. The spirit had not passed away, but the first freshness of many impressions had been ripened, I hope, into something better, but still into something soberer. He revived for me the delight of that new and strange relation to his fellow men which comes when a young man who thus far in his life has had others ministering to him, finds the conditions now reversed and other men are looking up to him for culture. There is the sober joy of responsibility. There is the surprised recognition of something which we have learned in some one of our schools of books or life, and counted useless, which now some man we meet welcomes when we give it to him as if it were the one thing for which he had been always waiting. There is the hopefulness that fears no failure. There is the pleasure of a new knowledge of ourselves as others begin to call out in us what we never knew was there. There is the joy of being trusted and responded to. There is the deepened sacredness of prayer and of communion with God when we go to Him, not merely for ourselves and for the great vague world, but for a people whom we have begun to love and call our own, while we know that they are His. There is the discovery of the better and devouter nature in men. There is the interest of countless new details and the inspiration of the noblest purpose for which a man can live. All these together make up the happiness and hope of those bright days in which a strong and healthy and devout young man is just entering the ministry of the Gospel.

I wish to speak to you today about the preacher in his work, and what I shall have to say will naturally divide itself into suggestions with reference to the nature, the method, and the spirit of that work.

Understanding Humanity

I must recur to what I said in the first lecture about the true character of preaching. Preaching is the communication of truth through a man to men. The human element is essential in it, and not merely accidental. There cannot really be a sermon in a stone, whatever lessons the stone may have to teach. This being so, we must carry out the importance of the human element to its full consequence. It is not only necessary for a sermon that there should be a human being to speak to other human beings, but for a good sermon there must be a man who can speak well, whose nature stands in right relations to those to whom he speaks, who has brought his life close to theirs with sympathy.

In every highest task there is an instinctive tendency of men to shirk and hide under the protection of some idea of fate. And very often we hear ministers trying to escape responsibility by vague and foolish statements that the truth is everything, and that it ought not to make any difference to a congregation how or from whom they hear it. It is a latent fatalism, a readiness to count out of the highest operations the play of human free will and choice, which lies at the bottom of such speeches.

The same reason which requires a man for a preacher at all requires as wise and strong and well-furnished, as skilful and as eloquent a man as can be found or made. The duty of making yourself acceptable to people, and winning by all manly ways their confidence in you, and in the truth which you tell, is one that is involved in the very fact of your being a preacher. And the dignity of the purpose gives dignity to many details which in themselves are trivial. The study of language and of oratory, which would belittle you if they were merely undertaken for your own culture, are noble when you undertake them in order that your tongue may be a worthier minister of God's truth; and the assiduous attention to people, and their tastes and habits and ways of thinking, which would be slavery if it had no object besides their pleasure or your own repute, is a lofty exercise, if it has for its purpose the finding out on which side of every man you can best bring to him the truth.

Here stands a man, and two other men are watching him. Both of them are studying his character. Both want to know what he thinks about, what his tastes are, how he spends his time. One of them is trying to find how he can best win from him a dollar or a vote. The other is trying to see what is his true way to preach the Gospel to that fellow man. There are the meanest and the noblest relations which any man can occupy towards his fellow man. The first is ignominious beyond description. It is a relation too low for any man to hold. A true man would rather starve than occupy it. But the other is a relation in which every man must stand who means to really preach to any brother. It is but the effort after what it is in our feeble power to attain of that knowledge of humanity which was in Him who "knew what was in man," and who, therefore, "spake as never man spake."

Pastor *and* Preacher

It follows from this that the work of the preacher and the pastor really belong together, and ought not to be separated. I believe that very strongly. Every now and then somebody rises with a plea that is very familiar and specious. He says, how much better it would be if only there could be a classification of ministers and duties. Let some ministers be wholly pastors. Let one class visit the flock, to direct and comfort them; and the other class stand in the pulpit. You will not go far in your ministry before you will be tempted to echo that desire. The two parts of a preacher's work are always in rivalry. When you find that you can never sit down to study and write without the faces of the people, whom you know need your care, looking at you from the paper; and yet you never can go out among your people without hearing your forsaken study reproaching you, and calling you home, you may easily come to believe that it would be good indeed if you could be one or other of two things, and not both; either a preacher or a pastor, but not the two together. But I assure you you are wrong.

The two things are not two, but one. There may be preachers here and there with such a deep, intense insight into the general humanity, that they can speak to men without knowing the men to whom they speak. Such preachers are very rare; and other preachers, who have not their power, trying to do it, are sure to preach to some unreal, unhuman man of their own imagination. There are some pastors here and there with such a constantly lofty and spiritual view of little things, that they can go about from house to house, year after year, and deal with men and women at their common work, and lift the men and women to themselves, and never fall to the level of the men and women whom they teach. Such pastors are rare; and other men, trying to do it, and never in more formal way from the pulpit treating truth in its larger aspects, are sure to grow frivolous gossips or tiresome machines.

The preacher needs to be pastor, that he may preach to real men. The pastor must be preacher, that he may keep the dignity of his work alive. The preacher, who is not a pastor, grows remote. The pastor, who is not a preacher, grows petty. Never be content to let men truthfully say of you, "He is a preacher, but no pastor;" or, "He is a pastor, but no preacher." Be both; for you cannot really be one unless you also are the other.

The Role of Pastor

Of the pastor's function considered by itself there is, I think, but very little to be said. I count of little worth all sets of rules, all teaching directly on the subject. The books that teach a pastor's duty except in the way of the most general suggestion are almost worthless. They have the fault which belongs to all books on behavior, which are needless for those who do behave well and useless for those who do not. The powers of the pastor's success are truth and sympathy together. "Speaking the truth and sympathy together." "Speaking the truth in love," is the golden text to write in the book where you keep the names of your people, so that you may read it every time you go to visit them.

Sympathy without truth makes a plausible pastor, but one whose hold on a parish soon grows weak. Men feel his touch upon them soft and tender, but never vigorous and strong. Truth without sympathy makes the sort of pastor whom people say that they respect but to whom they seldom go and whom they seldom care to see coming to them. But where the two unite, so far as the two unite in you, I think there will be nothing that will surprise you more than to discover how certain their power is. The man who has them cannot help saying the right word at the right time. You go to some poor crushed, and broken heart; you tell what truth you know, the truth of the ever ready and inexhaustible forgiveness, the truth of the unutterable love, the truth of the unbroken life of immortality; and you let the sorrow for that heart's sorrow which you truly feel, utter itself in whatever true and simple ways it will; then you come away sick at heart because you have so miserably failed; but by and by you find that you have not failed, that you really did bring elevation and comfort. You cannot help doing it if you go with truth and sympathy. This is the constant experience of the minister. This is the ground of confidence and hope with which he presses on from year to year.

The Importance of Being Frank

I am inclined to think, as I have already intimated that the trouble of much of our pastoral work is in its pettiness. It is pitched in too low a key. It tries to meet the misfortunes of life with comfort and not with inspiration, offering inducements to patience and the suggestions of compensation in this life or another which lies beyond, rather than imparting that higher and stronger tone which will make men despise their sorrows and bear them easily in their search for truth and nobleness, and the release that comes from forgetfulness of self and devotion to the needs of other people. The truest help which one can render to a man who has any of the inevitable burdens of life to carry is not to take his burden off but to call out his best strength that he may be able to bear it.

The pastorship of Jesus is characterized everywhere by its frankness and manliness. He meets Nicodemus with a staggering assertion of the higher needs of the spirit. The man who wants the inheritance divided is encountered with a strong rebuke of his presumptuous selfishness. And Simon Peter has the assurance of his forgiveness offered him in a demand for work. All three of these instances and many others are richly suggestive of contrasts with what many of the

ministers of Christ would do in the same circumstances. It is
the utter absence of sentimentality in Christ's relations with
men that makes his tenderness so exquisitely touching. It is
in the power, even in the effort, to awake the stronger nature
of mankind that our modern pastorship is apt to be deficient.
It ministers to women more than to men. It tries to soothe
with consolation more than to fire with ambition or to sting
with shame.

Influencing an Unheroic Church

Perhaps there will be no better place than this for me to
say that it is in the absence of the heroic element that our
current Christianity most falls short of the Christianity of
Gospel times. We keep still the heroic language, but does it
not often suggest strange incongruities? Have not the pictures
of some of our hymns, for instance, seemed sometimes
strangely out of keeping with the lips that sang them?   A
row of comfortable, self-contented, conservative gentlemen
and ladies standing up, for instance, and singing "Onward,
Christian soldiers, marching as to war," or "Hold the fort for
I am coming, Jesus signals still," reminds us all the more of
how unmilitary and unheroic are the lives they live. It is not
the mere difference of dress.

I doubt not the Christians in the catacombs, or the colliers
who listened to Whitefield when he preached at Bristol, might
have sung hymns that were built on the same imagery, and
nothing incongruous would have been suggested. And yet
they were as evidently men of peace as are our congregations. But they were conscious of and showed the true intenseness of spiritual warfare. They knew the fight within,
the terrible reality of the enemy, the terrible suspense of the
struggle, the glorious delight of triumph. No, it is the unheroic character of modern life and especially of modern
Christianity.

The life of Jesus Christ was radical. It went to the deep
roots of things. It claimed men's noblest and freest action.
We, if we are His ministers, must bring the heroic into the
unheroic life of men, demanding of them truth, breadth, brav-
ery, self-sacrifice, the freedom from conventionalities and an
elevation to high standards of thought and life. We must
bring men's life up to Him and not bring Him down to men's
life. This is the Christian pastor's privilege and duty.

Revealing Shame and Hope

It seems to me that a large part of the troubles and mistakes of our pastoral life come from our having too high an estimate of men's present condition and too low an estimate of their possibility. If this be true, then what we need to make us better pastors is more of the Gospel which reveals at once man's imperfect condition and his infinite hope. Jesus was the perfect pastor in the way in which He showed men what they were and what they might become. He never deceived and never discouraged them. The contact with His perfect humanity brought them at once shame and hope. And when He comes near to us now, when His spirit does His appointed work of taking Him and showing Him to us, the same power, combined of shame and hope, comes into our lives. Let that be the model of our pastorship.

The Pleasure of Preaching

But to return more definitely to preaching. I think that one of the preliminary considerations about it—one characteristic of it so prominent that we are sure that He who sent men out to preach must have designed it—is that which I have already once alluded to, the pleasure that belongs to it, the way in which it thoroughly interests the best parts of the man who does it. I remember, as I recur to it, how much I have already said about it, and may have yet to say; but it is much upon my mind. For I think there is something unhappy in the frequency with which ministers dwell upon their work as if it were full of hardships and disappointments.

Every power of man which has its natural and legitimate purpose brings two pleasures, one in the anticipation and attainment of its end, the other in its own exercise. There is a delight in exercising faculties as well as in doing work and in all the best activities of men the two will go together. This is all true of preaching. Its highest joy is in the great ambition that is set before it, the glorifying of the Lord and the saving of the souls of men. No other joy on earth compares with that. The ministry that does not feel that joy is dead. But in behind that highest joy, beating in humble unison with it, as the healthy body thrills in sympathy with the deep thoughts and pure desires of the mind and soul, the best ministries have always been conscious of another pleasure which belonged to the very doing of the work itself.

As we read the lives of all the most effective preachers of the past, or as we meet the men who are powerful preachers of the Word today, we feel how certainly and how deeply the very exercise of their ministry delights them. The best sermons always seem to carry the memory of the excited spring or quiet happiness, with which they are written or uttered. The soldier enjoys the battle as well as the victory. The carpenter enjoys the saw and plane as well as the prospect of the full-built house. When Wilberforce heard of Macaulay's first offer of a chance of public life, he was silent for a moment, and then his face lighted up and he clapped his hand to his ear and cried, "Ah, I hear that shout again. Hear! Hear! What a life it was!" In the case of the preacher this secondary pleasure, if I may call it so, consists in the enjoyment of close relationship with fellowmen and in the orator's delight in moving men. The fastidious man or the cold man loses a great deal of the stimulus and unfacing freshness of the ministry. Sometimes this pleasure grows very keen.

I always remember one special afternoon, years ago, when the light faded from the room where I was preaching and the faces melted together into a unit as of one impressive, pleading man, and I felt them listening when I could hardly see them. I remember this accidental day as one of the times when the sense of the privilege of having to do with people as their preacher came out almost overpoweringly. It is good to treasure all such enjoyment of the actual work of preaching. It bridges over the times when the higher enthusiasm flags, and it gives a deeper delight to it when it is strongest.

A Leader and a Brother

I think that as we study the preaching of Jesus we admire above almost everything the way in which He was at once the Leader and the Brother of the men He taught. He spake as one having authority always, but always His power was brought near to men by the complete way in which He made Himself one of them, by the evident reality with which He bore their sins and carried their sorrows. So that by as much as the Son of God was above men in His nature, by so much the more He came near to them in his sympathies and was a truer Son of Man than any of the wonderfully human prophets of the Old Testament, Isaiah, Jeremiah, or Ezekiel, to whom the same name is constantly applied.

Now when we compare the ordinary preacher's life with that of Jesus, I think we see how much more apt he is to have kept the position of leader than the position of brother of the people. At any rate, what we miss in a great deal of our preaching is that beautiful blending of the two whose power we recognize in the word and work of Jesus. We are the leaders of the people.

Woe to our preaching if in any feeble, false humility we abdicate that place. The people pass us by and pity us if they see us standing in our pulpits saying, "We know nothing particular about these things whereof we preach; we have no authority; only come here and we will tell you what we think, and you shall tell us what you think, and so perhaps together we can strike out a little light." That is not preaching. There has been pulpit talk like that, and men have always passed it by and hurried on to find some one who at least pretended to tell them the will of God. No, the preacher must be a leader, but his leadership must be bound in with his brotherhood.

It was as Man that Christ led men to God. It must be as men that we carry on the work of Christ and help men's souls to Him. This truth seems to me to lie at the bottom of all the best successes, and the forgetfulness of it at the bottom of all the worst failures of the ministry. There is no real leadership of people for a preacher or a pastor except that which comes as the leadership of the Incarnation came, by a thorough entrance into the lot of those whom one would lead.

The Limits of Leadership

And again, the limits of the preacher's leadership are very clear, and it is necessary that the young minister should know them. Sometimes a preacher finds himself—and oftener still, some foolish friends by his side will make him think himself—one of the wisest men, perhaps the wisest man in his small circle upon any of the ordinary topics of thought, upon art, or politics, or letters, or education. It is good for him to use his wisdom as it is for any other man. It is wrong for him to leave his wisdom unused as it is for any other man. He may do much good to the people, he may indirectly help his own peculiar mission by sharing his knowledge with them.

One of the most interesting pages of clerical life of which I know is Norman Macleod's account of his lectures to the weavers at Newmilns, on geology. Would that more of us were able to follow his example. All that is well; but we must know that there is nothing in our quality as preachers that gives us any claim to be authoritative guides to men in any of those things, neither in politics, nor in education, nor in science.

On one thing only we may speak with authority, and that is the will of God. Nor even in the details of religious thought need we aspire to be their guides. I do not want—and certainly I know that if I did want I never should be able—to make the people who listen to me accept every view of Christian truth which I utter before them. I have no reason to believe that what I utter is clothed with an infallibility. In much of what one preaches he is satisfied if men take home what he says as the utterance of one who has thought upon the subject of which he speaks and wishes them to think and judge. Surely he does not declare to them his belief about the method of the atonement, with the same authority with which he bids them repent of sin, and warns them that without holiness no man shall see the Lord. Such line of difference every true preacher draws, and freely lets men see where it runs. If you attempt to claim authority for all your speculations you will end by losing it for your most sure and solemn declarations of God's will.

Dealing With Criticism

One difficulty of the preacher's office is its subjection to flippant gossip, along with its exemption from severe and healthy criticism. There are people enough always to find out a minister's little faults, and let him hear of them; but it is wonderful how he can go on year after year, without being once brought up to the judgment-seat of sound intelligence, and hearing what is the real worth of the words that he is saying, and the work that he is doing. There are plenty of people to do for him the office of the man who Philip of Macedon kept in his service, to tell him every day before he gave audience, "Philip, remember thou art mortal," but hardly ever does he meet that sound and prompt investigation of his special work which comes to the author from his public, or the lawyer from his judge.

This makes for many men the worst possible condition to labor in—a constant fretting by small cavils, and no large estimation of the whole. It is like standing in a desultory dropping fire without being allowed to plunge into the battle, and to settle at once the question of life or death. It makes supremely essential to the minister that independence of men's judgments which can only come by the most absolute dependence on the judgment of the Lord by living "ever in the great Taskmaster's eye."

Dealing With Great Ideas

I should have liked to speak of one other danger of the preacher from his work. It is that which comes from the paralysis of great ideas. There are times which the vast thoughts of God stimulate us to action. There are other times when they seem to take all power of action out of us. These last times grow very frequent with some men, till you have the race of clerical visionaries who think vast, dim, vague thoughts, and do no work. It is a danger of all ardent minds. The only salvation, if one finds himself verging to it, is an unsparing rule that no idea, however abstract, shall be ever counted as satisfactorily received and grasped till it has opened to us its practical side and helped us somehow in our work. The spirit of practicalness is the consecration of the whole man, even the most ideal and visionary parts of him, to the work of life.

The Pastor's Methods

With regard to the second point of which I spoke, the methods of the preacher's work, there are two difficulties which beset us: one is the absence of method, and the other is the tendency to wrong methods. Let me say a few words to you on each of these.

Spontaneity vs. Organization

There is a certain air of spontaneousness, a certain dislike of rule and system which belongs to a great many ministers' fundamental conception of the work of preaching. Rightly studied and weighed, no doubt, the teachings of Christ and of the whole New Testament all look one way. They all involve the simple truth that he who works for God must work with his best powers; and since among the effective powers of man the powers of plan and arrangement stand very high, the whole of the New Testament really implies that he who preaches must lay out the methods and ways of preaching, as a merchant or a soldier lays out a campaign of the market or the battle-field. But at the same time there are many passages in the New Testament which seem to have in them something like a promise of immediate inspiration.

Christ bids His disciples: "Settle it, therefore, in your hearts not to meditate before what ye shall answer. For I will give you a mouth and wisdom which all your adversaries shall not be able to gainsay nor resist" (Luke 21:14-15). These words, and others like them, were spoken indeed to certain disciples, and in view of certain special emergencies of their life; but, with our vague unscientific notions about inspiration, they have been easily appropriated by many a poor uninspired creature who has found himself the subject of ordination; and a general impression of the piety of extemporaneousness has spread more widely and reached more thoughtful and intelligent men than we suppose. I think, too, that the revolt of Protestantism against the minute and overstrained organization of the Romish Church has had very much to do with the creation of that distrust of methodicalness which prevails so largely among preachers.

However it has come about, the fact is clear enough. Look at the way in which the pulpit teaches. I venture to say that there is nothing so unreasonable in any other branch of teaching. You are a minister, and you are to instruct these people in the truths of God, to bring God's message to them. All the vast range of God's revelation and of man's duty is open to you. And how do you proceed? If you are like most ministers there is no order, no progress, no consecutive purpose in your teaching. You never begin at the beginning and proceed step by step to the end of any course of orderly instruction. You float over the whole sea of truth, and plunge here and there, like a gull, on any subject that either suits your mood, or that some casual and superficial relationship with people makes you conceive to be required by a popular need.

No other instruction ever was given so. No hearer has the least idea, as he goes to your church, what you will preach to him about that day. It is hopeless for him to try to get ready for your teaching. I am sure that I may say (I suppose that this is partly the reason why as an Episcopalian I have been asked to lecture here) that I rejoice to see in many churches outside our own that to which we owe so much as a help to the orderliness of preaching, the observance of a church year with its commemorative festivals, growing so largely common. It still leaves largest liberty. It is no bondage within which any man is hampered. But the great procession of the year, sacred to our best human instincts with the accumulated reverence of ages—Advent, Christmas, Epiphany, Good Friday, Easter, Ascension, Whitsunday—leads those who walk in it, at least once every year, past all the great Christian facts, and, however careless and selfish be the preacher, will not leave it in his power to keep them from his people. The church year, too, preserves the personality of our religion. It is concrete and picturesque. The historical Jesus is forever there. It lays each life continually down beside the perfect life, that it may see at once its imperfection and its hope.

But not to dwell any longer on this special instance, the order and course of preaching, the same absence of method is apt to show itself everywhere in a preacher's life. Besides the reasons for it which I have already suggested, it comes from a feeble sense of responsibility. The mental and the moral natures have closer connections than very often we allow them, and traits which we think wholly intellectual are constantly revealing to us moral bases upon which they rest. We talk of clearness, for instance, as if it were purely a quality of style, but clearness in every speech addressed to men comes out of sympathy, which is a moral quality. So force implies conviction. And so the truest method involves conscientiousness. The intellectual and the spiritual belong together.

Logical arrangement of thought has real connection with a sincere desire to do right. The more you mean to do all the right, the more clearly your whole thinking processes will dispose themselves, and then, by the law of reaction, your orderly thinking will make it easier for you to do right. That which all men ought to remember, it behooves the minister more than all men not to forget; how closely the mental and moral natures are bound together in their characters and destinies.

A Call for Method and Order

On this high ground, and on a ground that perhaps is lower but still is sound, I urge upon you the need of method and order in your life and work. Do not be tempted by the fascination of spontaneousness. Do not be misled by any delusion of inspiration. The lower ground is the support which well-considered and settled methods of operation give to the higher powers in their weaker moments. No one dreads mechanical woodenness in the ministry more than I do. And yet a strong wooden structure running through your work, a set of well-framed and well-jointed habits about times and ways of work, writing, studying, relationship with people, the administration of charity and education, and the proportions between the different departments of clerical labor, is again and again the bridge over which the minister walks where the solid ground of higher motive fails him for a time. Routine is a terrible master, but she is a servant whom we can hardly do without. Routine as a law is deadly. Routine as a resource in the temporary exhaustion of impulse and suggestion is often our salvation. Coleridge told the story when he sang,

> There will come a weary day
> When, overtaxed at length,
> Both hope and love beneath
> The weight give way.
> Then with a statue's smile,
> A statue's strength,
> Patience, nothing loth,
> And uncomplaining, does
> The work of both.

But patience, while a strong power, is not quick-sighted, and works in ways and habits which have been made before.

Looking for a Panacea

Of *mistakes* of method as distinguished from *absence* of method in the ministry, experience has seemed to me to show that there is one comprehensive head under which a wonderfully large proportion of them all may be included. It is the passion for expedients. I know of no department of human activity, from the governing of a great nation to the doctoring of a little body, where the disposition is not constantly appearing to invent some sudden method or to seek some magical and concise prescription which shall obviate the need of careful, comprehensive study and long-continued application. But this disposition is nowhere so strong, I think, as in the ministry.

The bringing of truth, of Christ the Truth, to man, of the whole Christ to the whole man, you can think of no work larger in its idea than that. And evidently its methods must be as manifold as are the natures with which it deals. But we are constantly meeting people who seem to have epitomized all the needs of the church, all the requirements of the successful minister, into some one expedient, some panacea which, if it could only be applied, would overcome every obstacle and bring on at once the perfect day of preaching. These expedients are things good in themselves, making no doubt some very useful part of the great whole; but when they are magnified into solitary importance and offered as solutions of the difficulties that beset the Gospel, they are ludicrously insufficient.

Many a young minister today is staking his whole ministry on some one such idea. He attributes every defect to the imperfect apprehension of that idea in his community. He hopes for every good as that idea comes to be completely realized. He can expect no good without it. He can hardly conceive of any evil in connection with it. Perhaps his favorite idea is free churches; a good idea indeed, an idea without which there could have been no Christian church at all; an idea which beyond all doubt does represent the standard of Christianity, and to which Christian practice must some day return; but by no means the only idea of worship, nor suggesting by any means the only or the principal difficulty in the way of spreading the Gospel. You might break down every pew door and abolish every pew tax and yet wait to see your churches and the kingdom of God fill themselves full in vain.

Another's consuming thought is congregational singing. As you listen to him rushing hither and thither shouting the praises of his favorite method and dealing dreadful blows at the four-headed Cerberus which he detests, you are almost ready to believe that if all the people only could lift up their voices and sing the walls of wickedness must tumble into dust. It is a good and healthy agitation. It is well that we should break through the tyranny of old methods and really sing the praises of the Lord. But it is not going to do the work of casting out sin and winning righteousness. When the army goes into battle the bands must play, but they do not lead the host.

And so it is again with the hobby of inter-denominational relationship, of Christian union. It is well, and I would that we have more of it. But, to borrow the army simile again, no courtesies between two regiments ever yet defeated the other army. And so of the church sociable which tries to entice the passer-by to the altar of the Lord with the familiar but feeble odor of a cup of tea. And so with the children's church; one of the best and purest of the church's inventions for her work, but by no means enough to make a special and peculiar feature of in any congregation. It almost always weakens the preacher for his preaching to adults.

There is nothing so insignificant that some petty minister will not make it the Christian panacea. A young pastor said to me once, "Wherever else I fail, there is one point in which my ministry will be a success." "And what is that?" said I, expecting something sweet and spiritual. "In printing," he replied. He had devoted himself to setting forth elaborate advertisements, and orders of services, and Sunday school reward cards, and most complicated parish records, and I suppose his parish is strewn thick with those thick-falling leaves unto this day.

No! The clerical or parish hobby is either the fancy of a man who has failed to apprehend the great work of the Gospel, or the refuge of a man who has failed to do it. Its evils are endless. It makes a fantastic Christianity. It keeps us battering at one point in the long citadel of sin and lets the enemy safely concentrate all his force there to protect it. It robs us of all power of large appeal and confines the truth which we preach to some small class of people. It makes us exalt the means above the end, till we come to count the means precious, whether it attain the end or not. That is the death which many a parish life has died. As George Herbert has it,

> What wretchedness can give him any room
> Whose house is foul while he adores his broom?

But finally, and worst of all, the passion for expedients and panaceas narrows our standards of Christian life, and gives us false tests of what are Christians. It is possible to come to think that there can be no conversion in a rented pew; and that God will not hear the music of a choir, however devoutly it bears the praises of the people up to Him. Beware of hobbies. Fasten yourself to the center of your ministry; not to some point on its circumference. The circumference must move when the center moves.

The escape from the slavery of expedients is not in finding each one insufficient, and so changing it for another. The escape from despotism is never in a mere change of despots.

Some men's ministry has been occupied all through in the substitution of hobby for hobby year after year. Their history is made up of the record of the dynasties of successive expedients, following each other like the later emperors, each murdering his predecessor and murdered in his turn.

The escape must come in a larger human life for the minister. He must come into larger knowledge of men, and be in the truest and best sense a man of the world. He must get out of the merely ecclesiastical spirit; that is, he must cease to think of the church as a petty institution, to be carried on by fantastic methods of its own. It must seem to him what it is, the type and pattern of what humanity ought to be, so to be kept large enough that any man, coming from any exile where the homesickness of his heart has been awakened, may find his true and native place awaiting him. The preacher then will know all kinds of men, keeping his life large enough to enter into sympathy with them.

Let me make one special remark upon this head. Apart from its incidental advantage, to his style and manner, I think it is good, for a minister to do some work besides clerical work, and to write something besides sermons. But he must do it as a minister. And the proof of how large is his vocation, is that he can do it and yet be a minister in it all. He can write books, and yet be not a literary man but a minister. He can help the government, and yet be not a politician but a minister. There are bad ways, but there are also good ways in which a clergyman may carry his clerical character with him wherever he goes. It may be to your discredit, or to your credit, that strangers say of you, "I should know he was a minister." For the best minister is simply the fullest man. You cannot separate him from his manhood. Voltaire said of Louis XIV, "He was not one of the greatest men but certainly one of the greatest kings that ever lived." It would not be possible to say that of any minister. He who was one of the greatest of ministers must be one of the greatest of men.

Success in the Ministry

The faults of a minister's method are apt to be of the simplest sort; as his virtues are of no intricate or complicated kind, but the primary virtues of humanity. I cannot then pass by what, after all, has seemed to me to lie at the bottom of a very large part of the clerical failures and half-successes which I have witnessed. What is called a "success" in the ministry is, indeed, a curious sort of phenomenon, very hard to analyze. It is half clay, half gold. It is half secular and half religious, and the two halves are mingled so that it is impossible to separate them. There is too much of religious feeling in our communities to call a minister successful unless he seems to be doing a really spiritual work, and on the other hand there is too steady a watch kept upon economical considerations, to give the praise of success to mere spiritual devotion, unless it carries with it the signs of material prosperity.

The "successful minister" is a being of such mingled qualities that he leaves open room enough for many men who are not called successful, to be thoroughly good and nobly useful and very happy. But still this standard of success has its advantages. It is intelligible. And it brings at once forward the simplest of all causes of failure, and shows it to be the same that brings failure in every department of life. That cause is mere unfaithfulness, the fact of men not doing their best with the powers that God has given them. I think that it is hard to believe how common this trouble, underlying all troubles, is in the minister's life. I want to urge it upon you very earnestly.

While Some Fail: Unfaithfulness

You watch the career of some man who does not seem to succeed. You know his piety; you recognize his intelligence; you make all kinds of elaborate theories about what there is in his peculiar character that unfits him for effectiveness; you dwell on his fastidiousness, his reserve, the wonderful sensitiveness of his nature. You picture him to yourself writing exquisite sermons, full of thought, which the people are too coarse to comprehend. And then, with this picture of him in your mind, you come to know the habits of his life, and all your fine-spun pity scatters as you learn that, whatever other hindrances there may be, the hindrance that lies uppermost of all is that the man is not doing his best. His work is at loose ends; he treats his people with a neglect with which no doctor could treat his patients and no lawyer his clients; and he writes his sermons on Saturday nights. That last I count the crowning disgrace of a man's ministry. It is dishonest. It is giving but the last flicker of the week as it sinks in its socket, to those who, simply to talk about it as a bargain, have paid for the full light burning at its brightest. And yet men boast of it. They tell you in how short time they write their sermons, and when you hear them preach you only wonder that it took so long.

Ah! my friends, it is wonderful what a central power is the moral law. The primary fact of duty lies at the core of everything. Operations which we think have no moral character, move by the power which is coiled up in that spring. Derange it in any man, and his taste becomes corrupted, and his intellect suffers distortion. The first necessity for the preacher and the hod-carrier is the same. Be faithful, and do your best always for every congregation, and on every occasion.[1]

A very curious study in human nature is the way in which the moral sense sometimes suffers in connection with the highest spiritual experiences. A man who will cheat nowhere else will be a hypocrite in religion. A man who really wants to convert his brethren will sometimes try to do it by preaching other people's sermons as if they were his own. It is partly, I suppose, the vague sense of elevation which seems to have somewhat enfeebled the hold of the ordinary morality upon a man, as the earth's gravitation weakens for him who mounts among the stars. And in some men it is that demoralization which comes from feeling themselves in a place for which they are not fit, burdened with duties for which they have no capacity. And that, in political, or commercial, or clerical life, is the most demoralizing consciousness that a man can feel.

The Importance of Faithfulness

This question of faithfulness touches, I believe, almost all the difficulties in the way of constraint or dictation which a minister meets with from his people. I am apt to believe that

---

1. An unknown friend has called my attention to these good words of Cotton Mather, since this lecture was delivered. They are from *Ratio Disciplinae*, pp. 59 and 60.

"If churches hear of ministers boasting that they have been in their studies only a few hours on Saturday, or so, they reckon that such persons rather glory in their shame.

"Sudden sermons they may sometimes admire from their accomplished ministers, when the suddenness has not been a chosen circumstance. But as one of old, when it was objected against his public speeches (in matters of less moment than the salvation of souls), replied, 'I should blush at the incivility of treating so great and wise a people with anything but what shall be studied;' so the best ministers of New England ordinarily would blush to address their flocks without premeditation."

almost all the troubles between ministers and parishes are from the minister's folly if not from his fault. Not that there is not often enough blame upon the other side. But it seems to me reasonable that the minister, having an intense and more concentrated interest in his parish than any layman has, should have that measure of control which, wisely used, might hinder almost any trouble before it grew vigorous enough to enlist the angry interest of the people whose lives are largely occupied with other things.

There are such things as parish quarrels. If I am right, my friends, you will never have one in your parish which you might not have prevented, and never come out of one without injury to your character and your Master's cause. It is wonderful to me with what freedom a minister is left to do his work in his own way, if only his people believe in his scrupulous faithfulness.

Take, for instance, the matter of preaching old sermons. It is not good. A new sermon, fresh from the brain, has always a life in it which an old sermon, though better in itself, must lack. The trouble is in the prominence of that personal element in preaching of which I spoke in my first lecture. You may take the sermon off the shelf, and when you have brushed the dust off the cover it is the same sermon that you preached on that memorable day when you were all afire with your new line of study or with the spiritual zeal that was burning about you. You may reproduce the paper but you cannot reproduce the man, and the sermon was man and paper together. No, I would make as rare as possible the preaching of the same sermon to the same people. But what I wanted to say was this, that the main objection which the people have to the preaching of old sermons is in the impression that it gives them of unfaithfulness and idleness. Let a minister's whole life make any such suspicion impossible and there is no complaint.

The minister in whose faithfulness his people believe may use his own discretion. He must not play any tricks. He must not put old sermons to new texts. To put new sermons to old texts is better. But he may use his judgment, and those sermons, of which there is a certain class, which do not lose but rather gain by repetition, he may reproach again and again till they grow to be to people like their most cherished hymns or passages from some long-loved book of devotion.

Developing Good Habits

One of the most remarkable things about the preacher's methods of work is the way in which they form themselves in the earliest years of his ministry, and then rule him with almost despotic power to the end. I am a slave today, and so I suppose is every minister, to ways of work that were made within two or three years after beginning to preach. The newness of the occupation, that unexpectedness of everything to which I alluded when I began to speak to you this afternoon, opens all the life, and makes it receptive; and then the earnestness and fresh enthusiasm of those days serves to set the habits that a man makes them, to clothe them with something that is almost sacredness, and to make them practically almost unchangeable.

They are the years when a preacher needs to be very watchful over his discretion and his independence. When the clay is in the bank, it matters not so much who treads on it. And when the clay is hardened in the vase, it may press close upon another vase and yet keep its own shape. But when the clay is just setting, and the shape still soft, then is the time to guard it from the blows or pressures that would distort it forever. Be sure, then, that the habits and methods of your opening ministry are, first of all, your own. Let no respect, however profound or merited, for any hero of the pulpit make you submit yourself to him.

Let your own nature freely shape its own ways. Only be sure that those ways do really come out of your own nature, and not out of the merely accidental circumstances of your first parish. And let them be intelligent, not merely such as you happen into, but such as you can give good reasons for. And let them be noble, framed with reference to the large ideal and most sacred purposes of your work, not with reference to its minute conveniences. And let them be broad enough to give you room to grow.

It is with ideas and methods of work as it is with houses. To remove from one to another is wasteful and dispiriting; but to find the one in which we have taken up our abode unfolding new capacity to accommodate our growing mental family, is satisfactory and encouraging. It gives us the sense at once of settlement and progress. He is the happiest and most effective old man whose life has been full of growth, but free from revolution; who is living still in the same thoughts and habits which he had when a boy, but has found them as the Hebrews say that the Israelites found their clothes in the desert during the forty years, not merely never waxing old upon them, but growing with their growth as they passed on from youth to manhood.

I hope that I shall not have disappointed your expectation in what I have said about the preacher's methods by dwelling so largely upon principles, and going so little into details. It would be easy enough for any minister to amuse himself, and perhaps amuse you, by recitations from his diary. But it would not be good. I want to make you know two things: first, that if your ministry is to be good for anything, it must be your ministry, and not a feeble echo of any other man's; and, second, that the Christian ministry is not the mere practice of a set of rules and precedents, but is a broad, free, fresh meeting of a man with men, in such close contact that the Christ who has entered into his life may, through his, enter into theirs.

The Spirit of the Preacher

I have but a few words to add upon the spirit in which the preacher does his best work. After what I have been saying, my points will need no elaboration. Forgive me if I venture to put them in the simplest and strongest imperatives I can command.

First, *count and rejoice to count yourself the servant of the people* to whom you minister. Not in any worn-out figure but in very truth, call yourself and be their servant.

Second, *never allow yourself to feel equal to your work.* If you ever find that spirit growing on you, be afraid, and instantly attack your hardest piece of work, try to convert your toughest infidel, or try to preach on your most exacting theme, to show yourself how unequal to it all you are.

Third, *be profoundly honest.* Never dare to say in the pulpit or in private, through ardent excitement or conformity to what you know you are expected to say, one word which at the moment when you say it, you do not believe. It would cut down the range of what you say, perhaps, but it would endow every word that was left with the force of ten.

And last of all, *be vital, be alive, not dead.* Do everything that can keep your vitality at its fullest. Even the physical vitality do not dare to disregard. One of the most striking preachers of our country seems to me to have a large part of his power simply in his physique, in the impression of vitality, in the magnetism almost like a material thing, that passes between him and the people who sit before him. Pray for and work for fulness of life above everything; full red blood in the body; full honesty and truth in the mind; and the fulness of a grateful love for the Savior in your heart. Then, however men set their mark of failure or success upon your ministry, you cannot fail, you must succeed.

4

THE IDEA OF THE SERMON

I have dwelt long upon the preacher and his character because he is essential to the sermon. He cannot throw a sermon forth into the world as an author can his book, as an artist can his statue, and let it live thenceforth a life wholly independent of himself. That is the reason why sermons are not ordinarily interesting reading. At least that is one of the reasons. Now and then you do find a volume of sermons which, as it were, keep their author in them, so that as you read them you feel him present in the room. But, ordinarily, reading sermons is like listening to an echo. The words are there, but the personal intonation is gone out of them and there is an unreality about it all. Now and then you find sermons which do not suggest their ever having been preached and they give you none of this feeling. But they were not good sermons, scarcely even real sermons, when they were preached. In general it is true that the sermon which is good to preach is poor to read and the sermon which is good to read is poor to preach. There are exceptions, but this is generally true.

Whatever is in the sermon must be in the preacher first; clearness, logicalness, vivacity, earnestness, sweetness, and light must be personal qualities in him before they are qualities of thought and language in what he utters to his people. If you have your artist you have only to supply your marble and chisel with the mere technical skill, and you have your statue. If you have your preacher very little more is needed to set free the sermon which is in him. In this lecture and the next I want want to speak about the sermon. I make a division which will not be very precise, but may be of some service; and shall speak today more of the sermon in its general purpose and idea, and next Thursday more of the make and method of the sermon.

Persuasion, Not Art

It seems to me, then, that at the very outset the definite and immediate purpose which a sermon has set before it makes it impossible to consider it as a work of art, and every attempt to consider it so works injury to the purpose for which the sermon was created. Many of the ineffective sermons that are made owe their failure to a blind and fruitless effort to produce something which shall be a work of art, conforming to some type or pattern which is not clearly understood but is supposed to be essential and eternal. But the unreasonableness of this appears the moment that we think of it.

A sermon exists in and for its purpose. That purpose is the persuading and moving of men's souls. That purpose must never be lost sight of. If it ever is, the sermon flags. It is not always on the surface; not always impetuous and eager in the discourses of the settled pastor as it is in the appeals of the evangelist who speaks this once and this once only to the men he sees before him. The sermon of the habitual preacher grows more sober, but it never can lose out of it this consciousness of a purpose; it never can justify itself in any self-indulgence that will hinder or delay that purpose. It is always aimed at men. It is always looking in their faces to see how they are moved. It knows no essential and eternal type, but its law for what it ought to be comes from the needs and fickle changes of the men for whom it lives.

Now this is thoroughly inartistic. Art contemplates and serves the absolute beauty. The simple work of art is the pure utterance of beautiful thought in beautiful form without further purpose than simply that it should be uttered. The poem or the statue may instruct, inspire, and rebuke men, but that design, if it were present in the making of the poem or the statue, vitiated the purity of its artistic quality. Art knows nothing of the tumultuous eagerness of earnest purpose. She is supremely calm and independent of the whims of men. Phidias cast among a barbarous race must carve not some hideous idol which shall stir their coarse blood by its frantic extravagance, but the same serene and lofty beauty of Athene which he would carve at Athens. If it wholly fails to reach their gross and blunted senses, that is no disgrace to it as a work of art, for the artistic and the didactic are separate from one another.

And yet we find a constant tendency in the history of preaching to treat the sermon as a work of art. It is spoken of as if it were something which has a value in itself. We hear of beautiful sermons, as if they existed solely on the ground that "beauty is its own excuse for being." The age of the great French preachers, the age of Louis XIV, with its sermons preached in the salons of critical and skeptical noblemen, and of ladies who offered to their friends the entertainment of the last discovered preacher, was full of this false idea of the sermon as a work of art. And the soberer Englishmen, whether he be the Puritan praising the painful exposition to which he has just listened, or the churchman delighting in the polished periods of Tillotson or South, has his own way of falling into the same heresy.

I think it does us good to go back to the simple sermons of the New Testament. I do not speak of the perfect discourses of our Lord, though in them we should find the strongest confirmation of what I am now saying: but take the sermons of St. Peter, of St. Stephen, of St. Paul, and from them come down to the sermons which have been great as sermons ever since. Through all their variety you find this one thing constantly true about them: they were all valuable solely for the work they could accomplish. They were tools, and not works of art.

To turn a tool into a work of art, to elaborate the shape and chase the surface of the axe with which you are to hew your wood, is bad taste; and to give any impression in a sermon that it has forgotten its purpose and been shaped for anything else than which in the largest extent of those great words might be described as saving souls, makes it offensive to a truly good taste and dull to the average man, who feels an incongruity which he cannot define. The power of the sermons of the Paulist fathers in the Romish Church and of Mr. Moody in Protestantism lies simply here, in the clear and undisturbed presence of their purpose; and many ministers who never dream of such a thing, who think that they are preaching purely for the good of souls, are losing the power out of their sermons because they are trying, even without knowing it, to make them not only sermons, but works of art. There was an old word which I think has ceased to be used. Men used to talk of "sermonizing." They said that some good preacher was "a fine sermonizer." The word contained just this vice: it made the sermon an achievement, to be attempted and enjoyed for itself apart from anything that it could do, like a picture or an oratorio, like the Venus of Milo or the Midsummer-night's Dream.

Sermon Must Be Understood

And here lies the truth concerning the way in which really high truth and careful thought may be brought to a congregation. We hear a good deal about preaching over people's heads. There is such a thing. But generally it is not the character of the ammunition, but the fault of aim, that makes the missing shot. There is nothing worse for a preacher than to come to think that, he must preach down to people; that they cannot take the very best he has to give. He grows to despise his own sermons, and the people quickly learn to sympathize with their minister. The people will get the heart out of the most thorough and thoughtful sermon, if only it really is a sermon. Even subtlety of thought, the tracing of intricate relations of ideas, it is remarkable how men of no subtle thought will follow it, if it is really preached. But subtlety which has delighted in itself, which has spun itself fine for its own pleasure in seeing how fine it could be spun, vexes and throws them off; and they are right. Never be afraid to call upon your people to follow your best thought, if only it is really trying to lead them somewhere. The confidence of the minister in the people is at the bottom of every confidence of the people in the minister.

What I have been saying bears also on what we hear, every now and then, from the days of the "Spectator" down, the expression of a wish that moderate ministers, instead of giving people their own moderate thought, would recur to the good work which has been already done, and read some sermon of one of the great masters. There too, there is the "sermonizing" idea. The real sermon idea is lost. Such a practice coming into vogue would speedily destroy the pulpit's power. Not merely would it be a confession of incapacity, but the idea of speech, of present address for a present purpose, would disappear. I do not think we could anticipate any continual interest, scarcely any perpetual existence for the preaching work in case such an idea became prevalent and accepted.

Freedom From Modeling

The first good consequence of the emphatic statement that a sermon is to be considered solely with reference to its proper purposes will be in a new and larger freedom for the preacher. We make the idea of a sermon too specific, wishing to conform it to some preestablished type of what a sermon ought to be. There is nothing which a sermon ought to be except a fit medium of truth to men. There is no model of a sermon so strange and novel, so different from every pattern upon which sermons have been shaped before, that if it became evident to you that that was the form through which your message which you had to tell would best reach the men to whom you had to tell it, it would not be your right, nay, be your duty to preach your truth in that new form.

I grant that the accepted forms of preaching were shaped originally by a desire of utility, and only gradually assumed a secondary value and importance for their own sakes. That is the way in which every such superstitious value of anything originates. I grant, therefore, that the young preacher may well feel that a certain presumption of advantage belongs to those types of sermons which he finds in use. He will not wantonly depart from them. I am sure that all hearers of sermons will say: "Better the most abject conformity to rule than departure from rule for the mere sake of departure. Better the stiff movements of imitation than the fantastic gestures of deliberate originality." But what I plead for is, that in all your desire to create good sermons you should think no sermon good that does not do its work. Let the end for which you preach play freely in and modify the form of your preaching. He who is original for the sake of originality is as much governed by the type from which he departs as is another man who slavishly conforms to it; but he who freely uses the types which he finds, and yet compels them always to bend to the purposes for which he uses them, he is their true master, and not their slave. Such originality as that alone at once secures the best effectiveness of the preachers, and advances at the same time the general type and idea of the sermon, preserving it from monotony and making it better and better from age to age.

Now let me turn to some of those questions affecting the general idea of what a sermon ought to be, which are continually recurring, and say a few words on each.

Common Sermon Types

One of the most interesting of those questions, which appears in many forms, arises from the necessity of which I have already so much spoken, of mingling the elements of personal influence and abstract truth to make the perfect sermon. There are some sermons in which the preacher does not appear at all; there are other sermons in which he is offensively and crudely prominent; there are still other sermons which he is hidden and yet felt, the force of his personal conviction and earnest love being poured through the arguments which he uses, and the promises which he holds out.

Autobiographical Sermons

Of the second class of sermons, in which the minister's personality is offensively prominent, the most striking instance is what seems to me to have become rather common of late, and what I may call the autobiographical style of preaching. There are some preachers to whom one might listen for a year, and then he could write their biography, if it were worth the doing. Every truth they wish to teach is illustrated by some event in their own history. Every change of character which they wish to urge is set forth under the form in which that change took place in them. The story of how they were converted becomes as familiar to their congregation as the story of the conversion of St. Paul. It is the crudest attempt to blend personality and truth. They are not fused with one another, but only tied together.

It has a certain power. It is wonderful how interesting almost any man becomes if he talks frankly about himself. You cannot help listening to the garrulous unfolding of his history. And in the pulpit no doubt it gives a certain vividness, when a popular preacher whose people are already interested in, and curious about his personality, after enforcing some argument, suddenly turns, and instead of saying, after the pulpit manner, "But the objector will reply," briskly breaks out with, "Last Monday afternoon a man came into my study," or "A man met me in the street and said, Mr., this or that" (using his own name), "what do you make of this objection?" It gives a clear concreteness to the whole, and feeds that curiosity about each other's ways of living out of which all our gossip grows.

The evils of the habit are evident enough. Not to speak of its oppressiveness to the best taste, nor of the way in which its power dies out, as the much-paraded person of the minister grows familiar and unimposing, it certainly must have a tendency to narrow the suggested range of Christian truth and experience. In parishes where such strong prominence belongs to the preacher's personality, where the people are always hearing of how he learned this truth or passed through that emotion, all apprehension of thought and realization of experience narrows itself. It is expected in just that way which has been so often and so vividly pictured. It is distrusted if it comes in other forms. The rich variety and largeness of the Christian life is lost. There are some parishes which, in the course of a long pastorate, have become but the colossal repetition of their minister's personality. They are the form of his experience seen through a mist, grown large in size but vague and dim in outline. Every parishioner is a weakened repetition of the minister's ideas and ways.

I think that what a minister learns to rejoice in more and more is the endless difference of that Christian life, which is yet always the same. It shows him the possibility of a Christianity as universal as humanity, a Christianity in which the diversity and unity of humanity might both be kept. And any undue prominence of himself in his teaching loses the largeness on which the hope of this variety in unity depends.

Blending Preacher and Truth

There is something better than this. There is a fine and subtle infusion of a man into his work, which achieves what this crude fastening of the two together attempts, but fails to accomplish. Take, for instance, the sermons of Robertson. You will know, from allusions to them which I have already made, that I sympathize very fully with that high estimate which such multitudes of people have set upon those remarkable discourses. I think that in all the best qualities of preaching they stand supreme among the sermons of our time. And one of the most remarkable things about them is the way in which the personal force of the preacher, and the essential power of the truth, are blended into one strong impressiveness. The personality never muddies the thought.

I do not remember one allusion to his own history, one anecdote of his own life; but they are *his* sermons. The thought is stronger for us because he has thought it. The feeling is more vivid because he has felt it. And always he leads us to God by a way along which he has gone himself.

It is interesting to read along with the sermons the story of his life, to see what he was passing through at the date when this sermon or that was preached, and to watch, as you often may, without any suspicion of mere fancifulness, how the experience shed its power into the sermon, but left its form of facts outside; how his sermons were like the heaven of his life, in which the spirit of its life lived after it had cast away its body.

Tempering the Experiential

There have, indeed, been preachers and writers whose utterance of truth has fallen naturally in the forms of autobiography, and yet who have been at once strong and broad. You can gather all of Latimer's history out of his sermons, and Milton has given us a large part of his teaching in connection with the events of his own life. But ordinarily that is true in literature, and certainly in preaching which is true in life. It is not the man who forces the events of his life on you who most puts the spirit of his life into you. The most unreserved men are not the most influential. A reserved man who cares for truth, and cares that his brethren should know the truth, who therefore is always holding back the mere envelope of accident and circumstance in which the truth has embodied itself to him, and yet sending forth the truth with all the clearness and force which it has gathered for him from that embodiment, he is the best preacher, as everywhere he is the most influential man.

Try to live such a life, so full of events and relationships that the two great things, the power of Christ and the value of your brethren's souls, shall be tangible and certain to you; not subjects of speculation and belief, but realities which you have seen and known; then sink the shell of personal experience, lest it should hamper the truth that you must utter, and let the truth go out as the shot goes, carrying the force of the gun with it, but leaving the gun behind.

Sharing With a Congregation

There is something beautiful to me in the way in which

the utterance of the best part of a man's own life, its essence, its result, which the pulpit makes possible, and even tempts, is welcomed by many men, who seem to find all other utterance of themselves impossible. I have known shy, reserved men, who, standing in their pulpits, have drawn back before a thousand eyes veils that were sacredly closed when only one friend's eyes could see. You might talk with them a hundred times, and you would not learn so much of what they were as if you once heard them preach. It was partly the impersonality of the great congregation. Humanity, without the offence of individuality, stood there before them. It was no violation of their loyalty to themselves to tell their secret to mankind. It was a man who silenced them. But also, besides this, it was, I think, that the sight of many waiting faces set free in them a new, clear knowledge of what their truth or secret was, unsnarled it from the petty circumstances into which it had been entangled, called it first into clear consciousness, and then tempted it into utterance with an authority which they did not recognize in an individual curiosity demanding the details of their life.

Our race, represented in a great assemblage, has more authority and more beguilement for many of us than the single man, however near he be. And he who is silent before the interviewer pours out the very depths of his soul to the great multitude. He will not print his diary for the world to read, but he will tell his fellow men what Christ may be to them, so that they shall see, as God sees, what Christ has been to him.

Speculation and Frankness

I think, again, that this first truth of preaching, the truth that the minister enters into the sermon, touches upon the point of which I spoke in my last sermon the authority of the sermon. The sermon is God's message sent by you to certain of your fellow men. If the message came to your fellow men just as it came from God it must be absolutely true and must have absolute authority. If the fallible messenger mixes himself with his infallible message, the absolute authority of the message is in some degree qualified. But we have seen that the very idea of the sermon implies that the messenger must mingle himself with the message that he brings; and, as a mere matter of fact, we *know* that every preacher does declare the truth from his own point of view and follows his own judgment, enlightened by his study and his prayer, when he declares how the eternal truth applies to temporary circumstances. Some things which you say from the pulpit you know; other things are your speculations. This is true very largely of the anticipations and prophecies about the destiny of the Gospel, about the relations which the Gospel holds to the circumstances of special times in which ministers indulge.

John Wesley used to say that "infidels know, whether Christians know it or not, that the giving up witchcraft is in effect giving up the Bible." When we were children it used to be preached to us that the Bible must stand or fall with human slavery. And now we hear continually that this or that will happen to religion if such or such a theory of natural science should be accepted. Such prophecies are always bad. Tests which are not essential and absolute tests do great harm. But these are instances of the way in which speculations, personal opinions, prejudices, if you will, must attach themselves to any live man's utterance of the truth.

It is inevitable; and what must be the result? Either all speculation must be cut away and the sermon be reduced to the mere repetition of indisputable and undisputed truth; and the mere primary facts of Christianity which alone are held absolutely *semper, ubique et ab omnibus* must make the sum of preaching; or else the preacher must let the people clearly understand that between the facts that are his message and the philosophy of those facts which is his best and truest judgment there is a clear distinction. The first come with the authority of God's revelation. The others come with what persuasion their essential reasonableness gives them. Now the first method is impracticable. No man ever did it. No man who claims to preach nothing but the simple Gospel preaches it so simply that it has not in it something of his own speculation about it.

The other method is the only method. Even St. Paul came to it in his epistles. But how few preachers frankly adopt it! We cover all we say—our crude guesses, our ignorant anticipations—with a certain vague and undefined authority; and men, hearing themselves called on to believe them all, and seeing part of them to be untrue, really believe none of them in any genuine or hearty way. We stretch our authority to try to make it cover so much that it grows thin and will not decently cover anything at all.

Frankness is what we need, frankness to say, "This is God's truth, and this other is what I think." If we were frank like that, see what good things would come. The minister would have room for intellectual change and growth, and not have to steal them as if they were something to which he had no right. The people could hear many men preach, and hear them differ from each other, and yet not be bewildered and confounded. And every preacher, with the clearly recognized right, would have to accept the duty of being a thinker in the things of God.

The Doctrine Controversy

One of the most interesting questions which meet us as we try to form an idea of what the sermon ought to be, is that suggested by the occasional or constant outcry against the preaching of doctrine, and the call for practical sermons, or for what is called "preaching Christ only." Let me speak of this. I do not hold that the outcry is absurd. I do not think that it is one to which the preacher ought to shut his ears. It is a very blind and unintelligent cry, no doubt. All popular outcries are that. Every popular movement and demand has in general the same history. It begins with a vague discontent that never even attempts to give an account of what it means, and it passes on into three different manifestations of itself; one, an honest attempt by its own adherents to declare its philosophy and give an intelligible reason for it; another, an effort by those who dislike it to misrepresent and to defame it; and third, the adoption of its phrases by people who care little about it but like to affect an interest in whatever is uppermost. In this last stage the popular movement becomes a fashionable cant. There never was a stir and dissatisfaction, a dislodging and outreaching of men's minds which did not show itself in all these forms.

This current dissatisfaction with what is called doctrinal preaching appears in all three. At the bottom it is a discontent with something that the souls of men feel to be wrong. Then comes the endeavor of men to state the grievance, which is often very foolishly done, and would, if carried out, sweep away everything like positive Christianity together. Then comes the misrepresentation of the popular demand, which talks about it as if it all came of the spirit of indifference or unbelief. And then finally succeeds that which is the lowest degradation to which anything which might be an intelligent opinion can be reduced, the affectation which pretends to be in horror at anything like dogmatism, and repeats without meaning the praises of an undogmatic preaching.

Now the minister meets all of these. What shall he do? It is easy enough for him to expose the illogical reasoning, easy for him to see its misconceptions, easy for him to despise its cant, but it ought not to be easy for him to shut his ears to that out of which they all come, that deep, blind, unintelligent discontent with something which is evidently wrong. He must bring his intelligence to bear on that. It cannot tell what it means itself. He must find out what it means, and not be deterred by the offensiveness of any of its exhibitions from a careful understanding of its true significance.

For it does mean something, and what it means is this: that men who are looking for a law of life and an inspiration of life are met by a theory of life. Much of our preaching is like delivering lectures upon medicine to sick people. The lecture is true. The lecture is interesting. Nay, the truth of the lecture is important, and if the sick man could learn the truth of the lecture he would be a better patient, he would take his medicine more responsibly and regulate his diet more intelligently. But still the fact remains that the lecture is not medicine, and that to give the medicine, not to deliver the lecture, is the preacher's duty. I know the delusiveness of such an analogy. Let us not urge it too far; but let us own that the idea which has haunted the religious life of man, and which is not true, has had a serious and bad effect on preaching. That idea is that the tenure of certain truths, and not the possession of a certain character, is a saving thing. It is the notion that faith consists in the believing of propositions. Let that heresy be active or latent in a preacher's mind, and he inevitably falls into the vice which people complain of when they talk about doctrinal preaching. He declares truth for its own value and not with direct reference to its result in life.

It is not my place to argue here that the idea of faith from which such preaching comes is not the scriptural idea, not the idea of Jesus. But it does come within my region to point out the influence that a man's first idea of saving faith must have upon his whole conception of a sermon. The preacher who thinks that faith is the holding of truth must ever be aiming to save men from believing error and to bring them to the knowledge of what is true. The man who thinks that faith is personal loyalty must always be trying to bring men to Christ and Christ to men. Which is the true idea? That, as I said, it is not for me to discuss. But I may beg you to consider seriously what the faith was that Christ longed so to see in His disciples, and what that faith must be whose "trial" of education St. Peter says "is much more precious than of gold that perishes." Such words as those carry us inevitably into the realm of character, which we know is the one thing in man which God values and for which Christ labored and lived and died.

This does seem to me to make the truth about the preaching of doctrine very plain. The salvation of men's souls from sin, the renewing and perfecting of their characters, is the great end of all. But that is done by Christ. To bring them, then, to Christ, that He may do it, to make Christ plain to them, that they may find Him, this is the preacher's work. But I cannot do my duty in making Christ plain unless I tell them of Him all the richness that I know. I must keep nothing back. All that has come to me about Him from His Word, all that has grown clear to me about His nature or His methods by my inward or outward experience, all that He has told me of Himself, becomes part of the message that I must tell to those men whom He has sent me to call home to Himself. I will do this in its fulness. And this is the preaching of doctrine, positive, distinct, characteristic Christian truth. Only the truth has always character beyond it as its ulterior purpose. Not until I forget that, and begin to tell men about Christ as if that they should know the truth about Him, and not that they should become what knowing the truth about Him would help them be, were the final purpose of my preaching—not until then do I begin to preach doctrine in the wrong way which men are trying to describe when they talk about "doctrinal preaching."

The truth is, no preaching ever had any strong power that was not the preaching of doctrine. The preachers that have moved and held men have always preached doctrine. No exhortation to a good life that does not put behind it some truth as deep as eternity can seize and hold the conscience. Preach doctrine, preach all the doctrine that you know, and learn forever more and more; but preach it always not that men may believe it; but that men may be saved by believing it. So it shall be live, not dead. So men shall rejoice in it and not decry it. So they shall feed on it at your hands as on the bread of life, solid and sweet, and claiming for itself the appetite of man which God made for it.

The Sermon: A Harmonious Blend

I am inclined to think that the idea of a sermon is so properly a unit, that a sermon involves of necessity such elements in combination, the absence of any one of which weakens the sermon-nature, that the ordinary classifications of sermons are of little consequence. We hear of expository preaching and topical sermons, of practical sermons, or hortatory discourses, each separate species seeming to stand by itself. It seems as if the preacher were expected to determine each week what kind of sermon the next Sunday was to enjoy and set himself deliberately to produce it. It may be well, but I say frankly that to my mind the sermon seems a unit, and that no sermon seems complete that does not include all these elements, and that the attempt to make a sermon of one sort alone mangles the idea and produces a one-sided thing.

One element will preponderate in every sermon according to the nature of the subject that is treated, and the structure of the sermon will vary according as you choose to announce for it a topic or to make it a commentary upon some words of Christ or His apostles. But the mere preponderance of one element must not exclude the others, and the difference of forms does not really make a difference of sermons. The preaching which is wholly exposition men are apt to find dull and pointless. It is heat lightning that quivers over many topics but strikes nowhere. The preaching that is the discussion of a topic may be interesting, but it grows unsatisfactory because it does not fasten itself to the authority of Scripture. It tempts the preacher's genius and invention, but is apt to send people away with a feeling that they have heard him more than they have heard God. The sermon which only argues is almost sure to argue in vain, and the sermon which only exhorts is like a man who blows the wood and coal to which he has not first put a light. Either is incomplete alone; but to supplement each by the other in another sermon is certainly a very crude, imperfect way to meet the difficulty. It is better to start by feeling that every sermon must have:

- a solid rest on Scripture
- the pointedness which comes of a clear subject

- the conviction which belongs to well-thought argument, and
- the warmth that proceeds from earnest appeal.

I spoke of vagueness as the fault that most of all attended what is ordinarily called expository preaching. Besides this, there is the other fault of narrow view. I know that fault does not belong to it of necessity. I know that the expositor may refuse to become the mere ingenious interpreter of texts and the distiller of partial doctrines out of one petal of a great book or argument which is a symmetrical flower. He may insist on taking in the purpose of the whole Epistle as he comments upon one isolated chapter. He may claim light from the manifold radiance of the whole New Testament to let him see the meaning of a doubtful verse. But we all know the danger of the mere expositor of any book, whether that book be Shakespeare or the Bible. There is no reason why, in the Bible as in Shakespeare, the minute study of parts should not be dangerous to the conception of the whole. The same powers and the same weaknesses of the human mind are present in the sacred study as in what we call the profane study. The escape is not in the abandonment of minute and faithful study, but in the careful preservation of the larger purpose and spirit of the work.

Our literature abounds in illustrations of the difference. Compare the noble and vivid pages of Dean Stanley's *Jewish Church* with the labor of the ordinary textual commentator, and which is the true expositor of the Old Testament? The larger view in which the poetry and the essential truth reside comes in the attempt to grasp the topic of the whole. And so that preaching which most harmoniously blends in the single sermon all these varieties of which men make their classifications—the preaching which is strong in its appeal to authority, wide in its grasp of truth, convincing in the appeal to reason, and earnest in its address to the conscience and the heart, all of these at once—that preaching comes nearest to the type of the apostolical epistles, is the most complete and so the most powerful approach of truth to the whole man; and so is the kind of preaching which, with due freedom granted to our idiosyncrasies, it is best for us all to seek and educate.

Appealing to Heart, Conscience, and Reason

There is, indeed, another classification of sermons which

often occurs to me and which I think is not without its use. It belongs not to the mere form which a sermon takes, but to the side on which it approaches and undertakes to convince the human mind. Every reality of God may be recognized by us in its beauty, its righteousness, or its usefulness. I may see, for instance, of God's justice, either the absolute beauty of it, may stand in awe before it as the perfect utterance of the perfect nature, may desire to come near to it as the most majestic thing in the whole universe, may love it solely for itself, or I may be possessed with the relations which it holds to my own moral nature. It may impress me not so much as a quality in God as a relationship between God's life and mine. It may fill me with a sense of sin, make me realize temptation, and stir the depths of moral struggle in my life. Or, yet again, I may realize that justice as the regulative power of the universe, see how conformity to it means peace and prosperity from center to circumference of this vast order. I may rejoice in it not for what it is but for what it does. Of these three conceptions of God's justice, one appeals to the soul and its intuitions of eternal fitness, the second to the conscience and its knowledge of right and wrong, the third to the practical instinct with its love of visible achievement.

Now here we have the suggestions of three different sermons. The message which we have to bring is the same message, but we bring it to three different doors of the same manhood which it desires to enter. And one preacher will bring his message oftenest to one door, appealing mostly in his sermons to the soul, or to the conscience, or to the practical sense. And one congregation or one generation will have one door more open than the others, its circumstances in some way making it most approachable upon that side. Here is the free room for the personal differences of men to play within the great unity of the sermon idea.

Among the great French preachers there has always been drawn an evident distinction corresponding very nearly to this which I have defined. Massillon is the interpreter of the religious instinct, speaking to the heart. Bossuet is the preacher of dogma, appealing to the conscience. Bourdaloue is the preacher of morality, addressing himself to reason. Either of these sermons may be of the expository or of the topical sort. All of them are able to bring Christ in some one of His offices to men, as Priest, Prophet, or King. Each of them is capable of blending with another. There is no such distinction between

them that we may not find a great sermon here and there
where the three are met, and where Christ in His completeness
as the satisfaction of the loving heart, as the convicter and
guide of the awakened conscience, and as the hope and
inspiration of a laboring humanity, is perfectly set forth.
According to the largeness of your own Christian life will be
your power to preach that largest sermon. Only I beg you to
remember in what different ways sermons may all be
messages of the Lord. Let it save you from the monotonous
narrowness of one eternally repeated sermon. And, what is
far more important, let it keep you from ever daring to say
with cruel flippancy of some brother who brings his message
to another door of humanity from you, that he "does not
preach Christ."

Your Best Sermon

The best sermon of any time is the time's best utterance.
More than its most ingenious invention or its most highly
organized government, it declares the point which that time
has reached. So I think that a man's best sermon is the best
utterance of his life. It embodies and declares him. If it is
really his, it tells more of him than his casual intercourse
with his friends, or even the revelations of his domestic life.
If it is really God's message through him, it brings him out in
a way that no other experience of his life has power to do, as
the quality of the trumpet declares itself more clearly when
the strong man blows a blast for battle through it than when
a child whispers into it in play. Remember this, experience it
in yourself, and then, when you hear your brother preach,
honor the work that he is doing and listen as reverently as
you can to hear through him some voice of God. They say
that brother ministers make the most critical and least
responsive hearers. I have not found them so. I have found
them always fullest of sympathy. It would be much to their
discredit and excite serious suspicions of their work if their
mere familiarity with its details made them less ready to feel
its spirit and to submit to its power. It is not so. Do not begin
by thinking that it is so, and you will not find it so.

Approaching the Topics of Time

I should like to devote part of what time remains today to
some suggestions about the true subjects of sermons. I used a
few minutes ago the phrase "preaching Christ;" and, without

cant, it is Christ that we are to preach. But what is Christ? "The saving power of the world," we say. Where is His power, then, to reach? Wherever men are wrong; wherever men are capable of being better; wherever His authority and love can make them better. Wherever the abundance of sin has gone, there the abundance of grace must go. There you and I, as ministers of grace, are bound to carry it. I confess that at the very first statement of it this idea of Christ opens to me a range of the subjects, with which it is the preacher's duty and right to deal which seems to have no limit.

But let us go more into particulars. We hear today a great deal about how desirable it is that the pulpit, partly because it is, and partly that it may more fully be, a power, should deal more directly than it does with the special conditions of the time, with the special vices and the special needs of the days in which we live. It is urged that we ought to hear more often than we do now from our preachers concerning the right use of wealth, concerning the extravagance of society, concerning impurity and licentiousness, concerning the prevalent lack of thoroughness in our hurried life, concerning political corruption and misrule. I believe the claim is absolutely right. I believe no powerful pulpit ever held aloof from the moral life of the community it lived in, as the practice of many preachers, and the theory of some, would make our pulpit separate itself and confine its message to what are falsely discriminated as spiritual things.

But with regard to this interest of the pulpit in the moral conditions of the day, while I most heartily and even enthusiastically assert its necessity, I want to make one or two suggestions. The first is, that nowhere more than here ought the personal differences of ministers to be regarded. Some men's minds work abstractly, and others work concretely. One man sees sin as an awful, all-pervading spiritual presence; another cannot recognize sin unless he sees it incarnated in some special vicious act, which some man is doing here in his own town. One man owns holiness as an unseen spirit; to another, holiness is vague, but good deeds strike his enthusiasm and stir him to delight and imitation. Now, neither of these men must ask the other man to preach just in his way. The first man must not call the second a "mere moralist;" the second must not answer back by calling his accuser a "pietist." Granting that the preacher must attack the special sins around him, it is not true that every preacher, be the nature of his genius what it may, must be goaded and driven to it. It is good for us that there should be some men to preach, as it would not be well that all men should preach, of truth in its pure, invariable essence, and of duty in its primary idea, as it issues a yet undivided stream from the fountain of the will of God.

But again, the method in which the pulpit ought to approach the topics of the time is even more important. It seems to me to be involved, if we can find it there, in the perfectly commonplace and familiar statement that the visible, moral conditions of any life, or any age, are only symptoms of spiritual conditions which are the essential things. But what is the meaning and value of a symptom? Are there not two? A symptom is valuable, first as a sign and test of inward processes which it is impossible to observe directly, and it has a secondary value under the law of reaction, by which a wise restraint applied to the result may often tend to weaken and help destroy the cause. How, then, are symptoms to be treated? Always with reference to the unseen conditions which they manifest. They are to be examined as tests of what these conditions are, and they are to be acted upon, not for themselves, but in the hope of reaching those conditions in behind them.

Apply all this. You and I are preachers in the midst of a corrupt community. All kinds of evil practices are rife around us. We know—it is the first truth of the religion which we preach—that these evil practices are not the real essential evil. It is the heart estranged from God, the soul gone wrong, the unseen springs of manhood out of order, upon which our eye is always fastened, and to which alone we know the remedy can be applied. What have we, then, to do with these evil practices, which we see only as the outward and visible signs of an inward and spiritual disgrace? Just what I said above: First, honestly treat them as tests; honestly own that, so long as these exist, and wherever these exist, the spiritual condition is not right; frankly admit of any man, whatever his professions of emotional experience, whatever he believes, whatever he "feels," that if he does bad things he is not a good man. So cordially put the spiritual processes of which you preach within the judgment of all men who know a good life from a bad one. And in the second place strike at the symptom always for the sake of the disease. Aim at all kinds of vicious acts. Rebuke dishonesty, licentiousness, drunkenness, cruelty, extravagance, but always strike in the interest of the soul to which you are a messenger, of which your Master has given you part of the care.

Never let men feel that you and your gospel would be satisfied with mere decency, with the putting down of all vicious life that left the vicious character still strong behind. Surely such a protest against vice as this ought to be far more earnest, more uncompromising, more self-sacrificing than one that worked on lower motives and took shorter views. It can make no concessions. It strikes at all vices alike. It will not merely try to exchange one vice for another. It will hate vices more deeply in proportion as it realizes the depth of sin.

Do not these two methods of dealing with all symptoms describe the true attitude of the Christian preacher toward the evident vicious practices by which he is surrounded? Conceiving of them thus, he is neither the abstract religionist devoted to the fostering of certain spiritual conditions, heedless of how they show their worth or worthlessness in the moral life which they produce; nor is he the enlightened economist, weighing with anxious heart the evil of sins, but knowing nothing of the sinfulness of sin from which they come. He is the messenger of Christ to the soul of man always. His sermon about temperance, or the late election, or the wickedness of oppression, is not an exception, an intrusion in the current of that preaching which is always testifying of the spiritual salvation. He is ready to speak on any topic of the day, but his sermon is not likely to be mistaken for an article from some daily newspaper. It looks at the topic from a loftier height, traces the trouble to a deeper source, and is not satisfied except with a more thorough cure.

I do not know of any other principles than these which can be applied to the somewhat disputed question of political preaching. These seem to me sufficient. I despise, and call upon you to despise, all the weak assertions that a minister must not preach politics because he will injure his influence if he does, or because it is unworthy of his sacred office. The influence that needs such watching may well be allowed to die, and the more sacred the preacher's office is the more he is bound to care for all the interests of every child of God. But apply the principles which I laid down, and I think we have a better rule. See in the political condition the indication of the nation's spiritual state, and aim in all you say about public affairs, not simply at securing order and peace, but at making good men, who shall constitute a "holy nation." The first result of the application of these principles will be that only a true moral issue will provoke your utterance. You will not turn the pulpit into a place whence you can throw out your little scheme for settling a party quarrel or securing a party triumph. But when some clear question of right and wrong presents itself, and men with some strong passion or sordid interest are going wrong, then your sermon is a poor, untimely thing if it deals only with the abstractions of eternity, and has no work to help the men who are dizzied with the whirl and blinded with the darkness of today.

It was good to be a minister during the war of the Rebellion. A clear, strong moral issue stood out plain, and the preacher had his duty as sharply marked as the soldiers. That is not the case in the same clear way now. It will not ordinarily be so. But still, the ordinary talk about ministers not having any power in politics is not true. In a land like ours, where the tone of the people is of vast value in public affairs, the preachers who have so much to do in the creation of the popular tone must always have their part in politics.

Three Final Suggestions

I close this lecture with three suggestions, on which I had meant to dwell at large, but I have used up all my time.

1. You never can make a sermon what it ought to be if you consider it alone. The service that accompanies it, the prayer and praise, must have their influence upon it.

2. The sermon must never set a standard which it is not really meant that men should try to realize in life.

3. No sermon to one's own people can ever be conceived as if it were the only one. It must be part of a long culture, working with all the others.

And yet, in spite of all these definitions and suggestions, I beg you to go away believing that the idea of the sermon is not a complicated, but a very simple thing.

5
THE MAKING OF THE SERMON

I am to speak to you today about the making of a sermon. and if you compare their titles you will see in what relation this lecture and the last stand to each other, for the make of a sermon must always be completely dependent upon the idea of a sermon. The idea is perfectly supreme. It is the formative power to which all accidents must bow. If any rule of the composition or form contradicts the idea, it is rebellious and must be sacrificed without a scruple. I have heard sermons where it was evident that some upstart rule of form was in rebellion against the essential idea, and the idea was not strong enough to put the rebellion down, and the result was that the sermon, like a country in the tumult of rebellion, had neither peace nor power. What I say today, then, is in subordination to what I said before. Any law of execution which I may lay down that is inconsistent with the idea and purpose of preaching is an intruder and must be thrust aside.

The elements which determine the make of any particular sermon are three: the *preacher*, the *material*, and the *audience*; just as the character of any battle is determined by three elements: the gun (including the gunner), the ammunition, and the fortress against which the attack is made. The reason why a sermon preached last Sunday in the Church of St. John Lateran at Rome differed from the sermon preached in the First Congregational Church of New Haven must have been partly that the preacher was a different sort of man, partly that the truth which he wanted to preach was different, partly that the man he wished to touch and influence was different, at least in his conception. Make these three elements exactly alike, and all sermons must be perfectly identical. It is because these three elements are never exactly the same, and yet there always is a true resemblance, that we have all sermons unlike one another and yet a certain similarity running through them all. No two men are precisely similar, or think of truth alike, or see the men to whom they speak in the same light. Consequently the make of every man's sermon must be different from the make of every other man's.

The Preacher

Nay, we may carry this farther. No live man at any one moment is just the same as himself at any other moment, nor does he see truth always alike, nor do men always look to him the same; and therefore in his sermons there must be the same general identity combined with perpetual variety which there is in his life. His sermons will be all alike and yet unlike each other. And the making of every sermon, while it may follow the same general rules, will be a fresh and vital process, with the zest and freedom of novelty about it. This is the first thing that I wish to say. Establish this truth in your minds and then independence comes. Then you can stand in the right attitude to look at rules of sermon-making which come out of other men's experience. You can take them as helpful friends and not as arrogant masters.

I wish that not merely in sermon-writing but in all of life we could all come to understand that independence and the refusal to initiate and repeat other people's lives may come from true modesty as well as from pride. To be independent of man's dictation is simply to declare that we must live the special life which God has marked out for us and which He has indicated in the special powers which we discover in ourselves. We are fit for no other life. There can be nothing more modest than that. It is not pride when the beech-tree refuses to copy the oak. He knows his limitations. The only chance of any healthy life for him is to be as full a beech-tree as he can. Apply all that, and out of sheer modesty refuse to try to be any kind of preacher which God did not make you to be.

The Importance of Education

The lack of flexibility in the preacher, resulting in the lack of variety in the sermon, has very much to do with our imperfect education. The true result of education is to develop in the individual that of which I have been speaking, the clear consciousness of identity, together with a wide range of variety. The really educated man will be always distinctly himself and yet never precisely the same that he was at any other moment. His personality will be trained both in the persistency of its central stock and in its susceptibility and responsiveness to manifold impressions. He will have at once a stronger stand and a wider play of character. But an uneducated man will be either monotonously and doggedly the same, or else full of fickle alteration. The defects of our education are seen in the way in which it sometimes produces the narrow and obstinate specialist, sometimes the vague and feeble amateur in many works, but not often the strong man who has at once clear individuality and wide range of sympathy and action. This is the kind of man that the preacher above all ought to be. Education alone, thorough education, nothing but true, wise, devoted study, can make him so. Education alone gives a man at once a good stand and a good outlook. It is the Frenchman's rule for fencing, "*Bon pied, bon oeil,*" a good foot and a good eye.

As I begin to speak to you about literary style and homiletical construction, I cannot help once more urging upon you the need of hard and manly study; not simply the study of language and style itself, but study in its broader sense, the study of truth, of history, of philosophy; for no man can have a richly stored mind without its influencing the style in which he writes and speaks, making it at once thoroughly his own, and yet giving it variety and saving it from monotony.

I suppose the power of an uneducated man like Mr. Moody is doing something to discredit the necessity of study among ministers and to tempt men to rely upon spontaneousness and inspiration. I honor Mr. Moody, and rejoice in much of the work that he is doing, but if his success had really this effect it would be a very serious deduction from its value. When you see such a man, you are to consider both his exceptionalness and his limitations. In some respects he is a very remarkable and unusual man, and therefore not a man out of whom ordinary men can make a rule. And his work, valuable as it is, stops short at a clear line. He leaves undone what nothing but an educated ministry can do, and he who is most filled with thankfulness and admiration at that man's career ought to go the more earnestly to his books to try to be such a preacher as can help fulfil the work which the great revivalist begins.

"The Style Is the Man"

Every preacher's sermon style, then, ought to be his own; that is the first principle of sermon making. "The style is the man," said Buffon. Only we must remember that the man is not something invariable. He is capable of improvement. He is something different when he is filled with knowledge and affection and enthusiasm, from what he was in his first emptiness. The practical conclusion, then, that will come from our first principle will not be simply that every preacher is to accept himself just as he finds himself, and hope for nothing better; but rather this, that style is capable of indefinite cultivation, only that its main cultivation must come through the cultivation of the man; not by mere critical discipline of language, which at the best can only produce correctness, but by lifting the whole man to a more generous and exalted life, which is the only thing that can make a style truly noble.

I think, indeed, that the question as to wherein lies the power of a sermon style corresponds very largely with the question about the inspiration of the Scriptures. Various ideas have prevailed about the point in which was lodged that quality of the Bible which makes us separate it from other books and talk about it as inspired. One idea of inspiration puts it in the language, and supposes each word to be a dictation of the Holy Spirit. Another idea puts it in the writer, and supposes, with a profounder philosophy, that the power of exalted and truthful utterance was a truthful and exalted soul. Another idea puts it in the material. The history itself was full of God, and when men wrote that God-filled history their writings were different from other men's, more full of the divine atmosphere, because of the strange divine character of the things they wrote about.

And so the sermon comes forth peculiar. Wherein does its peculiarity reside? Is it that a certain language, certain forms of speech, belong there which do not belong to other literature? Is it that the sermon-writer is in a condition and an attitude that no other man ever quite assumes? Is it that the subjects with which the sermon deals are more solemn, and more touching, more divine than any others? No doubt all three ideas are true in their degrees, but no doubt, also, he who looks to the deepest truth in the matter will get the deeper power. He who aspires to the strength of truth and character will be a stronger man than he who tries to prevail by the finish and completeness of his language.

Selecting the Topic

The history of a particular sermon begins with the selection of a topic. Ordinarily, except in purely expository preaching, that comes before the selection of a text. And the ease and readiness of this selection depend upon the richness of a man's own life, and the naturalness of his conception of a sermon. I can conceive of but two things which should cause the preacher any difficulty in regard to the abundance of subjects for his preaching. The first is the sterility of his own mind, the second is a stilted and unnatural idea of what the sermon he is going to write must be.

Let the man's own mind be everywhere else except upon the things of God, let his own spiritual life be meager and unsuggestive, let him feel no developing power in his own experience, and I can see him sitting in despair or hurrying hither and thither in distraction, as the day approaches when he must talk of something, and he has nothing of which to talk. Or let him once get the idea that every sermon, or that any particular sermon, is to be a great sermon, a "pulpit-effort," as the dreadful epithet runs, and again he is all lost. Which of these quiet, simple, practical themes that offer themselves is suitable to bear the aspirations and contortions of his eloquence? The first of the difficulties I say no more about, only because I seem to have talked to you of nothing else than the way in which there must be a man behind every sermon, though, indeed, I do think that the most important, I had almost said the only important, thing in this matter of learning to preach. But I say no more of that just now. This other matter let me dwell on for a moment.

Preaching the Great Sermon

The notion of a great sermon, either constantly or occasionally haunting the preacher, is fatal. It hampers, as I said, the freedom of utterance. Many a true and helpful word which your people need, and which you ought to say to them will seem unworthy of the dignity of your great discourse. Some poor exhorter coming along the next week, and saying it, will sweep the last recollection of your selfish achievement out of the minds of people. Never tolerate any idea of the dignity of a sermon which will keep you from saying anything in it which you ought to say, or which your people ought to hear. It is the same folly as making your chair so fine that you dare not sit down in it.

There will come great, or at least greater sermons in every live minister's career, sermons which will stand out for vigor and beauty, distinctly above his ordinary work, but they will come without deliberation, the flowers of his ministry, the offspring of moments which found his powers at their best activity and him most regardless of effect. It is good and encouraging, it helps one's faith in human nature, and it has an influence to keep us from the pulpit's besetting follies, when we see how universally the deliberate attempt to make great sermons fails. They never have the influence, and they very seldom win the praise, that they desire. The sermons of which nobody speaks, the sermons which come from mind and heart, and go to heart and mind with as little consciousness as possible of tongue and ear, those are the sermons that do the work, that make men better men, and really sink into their affections. They are like the perfect days when no man says, "How fine it is," but when every man does his best work and feels most fully what a blessed thing it is to live.

I think, too, that this wrong notion about sermons has led to a great deal of the bad talk which is running about now among both clergymen and laymen about the excessive amount of preaching. "How is it possible," they say, "that any man should bring forth two strong, good sermons every week? It is impossible. Let us have only one sermon every Sunday; and if the people will insist on coming twice to the church, let us cheat them with a little poor music and a 'few remarks', and call it 'vesper service,' or let us tell a few stories to the Sunday school, and call it 'children's church'; but let us not preach twice to men and women. It is impossible." It is impossible, if by a sermon you intend a finished oration. It is as impossible to produce that twice as it is undesirable to produce it once a week. But that a man who lives with God, whose delight is to study God's words in the Bible, in the world, in history, in human nature, who is thinking about Christ, and man, and salvation every day—that he should not be able to talk about these things of his heart seriously, lovingly, thoughtfully, simply, for two half-hours every week, is inconceivable, and I do not believe it.

Cast off the haunting incubus of the notion of great sermons. Care not for your sermon, but for your truth, and for your people; and subjects will spring up on every side of you, and the chances to preach upon them will be all too few. I beg you not to fall into this foolish talk about too much preaching. It is not for us ministers to say that there is no need of more than one discourse a day. If you have anything to say, and say it bravely and simply, men will come to hear you. If you will preach as faithfully and thoughtfully at the second service as at the first, the second service will not be deserted. At any rate, it is our place to stand by our pulpits till men have deserted us, and not, for the sake of saving our own credit, to shut the church doors while they are still ready to come and hear.

Three Principles for Topic Selection

But to return more closely to our subject; having settled in general what topics may be preached upon, how shall the topic for a single sermon, the sermon for next Sunday, be selected? I answer that there are three principles which have a right to enter into the decision. They are the bent of the preacher's inclination, the symmetry and "scale" of all his preaching, and the peculiar needs of his people. I mention the three in the order in which they are apt to present themselves to the minister as he makes his choice. Reverse that order, begin with the last, and you have the elements of a right choice rightly arranged.

First comes the sympathetic and wise perception of what the people need; not necessarily what they consciously want, though, remember, no more necessarily what they do not want. This perception is not the sudden result of an impression that has come from some lively conversation which has sprung up on a parish visit, not the desire to confute the cavil of some single captious disputant; it is the aggregate effect of a large sympathetic relationship, the fruit of a true knowledge of human nature, combined with a special knowledge of these special people, and a cordial interest in the circumstances under which they live. That evidently is no easy thing to win. It requires of a minister that timeliness and that breadth which it is very hard to find in union with each other. It is not something to be picked up in the easy intimacy of parochial visiting. It may be helped there, but it must be born of an alert mind fully interested in the times in which it lives, and a devout soul really loving the souls with which it has to deal.

The second element of choice, the desire to preserve a symmetry and proportion in our preaching, of course comes in to modify the action of the first. Not merely by our present perception of what people need, but in relation to our whole scheme of teaching, to what has gone before and what is to come after, the subject of next Sunday is to be selected. I have suggested to you in another lecture how great a help the ancient calendar of the church year is in this respect. The prolonged and connected course of sermons is a safeguard against mere flightiness and partialness in the choice of topics.

The only serious danger about a course of sermons is, that where the serpent grows too long it is difficult to have the vitality distributed through all his length, and even to his last extremity. Too many courses of sermons start with a very vital head, that draws behind it by and by a very lifeless tail. The head springs and the tail crawls, and so the beast makes no graceful progress. I think that a set and formally announced course of sermons very seldom preserves both its symmetry and its interest. The system of long courses is apt to secure proportion at too great an expense of spontaneity. The only sure means of securing the result is orderliness in the preacher's mind; the grasp of Christian truth as a system, and of the Christian life as a steady movement of the whole nature through Christ to the Father.

Then comes the third principle *that a man can preach best about what he at that moment wishes to preach about,* the element of the preacher's own disposition. You can see why it should not be made the first element. It gives the freshness and joyousness and spring to the other two. You cannot think of a people listening with pleasure or vivacity to a sermon on a subject which they knew the minister thought they needed to hear about, and thought the time had come to preach about, but which they also knew that he did not care for, and did not want to preach upon. The personal interest of the preacher is the buoyant air that fills the mass and lifts it.

These three considerations, then, settle the sermon's topic. Evidently neither is sufficient by itself. The sermon preached only with reference to the people's needs is heavy. The sermon preached for symmetry is formal. The sermon preached with sole reference to the preacher's wish is whimsical. The constant consideration of all three makes preaching always strong and always fresh. When all three urgently unite to settle the topic of some special sermon I do not see why we may not prepare that sermon in a solemn exhilaration, feeling sure that it is God's will that we should preach upon that topic then; and, when it is written, go forth with it on Sunday to our pulpit, declaring, almost with the certainty of one of the old prophets: "The Word of the Lord came unto me, saying" (Jer. 1:4)

Let me add this, that the meeting of these various elements of choice is clearest when the selection is most deliberate. Always have the topic of your sermon in your mind as long as possible before you begin your preparation. Whatever else is hasty and extemporaneous, let it not be your decision as to what you will preach about.

Preparing the Sermon

The subject chosen, next will come the special preparation for the sermon. This ought to consist mostly in bringing together, and arranging, and illuminating a knowledge of the subject and thought about it which has already been in the possession of the preacher. I think that the less of special preparation that is needed for a sermon, the better the sermon is. The best sermon would be that whose thoughts, though carefully arranged, and lighted up with every illustration that could make them clearer for this special appearance, were all old thoughts, familiar to the preacher's mind, long a part of his experience.

Here is suggested, as you see, a clear and important difference between two kinds of preachers. One preacher depends for his sermon on special reading. Each discourse is the result of work done in the week in which it has been written. All his study is with reference to some immediately pressing occasion. Another preacher studies and thinks with far more industry, is always gathering truth into his mind, but it is not gathered with reference to the next sermon. It is truth sought for truth's sake, and for that largeness and ripeness and fulness of character which alone can make him a strong preacher. Which is the better method? The latter beyond all doubt.

In the first place, the man of special preparations is always crude; he is always tempted to take up some half-considered thought that strikes him in the hurry of his reading, and adopt it suddenly, and set it before his people, as if it were his true conviction. Many a minister's old sermons are scattered all over with ideas which he never held, but which once held him for a week, like the camps in other men's forests where a wandering hunter has slept for a single night. The looseness and falseness, the weakening of the essential sacredness of conviction which must come from years of such work, any one may see. And in the second place, the immediate preparation for a sermon is something that the people always feel. They know the difference between a sermon that has been crammed, and a sermon which has been thought long before, and of which only the form, and the illustrations, and the special developments, and the application of the thought, are new.

Some preachers are always preaching the last book which they have read, and their congregations always find it out. The feeling of superficialness and thinness attaches to all they do. The exegesis of a passage which the man never thought of till he began to preach about it may be clever and suggestive, but it inspires no confidence. I do not rest on it with even that amount of assurance which the same man's careful study would inspire. It is got up for the occasion. It is like a politician's opinions just before election.

But the strongest reason for the rule which I am stating comes from the very nature of the sermon on which I have dwelt so much. The sermon is truth and man together; it is the truth brought through the man. The personal element is essential. Now the truth which the preacher has gathered on Friday for the sermon which he preaches on Sunday has come *across* the man, but it has not come *through* the man. It has never been wrought into his experience. It comes weighted and winged with none of his personal life. If it is true, it is a book's truth, not a man's truth that we get. It does not make a full, real sermon.

If I am right in this idea, then it will follow that the preacher's must be a life of large accumulation. He must not be always trying to make sermons, but always seeking truth, and out of the truth which he has won the sermons will make themselves. I can remember how, before I began to preach, every book I read seemed to spring into a sermon. It seemed as if one could read nothing without sitting down instantly and turning it into a discourse. But as I began and went on preaching, the sermons that came of special books became less and less satisfactory and more and more rare.

Some truth which one has long known, stirred to peculiar activity by something that has happened or by contact with some other mind, makes the best sermon; as the best dinner comes not from a hurried raid upon the caterer's, but from the resources of a constantly well-furnished house. Constant quotations in sermons are, I think, a sign of the same crudeness. They show an undigested knowledge. They lose the power of personality. They daub the wall with untempered mortar. Here is the need of broad and generous culture. Learn to study for the sake of truth, learn to think for the profit and the joy of thinking. Then your sermons shall be like the leaping of a fountain and not like the pumping of a pump.

The Use of Scripture

For over six hundred years now it has been the almost invariable custom of Christian preachers to take a text from Scripture and associate their thoughts more or less strictly with that. For the first twelve Christian centuries there seems to have been no such prevailing habit. This fact ought to be kept in mind whenever the custom of a text shows any tendency to become despotic or to restrain in any way the liberty of prophesying. At the present day there can be no doubt that the change in the way of considering the Bible which belongs to our times has had an influence upon our feeling with regard to texts and our treatment of them. The unity of the Bible, the relation of its parts, its organic life, the essentialness of every part, and yet the distinct difference in worth and dignity of the several parts, these are now familiar ideas as they were not a few years ago.

There was a time when to many people the Bible stood, not merely a collection of various books, all equally the Word of God, all equally useful to men, but also as a succession of verses, all true, all edifying, all vital with the Gospel. A page of the Bible torn out at random and blown into some savage island seemed to have in it some power of salvation. The result of such a feeling was, of course, to clothe the single text with independent sacredness and meaning. It hardly mattered from what part of the Bible it might come. Solomon's Songs and St. John's Gospel were preached from as if they taught the same truth with the same authority. The cynical author of the Ecclesiastes was made to utter the same message as the hopeful and faithful St. Paul.

This is not the place to recount the causes for the change, nor to estimate its value or its dangers. Considered simply as it has affected the preacher's relation to the Bible, I think there can be no doubt of the improvement it has brought. It has made the single text of less importance. It has led men to desire an entrance into the heart and spirit of the Bible. It has made biblical study to consist, not in the weighing of text against text, but in the estimating of great streams of tendency, the following of great lines of thought, the apprehension of the spirit of great spiritual thinkers who "had the mind of Christ."

The single verse is no longer like a jewel set in a wall which one may pluck out and carry off as an independent thing. It is a window by which we may look through the wall and see richness it encloses. Taken out of its place it has no value. To enter thoroughly into the spirit of this new and better relation to the Bible seems to me to be all that the preacher needs to guide him with reference to the selection and the use of texts. Make them always windows. Go up and look through them and then tell the people what you see. Keep them in their places in the wall of truth. I would not say that it is not good to use them, though certainly there may be true sermons without them. They are like golden nails to hold our preaching to the Bible.

Whether the subject spring out of the text as stating the divine philosophy that underlies some Scripture incident, or the text spring out of the subject as describing some incident that illustrates divine philosophy, is unimportant. There are both kinds of sermons and both kinds are good. Only, as one rule that has no exceptions, let your use of texts be *real*. Never make them mean what they do not mean. In the name of taste and reverence alike, let there be no twists and puns, no dealing with the Word of God as it would be insulting to deal with the word of any friend. The Bible has suffered in the hands of many Christian preachers what the block of wood which the savage chooses for his idol suffers from its worshiper. The same selection which consecrates it as more sacred than other blocks of wood condemns it also to have all his ugly fancies and fantastic conceits painted and carved upon it. It is the most sacred and most hideous block of wood in the village. So the sacredness of the Bible has subjected it to a usage that no other book has received. Such a fantastic and irreverent way of manifesting our reverence has lasted too long. It is time that it were stopped. I beg you to do what you can to stop it. At least make your own use of the Bible reverent and true. Never draw out of a text a meaning which you know is not there. If your text has not your truth in it, find some other text which has. If you can find no text for it in the Bible, then preach on something else.

Matters of Style

I pass on to a few remarks, which will be more suggestions, about the style of sermons. The matter will control the style if it is free. The object of every training of style is to make it so simple and flexible an organ that through it the moving and changing thought can utter itself freely. I pity any man who writes the same upon all topics. He is evidently a slave to himself. To be yourself, yet not to be haunted by an image of yourself to which you are continually trying to correspond, that is the secret of a style at once characteristic and free. I go to hear a preacher whose style is peculiarly his own, and very often indeed I find him a slave to his own peculiarities. He must not think anything except what is capable of being said in a certain way.

A true style is like a suit of the finest chain armor, so strong that the thought can go into battle with it, but so flexible that it can hold the pencil in its steel fingers for the most delicate painting. For the acquisition of such a style no labor is too great. I think that it is good for every minister to write something besides sermons—books, articles, essays, at least letters; provided he has control of himself and still remains the preacher, and does not become an amateur in literature instead. If he can do it rightly, it frees him from the tyranny of himself, and keeps him in contact with larger standards.

Some of our noblest thinkers fail of effect for want of an organ of utterance, a free pulpit-style. The trouble with them, often, is that they never wrote anything but sermons. Indeed I do not think there is any such thing as a sermon-style proper. He who can write other things well, give him the soul and purpose and knowledge of a preacher and he will write you a good sermon. But he who cannot write anything well cannot write a sermon well, although we often think he can. To him who has no literary skill all subjects are alike. If you cannot swim, it matters not whether there be twenty or forty feet of water.

In a word, then, I should say, get facility of utterance where you can; in part at least, outside of sermon-writing. Make your style characteristic and forcible by never writing unless you have something that you really want to say; then let the changes of your truth freely play within it and shape its special forms. A style which is really a man's own will grow as long as he grows. One of the best things about Macaulay's life is his belief that as a writer he was improving to the last. It belonged to that vitality of which the man and the writing were both so full.

The range of sermon-writing gives it a capacity of various vices which no other kind of composition can presume to rival. The minister may sin in the same sermon by grandiloquence and meanness, by exaggeration and inadequacy. He needs a many-sided watchfulness, or rather a perfectly true literary nature, in order that he may do what Roger Ascham so quaintly and tellingly sums up thus: "In Genere Sublimi to avoid Nimium, in Mediocri to atteyne Satis, in Humili to eschew Parum." The way that he advises to do it is to study Cicero. Certainly, stated more generally, the true way is to know first what style is for, that it is an instrument and not an end, and then as an instrument to perfect it by every noble intimacy and laborious practice.

It would be impossible to speak of this matter of style without saying something of the danger of imitation and the way to guard against it. It is connected with that personalness of the work of preaching about which I have said so much. A successful preacher is not like a successful author. He stands out himself more prominently through his work.

Men realize him more and feel in themselves the same powers by which he has succeeded. A mere finished result such as the author gives us in his book does not excite the desire of imitation like the sight of the process going on in personal action before us in the pulpit. This is the reason why those preachers whose power has in it the largest element of personality are the richest in imitators. There are some strong voices crying in the wilderness who fill the land with

echoes. There are some preachers who have done noble work
of whom we are often compelled to question whether the
work that they have accomplished is after all greater than the
harm that they have innocently done by spoiling so many
men in doing it. They have gone through the ministry, as a
savage goes through the forest, blazing his way upon the
trees that stand around him, so that you can tell as you travel
through the land just where they have been by the tones of
voice and the turns of sentences which they have left behind
them. They leave their imitators behind them when they die,
and in a sense which is not pleasant, "being dead, yet speak."
Often the circle of one man's influence widens, growing
feebler and feebler until it meets the wave that is spreading
from another center, another popular pulpit, and only there
they obliterate each other, and calmness is restored and
freedom to be one's self is reasserted.

Two Dangers of Imitation

The dangers of imitation are two—one positive, the other
negative. There is evil in what you get from him whom you
imitate and there is a loss of your own peculiar power. The
positive evil comes from the fact that that what is worst in
any man is always the most copiable. And the spirit of the
copyist is blind. He cannot discern the real seat of the power
that he admires. He fixes on some little thing and repeats
that perpetually, as if so he could get the essential greatness
of his hero. There is a passage in Macaulay's diary which is
full of philosophy. "I looked through——," he says. "He is, I
see, an imitator of me. But I am a very unsafe model. My
manner is, I think, and the world thinks, on the whole a good
one, but it is very near to a very bad manner indeed, and
those clear characteristics of my style which are the most
easily copied are the most questionable." All this is very true
of ministers. There is hardly any good pulpit-style among us
which is not very near to a very bad style indeed, and the
most prominent characteristics are very often the most
questionable.

The obtuseness of the imitator is amazing. I remember
going years ago with an intelligent friend to hear a great
orator lecture. The discourse was rich, thoughtful, glowing,
and delightful. As we came away my companion seemed
meditative. By and by he said, "Did you see where his power
lay?" I felt unable to analyze and epitomize in an instant

such a complex result, and meekly I said, "No, did you?" "Yes," he replied briskly, "I watched him and it is in the double motion of his hand. When he wanted to solemnize and calm and subdue us he turned the palm of his hand down; when he wanted to elevate and inspire us he turned the palm of his hand up. That was it." And that was all the man had seen in an eloquent speech. He was no fool, but he was an imitator. He was looking for a single secret for a multifarious effect. I suppose he has gone on from that day to this turning his hand upside down and downside up and wondering that nobody is either solemnized or inspired.

The negative evil of imitation, the loss of a man's own personal power, is even more evident and more melancholy. If it were only the men who were incapable of any manner of their own that caught up other people's manners, it would not be so bad, but often strong men do it. Men imitate others who are every way their inferiors, and so some pretentious blockhead not merely gives us himself, but loses for us the simple and straightforward power of some better man, as a log of wood lodged just in the neck of the channel stops the water of a free, live stream.

I am convinced that the only escape from the power of imitation when it has once touched us—and remember it often touches us without our consciousness; you and I may be imitating other men today and not at all aware of it—lies in a deeper seriousness about all our work. What we need is a fuller sense of personal responsibility and a more real reverence for the men who are greater than we are. Give a man real personal sense of his own duty and he must do it in his own way. The temptation of imitation is so insidious that you cannot resist it by the mere determination that you will not imitate. You must bring a real self of your own to meet this intrusive self of another man that is crowding in upon you. Cultivate your own sense of duty. The only thing that keeps the ocean from flowing back into the river is that the river is always pouring down into the ocean.

And again if you really reverence a great man, if you look up to and rejoice in his good work, if you truly honor him you will get at his spirit, and doing that you will cease to imitate his outside ways. You insult a man when you try to catch his power by moving your arms or shaping your sentences like his, but you honor him when you try to love truth and do God's will the better for the love and faithfulness which you see in him. So that the release from the slavery of superficial imitation must come not by a supercilious contempt, but by a profounder reverence for men stronger and more successful than yourself.

Written Sermons or Unwritten Sermons?

With regard to the vexed question of written or unwritten sermons I have not very much to say. I think it is a question whose importance has been very much exaggerated, and the attempt to settle which with some invariable rule has been unwise, and probably has made stumbling speakers out of some men who might have been effective readers, or stupid readers out of men who might have spoken with force and fire. The different methods have their evident different advantages.

In the written sermon the best part of the care is put in where it belongs, in the thought and construction of the discourse. There is deliberateness. There is the assurance of industry and the man's best work. The truth comes to the people with the weight that it gets from being evidently the preacher's serious conviction. There is self-restraint. There is some exemption from those foolish fluent things that slip so easily off the ready tongue. The writer is spared some of those despairing moments which come to the extemporaneous speaker when a wretched piece of folly escapes him which he would give anything to recall but cannot, and he sees the raven-like reporters catch the silly morsel as it drops. Whatever may be said about the duty of labor upon extemporaneous discourses, the advantage in point of faithfulness will no doubt always be with the written sermon. King Charles II used to call the practice of preaching from manuscript which had arisen during the civil wars, "this slothful way of preaching," but he was comparing it probably with the method of preaching by memory, the whole sermon being first written and then learned by heart, a method which some men practice, but which I hope nobody commends.

On the other hand, the extemporaneous discourse has the advantage of alertness. It gives a sense of liveliness. It is more immediately striking. It possesses more activity and warmth. It conveys an idea of steadiness and readiness, of poise and self-possession, even to the most rude perceptions. Men have an admiration for it, as indicating a mastery of powers and an independence of artificial helps. A rough backwoodsman in Virginia heard Bishop Meade preach an extemporaneous sermon, and, being somewhat unfamiliar with the ways of the Episcopal Church, he said, "he liked him. He was the first one he ever saw of those petticoat fellows that could shoot without a rest."

It is easy thus to characterize the two methods, but, when our characterizations are complete, what shall we say? Only two things, I think, and those so simple and so commonplace that it is strange that they should need to be said, but certainly they do. The first is that two such different methods must belong in general to two different kinds of men; that some men are made for manuscripts, and some for the open platform; that to exclude either class from the ministry, or to compel either class to use the methods of the other would rob the pulpit by silencing some of its best men. The other remark is that almost every man, in some proportion, may use both methods; that they help each other; that you will write better if you often speak without your notes, and you will speak better if you often give yourself the discipline of writing. Add to these merely that the proportion of extemporaneous preaching may well be increased as a man grows older in the ministry, and I do not know what more to say in the way of general suggestion. The rest must be left to a man's own knowledge of himself and that personal good sense which lies behind all homiletics.

Audience Awareness

But there is one thing which I want very much to urge upon you. The real question about a sermon is, not whether it is extemporaneous when you deliver it to your people, but whether it ever was extemporaneous, whether there ever was a time when the discourse sprang freshly from your heart and mind. The main difference in sermons is that some sermons are, and other sermons are not, conscious of an audience. The main question about sermons is whether they feel their hearers. If they do, they are enthusiastic, personal, and warm. If they do not, they are calm, abstract, and cold. But that consciousness of an audience is something that may come into the preacher's study; and if it does, his sermon springs with the same personalness and fervor there which it would get if he made it in the pulpit with the multitude before him. I think that every earnest preacher is often more excited as he writes, kindles more than with the glow of sending truth to men than he ever does in speaking; and the wonderful thing is that that fire, if it is really present in the sermon when it is written, stays there, and breaks out into flame again when the delivery of the sermon comes. The enthusiasm is stowed away and kept. It is like the fire that was packed away in the coal-beds ages ago and comes out now to give us its undecayed and unwasted light.

As you preach old sermons, I think you can always tell, even if the history of them is forgotten, which of them you wrote enthusiastically, with your people vividly before you. The fire is in them still. François Fénelon had a favorite maxim that anything which was truly written with enthusiasm could be quickly learned even by some one else than its author. It is the same idea: that which once has true life in it never dies. Believe me, this is the most important principle about the matter. It differs, no doubt, in different subjects.

Some kinds of discourses we can never write. They must be made as we deliver them. Others we may better write, if we can write with the people there before us. Some medicines you must mix on the spot; others you may mix beforehand and they will keep their power. Only be sure that you are a true preacher, that you really feel your people, and the details of method may be settled by minute and personal considerations, by your special fitness, in some degree even by your peculiar taste. I really think that you will be surprised to see how often this idea describes the secret of some power in a sermon which you have found it hard to discover while you have felt it very deeply.

The minister who reads his manuscript had you with him as he wrote those pages. In the calm air of his study, sacred with the thought and prayer of years, nothing came in between him and you; and so the accidents of the paper and the reading amount to nothing. The sermon still speaks to you. But sometimes to an extemporaneous preacher his very extemporaneousness proves a dull, dead cloud, which wraps itself around him, and separates him from the people who are crowded up close about his feet. The struggles of thought are on him. He is busy with the choice of words. His mind is watching its own action as it seizes on thought after thought. There is a process of memory and a process of anticipation going on all the time which prevent his perfect occupation in the present set. He is forced to recollect himself, and so he does not feel the people. This, I am sure, is a true account of what is no unusual condition of the extemporaneous preacher's mind.

I think that the best sermons that ever have been preached, taking all the qualities of sermons into account, have probably been extemporaneous sermons, but that the number of good sermons preached from manuscript have probably been far greater than the number of good sermons preached extemporaneously; and he who can put those two facts together will arrive at some pretty clear and just idea of how it will be best for him to preach.

Using Illustrations

Let me offer only a few suggestions upon one or two other points, and first with regard to illustrations. The Christian sermon deals with all life, and may draw its illustrations from the widest range. The first necessity of illustration is that it should be true, that is, that it should have real relations to the subject which it illustrates. An illustration is properly used in preaching either to give clearness or to give splendor to the utterance of truth. Both objects, I believe, are legitimate. Ruskin says that "all noble ornament is the expression of man's delight in God's work." And so I think that we confine too much the office of illustration if we give it only the duty of making truth clear to the understanding, and do not also allow it the privilege of making truth glorious to the imagination. Archbishop Whately's illustrations are of the first sort, Jeremy Taylor's of the second. The ornament that fills his sermons is almost always the expression of man's delight in God's truth. But both sorts of illustration, as you see, have this characteristic; they exist for the truth. They are not counted of value for themselves. That is the test of illustration which you ought to apply unsparingly. Does it call attention to or call attention away from my truth? If the latter, cut it off without a hesitation. The prettier it is the worse it is. Here as everywhere the love of truth for itself is the only salvation. Love the truth, and then, for your people's good and for your own delight, make it as beautiful as you can.

Old Testament Illustrating the New

As to the subjects from which illustrations may be drawn, I cannot but think that it would be well if we made a much greater use of the history of the Old Testament to illustrate the Gospel of the New. And for these reasons; *first, that the two have an essential connection with each other* and so they come together with peculiar sympathy and fitness; *second, that the very antiquity of that history makes it timeless and passionless*, as it were, and so enables us to use it purely as ornament or illustration, without the danger of its introducing side issues from its own life; and *thirdly, we should thus revive and preserve people's acquaintance with the Old Testament*, which is always falling into decay. The second of these reasons shows where the weak spot is in the illustration drawn from the events of the current hour, which is otherwise so strong and vivid. It is difficult to make it serve purely as an illustration. It brings in its own associations and prejudices. It is too alive.

It is as if you made the cornice of your house out of wood with so much life in it that it sprouted after it was up, and hid with its foliage the architecture which it was intended only to display. It was hard during the rebellion to illustrate the Christian warfare by the then familiar story of the soldier's life without hearing through the sermon the drums of the Potomac, and seeing the spires of Richmond quite as much as the walls of the New Jerusalem in the distance. Besides this, an over eagerness to catch the last sensation to decorate your sermon which gives a certain cheapness to your pulpit work. With cautions such as these in mind, we cannot still afford to lose the freshness and reality which comes from letting men see the eternal truths shining through the familiar windows of today, and making them understand that the world is as full of parables as it was when Jesus painted the picture of the vineyard between Jerusalem and Shechem, or took his text from the recent terrible accident at Siloam.

Organizing Sermons

One prevalent impression about sermons which prevails now in reaction from an old and disagreeable method is, I think, mistaken. In the desire to make a sermon seem free and spontaneous there is a prevalent dislike to giving it its necessary formal structure and organism. The statement of the subject, the division into heads, the recapitulation at the end, all the scaffolding and anatomy of a sermon is out of favor, and there are many very good jests about it. I can only say that I have come to fear it less and less. The escape from it must be not negative but positive. The true way to get rid of the boniness of your sermon is not by leaving out the skeleton, but by clothing it with flesh. True liberty in writing comes by law, and the more thoroughly the outlines of your work are laid out the more freely your sermon will flow, like an unwasted stream between its well-built banks. I think that most congregations welcome, and are not offended by clear, precise statements of the course which a sermon is going to pursue, carefully marked division of its thoughts, and, above all, full recapitulation of its argument at the close. A sermon is not like a picture which, once painted, stands altogether before the eye. Its parts elude the memory, and it is good before you close to gather all the parts together, and as briefly as you can set them as one completed whole before your hearer's mind. Leave to the ordinary Sunday school lesson its unquestioned privilege of inconsequence and incoherence. But give your sermon an orderly consistent progress, and do not hesitate to let your hearers see it distinctly, for it will help them first to understand and then to remember what you say.

Of oratory, and all the marvellous mysterious ways of those who teach it, I dare say nothing. I believe in the true elocution teacher, as I believe in the existence of Halley's comet, which comes into sight of this earth once in about seventy six years. But whatever you may learn or unlearn from him to your advantage, the real power of your oratory must be your own intelligent delight in what you are doing. Let your pulpit be to you what his studio is to the artist, or his court room to the lawyer, or his laboratory to the chemist, or the broad field with its bugles and banners to the soldier; only far more sacredly let your pulpit be this to you, and you have the power that is to all rules what the soul is to the body. You have enthusiasm which is the breath of life.

I have spoken today about the making of a sermon. I alluded at the beginning of one lecture to a young man whom I saw just entering on his work. Today I have been thinking of one whom I knew—nay, one whom I know—who finished his preaching years ago and went to God. How does all this seem to him?—these rules and regulations of the preacher's art, which he once studied as we are studying them now. Let us not doubt, my friends, that while he has seen a glory and strength in the truth which we preach such as we never have conceived, he has seen also that no expedient which can make that truth a little more effective in its presentation to the world is trivial, or undignified, or unworthy of the patient care and study of the minister of Christ.

6
THE CONGREGATION

I have said what I had to say about the preacher and about the sermon. Today I want to speak to you about the congregation. There is something remarkable in the way in which a minister talks about "my congregation." They evidently come to seem to him different from the rest of humankind. There is the rest of our race, in Europe, Asia, Africa, and America, and the Islands of the Sea, and then there is "my congregation." A man begins the habit the moment he is settled in a parish.

However young, however inexperienced he may be, he at once takes possession of that fraction of the human family and holds it with a sense of ownership. He immediately assumes certain fictions concerning them. He takes it for granted that they listen to his words with a deference quite irrespective of the value of the words themselves. He talks majestically about "what I tell my congregation," as if there were some basis upon which they received his teachings quite different from that upon which other intelligent men listen to one who takes his place before them as their teacher. He supposes them to be subject to emotions which he expects of no one else. He thinks that, in some mysterious way, their property as well as their intelligence is subject to his demand, to be handed over to him when he shall tell them that he has found a good use to which to put it. He imagines that, though they are as clear-sighted as other people, little devices of his which are perfectly plain to everybody else impose upon them perfectly. He talks about them so unnaturally that we are almost surprised when we ask their names and find that they are men and women whom we know, men and women who are living ordinary lives and judging people and things by ordinary standards, with all the varieties of character and ways which any such group must have, whom he has separated from the rest of humanity and distinguished by their relation to himself and calls "my congregation."

I think that a good deal of the unreality of clerical life comes from this feeling of ministers about their congregations. I have known many ministers who were frank and simple and unreserved with other people for whom they did not feel a responsibility, but who threw around themselves a cloak of fictions and reserves the moment that they met a parishioner. They were willing to let the stranger clearly see that there were many things in religion and theology which they did not know at all, many other questions on which they were in doubt, points of their church's faith which they thought unimportant to salvation, methods of their church's policy which they thought injudicious. All this they would say freely as they talked with the wolf over the sheepfold wall, or with some sheep in the next flock; but in their own flock they held their peace, or said that everything was right, and never dreamed that their flock saw through their feeble cautiousness. The result of all this has sometimes been that parishioners have trusted other men more than their minister just because he was their minister, and have gone with their troublesome questions and dark experiences to some one who should speak of them freely because he should not feel that he was speaking to a member of his congregation.

It is easy to point out what are the causes of this feeling which we thus see has its dangers. The bad part in it is a love of power. The better part is an anxious sense of responsibility, made more anxious by the true affection which grows up in the preacher's heart. It is almost a parental feeling in its worse as in its better features, in its partialness and jealousy as well as in its devotion and love. But besides these, there is another element in the view which the preacher takes of his congregation which I beg you to observe and think about. It is the way in which he assumes a difference in the character of people when they are massed together from any which they had when they were looked at separately. This is the real meaning of the tone which is in that phrase "my congregation." It is to the minister a unit of a wholly novel sort. There is something in the congregation which is not in the men and women as he knows them in their separate humanities, something in the aggregate which was not in the individuals, a character in the whole which was not in the parts. This is the reason why he can group them in his thought as a peculiar people, hold them in his hand as a new human unity, his congregation.

And no doubt he is partly right. There is a principle underneath the feeling by which he vaguely works. A multitude of people gathered for a special purpose and absorbed for the time into a common interest has a new character which is not in any of the individuals which compose it. If you are a speaker addressing a crowd you feel that. You say things to them without hesitation that would seem either too bold or too simple to say to any man among them if you talked with him face to face. If you are a spectator and watch a crowd while some one else is speaking to it, you can feel the same thing. You can see emotions run through the mass that no one man there would have deigned to show or submitted to feel if he could have helped it. The crowd will laugh at jokes which every man in the crowd would have despised, and be melted by mawkish pathos that would not have extorted a tear from the weakest of them by himself. Imagine Peter the Hermit sitting down alone with a man to fire him up for a crusade.

Probably all this is less true of one of our New England audiences than of any other that is ever collected in our land. In it every man keeps guard over his individuality and does not easily let it sink in the character of the multitude. And yet we are men and women even here, and the universal laws of human nature do work even among us. And this is a law of nature which all men have observed. "It is a strange thing to say," says Arthur Helps in *Realmah*, "but when the number of any public body exceeds that of forty or fifty, the whole assembly has an element of joyous childhood in it, and each member revives at times the glad, mischievous nature of his schoolboy days." Canning used to say that the House of Commons as a body had better taste than the man of the best taste in it, and Macaulay was much inclined to think that Canning was right.

The Elements of a Congregation

What are the elements of this new character which belongs to a congregation, a company of men? Two of them have been suggested in the two instances which I have just quoted—the spontaneousness and liberty, and the higher standard of thought and taste. It is not hard to see what some of the other elements are. There is no doubt greater receptivity than there is in the individual. Many of the sources of antagonism are removed. The tendency to irritation is put to rest. The pride of argument is not there; or is modified by the fact that no other man can hear the argument, because it cannot speak a word, but must go on in a man's own silent soul. It is easier to give way when you sit undistinguished in an audience, and your next neighbor cannot see the moment when you yield. The surrender loses half its hardness when you have no sword to surrender and no flag to run down. And, besides this, we have all felt how the silent multitude in the midst of which we sit or stand becomes ideal and heroic to us. We feel as if it were listening without prejudice, and responding unselfishly and nobly. So we are lifted up to our best by the buoyancy of the mass in which we have been merged. It may be a delusion. Each of these silent men may be thinking and feeling meanly, but probably each of them has felt the elevation of the mass about him of which we are one particle, and so is lifting and lifted just as we are. Who can say which drops in the great sweep of the tide are borne, and which bear others toward the shore, on which they all rise together?

This, then, is the good quality in the character of the congregation. It produces what in general we call responsiveness. The compensating quality which takes away part of the value of this one is its irresponsibility. The audience is quick to feel, but slow to decide. The men who make up the audience, taken one by one, are slower to feel an argument or an appeal to their higher nature, but when they are convinced or touched, it is comparatively easy to waken the conscience, and make them see the necessity of action. I have often heard the minister's appeals compared to the lawyer's addresses to the jury. "Look," men say, "the lawyer pleads, and gets his verdict. You plead a hundred times. You argue week after week, and men will not decide that Christianity is true, nor steadfastly resolve to lead a new life." The fallacy is obvious. We are like lawyers pleading before a jury which in the first place feels itself under no compulsion to decide at all; and in the second place, if it decides as we are urging it, must change its life, break off its habits, and make new ones, which it does not like to contemplate. There is no likeness between it and that body of twelve men who cannot go home till they decide one way or the other, and who have no selfish interest to bias their decision. No wonder that our jury listens to us as long as it pleases, perhaps trembles a little when we are most true and powerful, and then, like Felix, who was both judge and jury to St. Paul, shuts up the court, and departs with only the dimmest feelings of responsibility, saying, "Go thy way for this time. I will hear thee again of this matter."

The Congregation and the New Nature

The result of all this is that in the congregation you have something very near the general humanity. You have human nature as it appears in its largest contemplation. Personal peculiarities have disappeared and man simply as man is before you. This is a great advantage to the preacher. "It is more easy to know man in general than to know a man in particular," said La Rochefoucauld. If in the crowd to whom you preach you saw every man not merely in general but in particular, if each sat there with his idiosyncrasies bristling all over him, how could you preach? There are some preachers, I think, who are ineffective from a certain incapacity of this larger general sight of humanity which a congregation ought to inspire. It has been said of the French preachers that Bossuet knew man better than men, but Fénelon knew both man and men. There are some preachers who seem to know men, but hardly to know or to be touched by man at all. They are ready with special sympathies and with minute advice in the dilemmas of detail which men encounter; but the sight of their race does not rouse them, and they are not able to bring to bear upon a people those universal and eternal motives of the highest human action which, however they may distribute themselves into special motives for special acts, still have a real unity and are the springs of many goodnesses of many kinds. Such men may have a certain fitness to be the spiritual advisers of individuals, but it is not easy to see how they can be powerful preachers to mankind.

I think that it is almost necessary for a man to preach sometimes to congregations which he does not know, in order to keep this impression of preaching to humanity, and so to keep the truth which he preaches as large as it ought to be. He who ministers to the same people always, knowing them minutely, is apt to let his preaching grow minute, to forget the world, and to make the same mistakes about the Gospel that one would make about the force of gravitation if he came to consider it a special arrangement made for these few operations which it accomplishes within his own house. I think there are few inspirations, few tonics for a minister's life better than, when he is fretted and disheartened with a hundred little worries, to go and preach to a congregation in which he does not know a face. As he stands up and looks across them before he begins his sermon, it is like looking the race in the face. All the nobleness and responsibility of his vocation comes to him. It is the feeling which one has had sometimes in travelling when he has passed through a great town whose name he did not even learn. There were men, but not one man he knew; houses, shops, churches, bank, postoffice, business and pleasure, but none of them individualized to him by any personal interest. It is human life in general, and often has a solemnity for him which the human lives which he knows in particular have lost. And this is what we often find in some strange pulpit, facing some congregation wholly made up of strangers.

But this should be occasional. A constant travelling among unknown towns would no doubt weaken and perhaps destroy our sense of humanity altogether. There can be no doubt that it is good for a man that his knowledge of a congregation should be primarily and principally the knowledge of his own congregation, certain dangers of a too exclusive relationship being obviated by preaching sometimes where the people are all strange. It is remarkable how many of the great preachers of the world are inseparably associated with the places where their work was done, where perhaps all their life was lived. In many cases their place has passed into their name as if it were a true part of themselves. Chrysostom of Constantinople, Augustine of Hippo, Savonarola of Florence, Baxter of Kidderminster, Arnold of Rugby, Robertson of Brighton, Chalmers of Glasgow, and in our New England a multitude of such associations which have become historic and compel us always to think of the man with the place and of the place with the man. Everywhere a man must have his place. The disciples are sometimes set before us as if our pastoral life of modern times were an entire departure from their methods; and yet they had their pastorates. Think of St. Paul at Ephesus. Think of St. John in the same city. Think of St. James at Jerusalem. The same necessity, may we not say, which required that the Incarnation should bring divinity, not into humanity in general, but into some special human circle, into a nation, a tribe, a family, requires that he who would bear fruit everywhere for humanity should root himself into some special plot of human life and draw out the richness of the earth by which he is to live at some one special point.

There is nothing better in a clergyman's life than to feel constantly that through his congregation he is getting at his race. Certainly the long pastorates of other days were rich in the knowledge of human nature, in a very intimate relation with humanity. These three rules seem to have in them the practical sum of the whole matter. I beg you to remember them and apply them with all the wisdom that God gives you. First. *Have as few congregations as you can.* Second. *Know your congregation as thoroughly as you can.* Third. *Know your congregation so largely and deeply that in knowing it you shall know humanity.*

I have lingered too long upon the congregation as a whole. Let me go on to speak of that which appears to every minister as he takes a certain congregation to be his congregation and comes to know them very well. Then the unity in which he saw them the first time he stood before them breaks up, and they are divided into various classes. Between that one great gathering which fills the house and the individuals of whom it is composed there are divisions into various groups, which, with certain modifications here and there, appear in every congregation in the land. Let us see what they are.

Congregation Within the Congregation

First and most prominent in every congregation there are some persons who peculiarly represent it to the world. They live in the church, as it were. Their whole life is bound up in its interests. They may be church officers or not. They are part of its history and of its present life. The congregation goes by their name almost as readily as, in your congregational fashion, by the minister's. They are the persons to whom every new enterprise in church life looks first for approval and then for the means of its execution. They are what are sometimes called the "pillars of the church." And such people are very valuable. Often their lives are very noble and devoted. There are people so prominently representative of churches whose life is as truly a consecrated life, with an ordination of its own, as any minister's. They give a solidity and permanence to the congregation, preserve its continuity and identity in the midst of the continual changes of these parts of it which are less firmly fixed. They gather their strength about the minister. They save him from falling into that heresy which has beset all Christian history and been the fruitful source of many kinds of woes, the heresy that the clergyman is the church. They constantly remind him that the people are the church, and that he is the church's servant. I recognize the value of this element in the congregation very heartily. I think that every parish needs such laymen. It would be a very loose and incoherent thing without them.

But still I want you to notice the dangers that may come in connection with the special prominence and special usefulness of a few members of the church. There is chance always of the church becoming a sort of club, providing for the wants, perhaps, indeed, the highest spiritual wants, of a few, but forgetting that it has the world about it and was meant for all men. This is a danger which belongs to the very fact of a recognized body called the congregation. It is a danger which is intensified when in the center of that body there is a core which emphasizes all its qualities and spirit, the congregation of the congregation. The congregation ought to be exclusive only, as our old professor of theology used to say of the Gospel, as the light in the Pharos was covered with glass merely that it might burn the more brightly and shed the more light abroad. Remember this danger.

Give much time and thought and care to the outskirts of your parish, to its loose and ragged fringes; seek the people who just drift within your influence, and who will drift away again, if your kind, strong hand is not upon them. Do not spend too much time in the safe sheepfold where the ninety-nine are secure, while there are sheep upon the mountains. Be sure that nothing will make the core and heart of your congregation so solid as a strong drawing inward of its loose circumference. The strong and settled men of your church will value you and your usefulness to them more highly if they see you busy among the wretched, the careless, and what men dare to call the worthless souls.

And there is another danger, I think, which the congregation in the congregation brings with it. The laymen who are most active and interested in church life are very often not the most receptive hearers. They are apt to take a few truths for settled, and, realizing them very fully, using them in their church work constantly, to ask no more, indeed to be hardly open to any more. They are half clergymen, half laymen, without the full receptivity and mental enterprise which belongs to either. This is the reason why they sometimes become dogmatic, and not merely do not care themselves to speculate or learn, but, with an honest and narrow fear, begrudge the clergy and their fellow laymen an eagerness for truth which overruns their own settled lines. The strongest bigotry is often found among theological laymen rather than among clergymen. The pillars of the church are apt to be like the Pillars of Hercules, beyond which no man might sail. Dean Stanley, in an essay upon the connection of church and State, says of the lay element in church synods; "The laymen who as a general rule figure in such assemblies do not represent the true lay mind of the church, still less the lay intelligence of the whole country. They are often excellent men, given to good works, but they are also usually the partisans of some special clerical school; they are, in short, clergymen under another form rather than the real laity themselves." He is writing on an English subject, but his words describe a danger which we in America can recognize, and which makes us glad to go on and find in the congregation other elements besides this most valuable, this indispensable one of which I have been speaking.

The Skeptic

To pass at once, then, to the other extreme, there is in very many, if not in all, congregations in these days what we may call the supercilious hearer. He is a man who for some reason comes to church, but is out of sympathy with what goes on there. He is skeptical about the truth of what we believe and preach. You come to know that hearer. You are sure that he is critical. You are aware that some safe, sonorous, and unmeaning statements, which some of your people will take because they have the right words in them and the true ring about them, he seizes on the moment that they fall from your lips and tears their flimsiness to pieces in his merciless mind.

Sometimes your heart has sunk as you have said some foolish thing and not dared to look him in the face, but felt sure that it has not escaped him. In one of his Lent discourses Massillon upbraids such hearers. "It is not to seek corn," he says, "that you come into Egypt. It is to seek out the nakedness of the land. *Exploratores Estis, ut videatis infirmiora terrae hujus venistis.*"

Now, such an element in a congregation, though it may be very small, cannot but influence the preacher. What shall he think about it? He ought to start, it seems to me, by feeling that the very presence of such men in church means something. They have not come wholly, certainly they will not come continually, for the malicious reason which Massillon ascribes. There is some better and deeper cause, even though the man is not conscious of it himself. The preacher has a right to believe this, and so the man's presence may become not an embarrassment but an inspiration. And then, when this is gained, he may become a help in other ways. He keeps the atmosphere of the church fresh. He makes you aware as you preach of the unbelief which you have no right to forget. He incites you with the sense of difficulty and the consciousness of criticism. A parish of critics would be killing, but a critic here and there is a tonic. He keeps the walls of your church from growing so solid that as you preach you cannot, as you ought, look through them as if they were glass, and preach in the present remembrance of the multitudes who never come to church, and do not know your truth, and yet for whom your truth is just as true and might be just as helpful as it is to you. This man makes all this real to you. He compels you to remember it.

It is strange how the general skepticism about us may not put us out, or disturb us at all, while a special case close by us will excite us and waken all our powers. It is like the way in which you can go on with your private work or thought, perfectly well, perhaps all the better, for the general roar of the city, while a single hammer clanging under your window distracts you and compels you to hear it. How shall such a critic enter into your preaching? What influence shall it have upon your sermon to know that he is there? The influence, I should say, of making the whole sermon more true and conscientious, more complete in the best qualities that belong to all good sermons. But not the influence of changing the sermon's essential character. Preach the Gospel all the more seriously, simply, mightily if you can, because of the unsympathetic criticism that it has to meet, but let it be the same Gospel which you would pour into ears hungry to receive it.

The two faults that you have to avoid in preaching to unbelief are, defiance and obsequience. One makes the unbeliever hate your truth, and the other makes him despise it. Be frank, brave, simple. There is nothing the unbeliever honors like belief. Let the influence of your supercilious and skeptical audience be primarily upon yourself, making you more serious and eager, then let it come indirectly into your sermon, not changing its topic, but filling it with a stronger power of conviction and of love. Of course, I am speaking now, not of the sermons in which one specially deals with some special phase of skepticism, but only of the general tenor of a man's preaching in view of this part of his congregation.

The Habitual Attender

The next element in the congregation of which I wish to speak is less interesting than these two; perhaps, also, more puzzling. In every congregation there are many people who come to church, as it seems, purely from habit. As with the supercilious hearers, it is hard to tell why they come, but not now because of any positive reason why they should not, but merely from the absence of any reason why they should. Such a hearer seems to be docile, but his docility consists in never doubting or denying what you say. He has probably grown up in the church.

There is more or less of the notion of respectability attaching to that mysterious impulse which every Sunday turns his steps towards the sanctuary. Probably if you could get deep enough, deeper than his own consciousness of its causes, you would find that some vague fear had something to do at least with the origin, perhaps with the continuance of this strange habit. He is no unusual sight. He comes and goes in all our churches. In many churches it seems as if such as he made up a large part of the congregation. Now what shall we say of him? First of all, certainly, as we said of the critic, that we have a right to believe that we have not wholly fathomed the secret of his presence. At least we may hope that, however unconsciously and vaguely, the spirit of the place has reached him. Hoping this, you may expect to see the unconscious impulse develop into a conscious seeking, if you can intensify the spirit of the place, and make it more positive about him. The form in which the change takes place will vary according to his character. It may be sudden and vehement; a conversion as true and picturesque as any that comes to one who, after years of brutal ignorance, hears for the first time the story of the Savior. Or it may be very gradual, the slow, still drawing to a focus and quickening into fire of that heat which he has been absorbing, without knowing it, so long.

There are two effects of every sermon, one special, in the enforcement of a single thought, or the inculcation of a single duty; the other general, in the diffusion of a sense of the beauty of holiness and the value of truth. To the second of these effects this routine listener has been susceptible during many a service and sermon that seemed to pass across him like the wind. However the awakening comes, there is no happier sight for any minister to see. It puts new vigor into him, makes him believe his truth by one more evidence, and teaches him that lesson which the preacher must know, but which he can only learn thoroughly out of experiences such as this, that it is not his business to despair of anybody.

Perhaps, so far as the minister is concerned, this is the final cause of this most discouraging being's presence in the congregation. He furnishes the minister now and then with an encouragement such as nobody but himself could furnish. And, in the meantime, sitting there with the calm countenance which has faced so many sermons, if anything could sting the jaded and commonplace minister into freshness and pointedness, it would seem as if it must be this man's presence. He shames you and inspires you. He makes you feel your responsibility, and makes you eager not to boast of it. He reminds you of your duty and your feebleness. He rebukes anything fantastic or unreal in your preaching. He tempts your plainest, and directest, and tersest truth. There is a prayer in an old Russian liturgy which always seemed to me the very model of the minister's prayer, which I wish that all of us ministers could learn to pray continually, and which this man in your congregation makes you pray with double earnestness—"O, Lord and Sovereign of my Life, take from me the spirit of idleness, despair, love of power, and unprofitable speaking."

The Seekers

But from these classes let us turn to that part of a congregation which constitutes its chief and most inspiring interest. I mean those who in any way are to be characterized as earnest seekers after truth. It is the element that calls out all that is best in a preacher. Very often as we read Christ's teachings, we can almost feel His eye wandering here and there across the motley crowd around Him, till He finds some one man evidently in earnest, and then the discourse sets towards him, and we almost feel the Savior's heart beat with anxiety to help some poor forgotten creature, who has long since passed out of the memory of man, but in whom on that day so long ago He saw a seeker. And we may say with certainty that any man who has not in him the power of quick response to the appeal of spiritual hunger lacks a fundamental quality of the true preacher. There are some men who cannot see bodily pain without a longing to relieve it which begets an ingenuity in relieving it, out of which springs all the best refinements of the doctor's art. There are other men who, just in the same way, perceive the wants and longings of men's souls, and in them is begotten the holy ingenuity which the true preacher uses. The soul quickens the mind to its most complete fertility.

I do not subdivide this class. It includes the whole range of personal earnestness. The heart just conscious of some need, yet ignorant of what it is, dissatisfied and restless, not alone from the unsatisfactoriness of earthly things, but likewise from a true attraction which comes to it from a higher life, this heart is close beside another which has long known the truth and long rested on the love of Christ, but yet is always craving a deeper truth and a more unhindered love. The two hearts belong together. They help to throw the same kind of spirit into the congregation. They send up the same kind of inspiration to the preacher. It is good always to think of these two hearts together, to count your congregation, not by the point in Christian attainment which you conceive them to have reached, but by the spiritual desire and eagerness which you can perceive in them. We may mistake the first. We can hardly be mistaken about the second. Here must be the preacher's real encouragement. Behind all tests which the church-membership lists and the contribution boxes can furnish, there lies the knowledge, which comes out of all his anxious intercourse with them, whether these men and women to whom he preaches are seeking for more truth and higher life. It seems as if one of the ways in which the Lord's beatitude about the hungerers and thirsters after righteousness came true was by the power to help them which the very sight of their thirst and hunger gave to those whom God had sent to be their feeders.

And I believe that the proportion of this class in the general congregation is much greater than we are apt to imagine. In all life, and nowhere more than in what we say about the church and its work, cynical and disparaging ideas are capable of much more clever, epigrammatic statement than hopeful ideas. So they have easy currency and impose on people. It is easy to draw the picture of the faithless or frivolous elements in a congregation till it appears as if the whole company which meets every Sunday were in an elaborate conspiracy to make sport of itself, as if a crowd of people came together to criticise what none of them believed, and to endure with half-concealed impatience what none of them cared anything about. But such a picture, the more cleverly and sweepingly it is drawn, evidently disproves itself. If that were the congregation, evidently there would not long be any congregation. If that were what their meeting meant, evidently they would not meet again and again year after year. No mere momentum of a past impulse could carry along so dead a weight. No, there is in the congregation as its heart and soul a craving after truth. Believe in that. Let it give an expectant look to the whole congregation in your eyes. Let it fill your study as you write at home. And if among the elements which make up your great congregation you grow bewildered and cannot tell to which one you ought to write or speak, I do not hesitate at all to say let it be this one. This is the spirit to which if you speak you will be sure to speak most universally.

One sermon here and there to those who are entirely indifferent, beating their sleepy carelessness awake; one sermon here and there to those who are scornfully skeptical, showing them if you can how weak their superciliousness is, a sermon fired if need be with something of "the scorn of scorn;" one sermon here and there perhaps for those rare few whose life seems to have mastered truth and bathed itself in love, a sermon of congratulation and of peace; but almost all your sermons with the seekers in your eye. Preaching to them you shall preach to all. The indifferent shall be awakened into hope; the scornful shall feel some sting of shame; and before those who are most conscious of what God has done for them shall open visions of what greater things He yet may do, and like St. Paul they may forget the things behind and press forward with a new desire.

It is from the recognition of this element in the congregation that the minister's perception of the necessary variety of Christian life proceeds. All earnestness emphasizes individuality. So long as you see no personal anxiety in your people's eyes, you may calmly form your own plans about them, make up your mind what they are to be made, and go to work to make them that with certain expectation that they will take your truth in just your way, and shape their lives into the mold which you lay before them as if it showed the only shape of Christian character. But when you feel the anxious wish of men and women really seeking after truth, when the cry "What must I do to be saved?"sounds in your quickened ears from all the intent and silent pews, then is the time when you really learn how wide and various salvation is.

The revival and the inquiry room must always widen a man's conception of Christianity, and they are only the emphatic expressions of what is always present and may always be felt to every congregation.

A minister once said to me how strange it seemed to him that he had been preaching one truth in one language for years and yet the people who came to him moved by the truth he taught never conceived it in his form, nor used, as they told him their experience, the language in which he had set the truth before them. It troubled him. It made him wonder whether the language he had used was wrong and false; perhaps, also, whether the truth which they stated so differently really was the same truth which he had tried to teach them. To me it rather showed that there must have been truth and noble reality about his words, a genuinely feeding power, that men should have taken them as they take the healthy corn out of the fields and turn it into all kinds of strength and work. However that may have been, the more truly you think of your congregation as seekers after salvation, to whom you are to open the sacred doors, the more ready you will be to see each entering into a salvation peculiarly his own. You will be glad and not sorry when a man tells you what God has done for him, and only gradually you find that it is the truth which you told him, transformed into some new shape of which you never dreamed, that is the new treasure of his life.

The Make-up of the Congregation

These, then are the elements which make up the congregation. They are the constant factors. In order to realize the congregation entirely, we must think of it as not closed, but open, and always including some people who as mere strangers have wandered in and taken their seats among the people who are always there. They suggest the outside world. Their unfamiliar faces remind the preacher of the general humanity. They are not classified at all. They are simply men and women.

I think it is a great advantage to a congregation that it should have such an element. They are to a congregation what the few people who came into contact with Jesus who were not Jews—such as the Syrophenician woman, and the Centurion, and the Greeks, who asked to see Him—were to Christ's disciples. They kept men's conception of His ministry from closing in tightly to the Jewish people.

This is the danger of the country parish, where you know everybody who comes into the church. You forget the mission to the world. I know no safeguard against such forgetfulness but a deep sense of the general humanity of the people underneath their special characters, which shall make them true specimens of the race, as well as the distinct individuals, whose faces, names, and ways you know.

These are the elements, then. Now mingle these elements in your mind, and ask what sort of body they make. What will be the general characteristics of this assemblage, so heterogeneous and yet with such a true unity in it, which we call the congregation?

It has the genuine solidity which comes from certain fundamental assumptions.

- It is gathered as a Christian gathering.
- It is not loose and incoherent, like the multitude who stood about Paul on the Hill of Mars, merely asking in general for what is new, or, more earnestly, for what is true.
- It has a positive character.

- It accepts a positive authority.
- It is alert and questioning.

The truth which it desires is open to abundant varieties of conception and application. It is this combination of solidity with vitality, this harmonizing of settled conditions with constant activity and growth, which makes, I think, the most marked character of the Christian congregation:

- It is an institution pervaded with individual life.
- It is an assembly of individuals to which has been given something of the coherence of an institution.
- It is the home at once of faith and thought.

Try to keep all of this character in your congregation. Remember both its institutional character and its individual character. Do not try to make it a highly organized machine, nor to let it merely dissipate into an audience. Make it one without losing its oneness. Let it be full of the spirit of authoritative truth, and at the same time of personal responsibility for thought and action.

The Congregation as People

If we look at the Christian congregation in another and perhaps a simpler way, it stands as perhaps the best representative assembly of humanity that you can find in the world. Men, women, and children are all there together. No age, no sex must monopolize its privileges. All ministrations to it must be full at once of vigor and of tenderness, the father's and the mother's touch at once. Riches and poverty meet indifferently in the idea, however it may be in the reality, of the congregation. Even learning and ignorance are recognized as properly meeting there. However difficult it may be to do it, it is clearly recognized that men ought to preach so that the wisest and the simplest alike can understand and get the blessing.

Here, then, is pure humanity. What other assembly so brings us together on the simple warrant of our race? This is what I always think is meant by that record of the ministry of Jesus, "The common people heard Him gladly." It was not the poor because of some privilege that belonged to their poverty. It was those, rich or poor, wise or rude, in whom the fundamental elements of human life were unclouded by artificial culture. Pharisee or publican, fisherman, or philosopher, if they had not forgotten to be men, they were still "common people," and heard the human Savior gladly. It was to their humanity He preached, and nothing that He knew of God was too precious to be brought, if He could bring it, to their understanding.

Preach to this same humanity, and you too will give it your best. Trust the people to whom you preach more than most ministers do. Begin your ministry by being sure that if you give your people your best thought, it will be none too good for them. They will take it all. Only be sure that it is real, and that you are giving it to them for their best good, and that it is what, if they did receive it, would do them good, and then give them the very best and truest that you know. For one minister who preaches "over people's heads" there are twenty whose preaching goes wandering about under men's feet, or is flung off into the air, in the right intellectual plane perhaps, but in a wholly wrong direction.

Not that there must not be discrimination; only it must not be in the quality of your thought. Never your best thought for the old, your cheap thought for the children; never your best thought for the rich and poor thought for the poor. The best that you can give is not too good for any one; but in that giving of the best there is need for the most true and delicate discrimination as to how it shall be given, and which part of it shall be given to this congregation and which to that. It is not a matter of rule. It belongs to wise and sympathetic instinct. To cultivate that instinct, to learn to feel a congregation, to let it claim its own from him, is one of the first duties of a minister. Until you do that you may be a great expounder, a brilliant "sermonizer," but you cannot be a preacher. Never to be tempted to profoundness where it would be thrown away; never to be childlike when it is manly vigor that you need; never to be dull when you mean to be solemn, nor frivolous when you mean only to be bright; this comes from a very quick power of perception and adaptation.

Our work has always had some curious connections with the art of fishing. Let me quote you from Isaak Walton what Piscator says to Venator while they sit by the stream-side at breakfast, on the morning of the first lesson in trout fishing. I was struck by its appropriateness to the subject of discrimination in preaching. It may help you, if you remember it, when you come to "fish for trout with a worm" yourself, and may make no unfit rule for real timeliness in the pulpit. "Take this for a rule," he says; "when you fish for trout with a worm, let your line have so much and not more lead than will fit the stream in which you fish; that is to say, more in a great troublesome stream than in a smaller that is quieter; as near as may be so much as will sink the bait to the bottom and keep it still in motion and not more." Weight and movement, these are what we need in fishing and in preaching.

The Help and Danger of the Congregation

The congregation being what it is, let me ask in the few moments that remain today, what it can do for the preacher, both in the way of help and in the way of danger.

In the way of help, it brings him the inspiration of its numbers, the boldness and freedom of its mitigated personality, and the larger test of his work. It is not safe to judge of the effect of your work by any one individual; but when a congregation pronounces on it, not by the unreliable witness of praise, but by the testimony of its evidently changed condition, its higher life, its more complete devotion, it is never wrong. Do not despise the witness that even the meanest of your people bear to your faithfulness or unfaithfulness. When it really rains, the puddles as well as the ocean bear witness of the shower. Trust your people's judgment on your work; what they say about it, a good deal; but what it does upon them, much more.

And I cannot *help* bearing witness to the fairness and considerateness which belong to this strange composite being, the congregation. His insight is very true, and his conscience on the whole is very right. If he sees that his minister is totally devoted to him, and giving his life up to his work, he stands by that minister of his and provides for him abundantly. If he sees that his minister is taking good care of his own interests, he lets him do it as he would let any other man, and does not trouble himself about it, as there is no reason that he should. Whether the minister feels the congregation or not, the congregation feels the minister. Often the horse knows the rider better than the rider knows the horse.

There may be exceptions which would not justify my confidence. In all these lectures, I am only giving you the impressions which have come out of my own experience. I am sure it will be well if you can never allow yourself to complain that your congregation neglect you without first asking yourself whether you have given them any reason why they should attend to you.

Indeed, the *danger* of the congregation to the minister comes more from their indulgence than from their opposition. The feeling of the strongest ministers about the superficialness of clerical popularity is very striking. Nothing seemed to vex Robertson so much as to be talked of as the idol of the crowd. Indeed, he is absolutely morbid about it, and hates that to which he need only have been indifferent. It would seem as if mere popularity, to a man of any independence, was the driest of all Dead Sea fruits. And there is reason why it should be so. It is the worst and feeblest part of your congregation that makes itself heard in vociferous applause, and it applauds that in you which pleases it.

Robertson, in one of his letters, says of a friend: "He has lost his power, which was once the greatest that I ever knew. The sentimental people of his congregation attribute it to an increase of spirituality, but it is in truth, a falling-off of energy of grasp." These words suggest the cause of many a minister's decay, the Capua where many a preaching Hannibal has been ruined. *"Turba est argumentum pessimi,"* says Seneca.

There are certain other causes which help to produce the impression, but still there is truth in the belief that much of the best thinking and preaching of the land is done in obscure parishes and by unfamous preachers. The true balance, if we could only reach and keep it, evidently is in neither courting nor despising the popular applause, to feel it as every healthy man feels the approval of his fellowmen, and yet never to be beguiled by it from that which is the only true object of our work, God's truth and men's salvation. And remember this, that the only way to be saved from the poison of men's flattery is to be genuinely devoted to those same men's good. If you really want to drag a man out of the fire, you will not be distracted into self-conceit by his praises of the grace and softness of the hand that you reach out to him. You will say, "Stop your compliments and take hold."

The Popularity Question

The subject of the popularity of ministers is indeed a curious one, and may well merit a few moments' study. We hardly realize, I believe, how far the desire for popularity in this time and land has taken the place of the ambition for preferment which we read of in English clerical history, and which has so strongly and so justly excited our dislike. He who used there to seek the favor of a bishop, or some other patron, bids here for the liking of the multitude. It is a question hardly worth the asking, which ambition calls out the lower arts or does the greater mischief. Both are very bad. To set one's heart on being popular is fatal to the preacher's best growth. To escape from that desire one needs to know that the men who are in no sense popular favorites do much of the very best work of the ministry.

In all work there seems to be generally two classes of workers, one whose processes of working are apparent, the other whose results only appear. Now most popular preachers seem to me to belong to the first class, and to owe their popularity to that characteristic. Not only what they do, but the way in which they do it, interests people. It is not only the power of the truth which they declare: it is the eloquence of the sermons in which they declare it. It is not only the gracious influence they exercise; it is their gracious way of exercising it, the smile, the tone, the transparent vision of the kindly heart. Let a man understand this, and it will certainly require no very profound philosophy or devotion for him to let the popularity go if he can do the work. The popularity is an accident; the power is essential.

And no doubt, the absence of lively popular favor has an influence in enabling a minister to apprehend the larger indications of the successful working of his truth. The people's applause emphasizes the small success, and tempts a man to be content with that. He who works in silence becomes aware of the larger movements of the truth and the surer conquests of the power of God. The small signs fail; there is no glitter in the arms, no shout of triumph anywhere, but often the very silence lets one hear more clearly the great progress that is going on all over the field.

Again, there is great difference in men according as they seem to possess or to lack themselves the qualities and conditions which they try to create in other people. Some men are all afire themselves, and seem to fire others by contagion; other men appear cold, but send forth fire from their very coldness. Some men are full of movement, and so make others move. Other men seem sluggish, and yet awaken others to a vitality which they do not seem to possess themselves.

> The enormous axle-tree
> That whirls (how slow itself!) ten thousand spindles.

In general, the popularity, the quick general sympathy and admiration, will go with the first class of men. The others will do their work in quietness, with much power but not much observation.

Be Yourself

To be your own best self for your people's sake, that is the true law of the minister's devotion. *"Loquendum ut multi, sapiendum ut pauci"*— the thought of the few in the speech of the many—that describes a popular power which any preacher has not only the right but the duty to cover.

The whole of the relation, then, between the preacher and the congregation is plain. They belong together. But neither can absorb or override the other. They must be filled with mutual respect. He is their leader, but his leadership is not one constant strain, and never is forgetful of the higher guidance upon which they both rely. It is like the rope by which one ship draws another out into the sea. The rope is not always tight between them, and all the while the tide on which they float is carrying them both. So it is not mere leading and following. It is one of the very highest pictures of human companionship that can be seen on earth. Its constant presence has given Christianity much of its noblest and sweetest color in all ages. It has much of the intimacy of the family with something of the breadth and dignity that belongs to the state. It is too sacred to be thought of as a contract. It is a union which God joins together for purposes worthy of His care. When it is worthily realized, who can say that it may not stretch beyond the line of death, and they who have been minister and people to each other here be something holy and peculiar to each other in the City of God forever?

7

THE MINISTRY
FOR OUR AGE

I am to speak to you today upon the preacher in his special relation to our own time. There is a strange sound, perhaps, when we think about it, in the very suggestion that the preacher of the Gospel is to be something special with reference to the special time in which he lives. For we have dwelt upon the one universal and eternal message which the preacher is sent to carry to the world. That message never changes. The identity of Christianity lies in its identity. Nay, the identity of man is bound up with it; and so long as man is what he is, what God has to say to him by His servants will certainly always be the same. And so the preacher, as the bearer of that message, must have his true identity, must stand before men in essentially the same figure and speak with essentially the same voice in all the ages. Where, then, does the adaptation of a preacher in his own age come in? The best answer, perhaps, would be, by way of illustration in the position which every live and cultivated man holds with reference to the time he lives in.

A Man for This Time

He is, in the first place, a man in universal human history. His are the rights, the duties, and the standards which belong to all men simply as men. In proportion as he is a strong, wise man this larger life is real to him. He knows that he will live his special life more healthily for himself and more helpfully to his brethren, not by forgetting, but by remembering his place in the general and continuous humanity. It will keep his sight truer. Many times it will preserve his independence when it is in danger from the fleeting passions of the hour. But yet he lives the special life. He is a man of his own day, thoroughly interested in the questions that are exciting men around him, pained by the troubles, delighted by the joys, and busy in the tasks of his own time. His broad humanity and broad culture make him a man of all days; his keen life and quick sympathies and healthy instincts and real desire for work make him a man of his own day.

We can all see the ideal completeness of such a life. Whenever we have seen a man at all attaining it we have felt how complete he was. The incompleteness of men comes as they fall short of this on one side or the other. The man who belongs to the world but not to his time grows abstract and vague, and lays no strong grasp upon men's lives and the present causes of their actions. The man who belongs to his time but not to the world grows thin and superficial.

A Preacher for This Time

And just exactly this is true about the preacher. There are the constant and unchanging needs of men, and the message which is addressed to those needs and shares their unchangeableness; and then there are the ever-varying aspects of those needs to which the tone of the message, if it would really reach the needy soul, must intelligently and sympathetically correspond. The first of these comes of the preacher's larger life, his study of the timeless Word of God, his relationship with God in history, his personal communion with his Master, and the knowledge of those depths of human nature which never change whatever waves of alteration may disturb the surface. The second comes from a constantly alert watch of the events and symptoms of the current times, begotten of a deep desire that the salvation of the world, which is always going on, may show itself here and now in the salvation of these particular men to whom the preacher speaks. If we leave out the difference of natural endowments and of personal devotedness, there is nothing which so decides the different kinds as well as the different degrees of ministers' successes as the presence or absence of this balance and proportion of the general and special, the world-consciousness and the time-consciousness.

Those Who Fail

The abstract reasoner, laying his deep trains of thought which run far wide of the citadels where sin is now entrenched, and never shatter a stone of present wickedness with their ponderous explosions, whatever other good things he may do, fails as a preacher to men. The mere critic of the time who, with no deep principles and no long hopes, goes on his way merrily or fiercely lopping off the ugly heads of the vices of the time with his light switch or valiant sword, he, too, fails in his work, and by and by is wearied and distressed as he finds the surface character of all the reformation to which he brings his converts. It is the first sort of preaching that wearies men when they complain of what they call a very profound but a very dull sermon. The second is what makes people dissatisfied with a sense of unthoroughness as they come home still mildly tingling from what they call a sensational sermon. The first man has aimed at truth without caring for timeliness. The second man has been so anxious to be timely that he has perhaps distorted truth, and certainly robbed her of her completeness.

Truth and timeliness together make the full preacher. How shall you win such fulness? Let me say one or two general words, and leave particulars of the method to come out, if they may, all through the lecture. First, seek always truth first and timeliness second, never timeliness first and truth second. Then let your search for truth be deliberate, systematic, conscientious. Let your search for timeliness consist rather in seeking for strong sympathy with your kind, a real share in their occupations, and a hearty interest in what is going on. And yet again; let the subjects of your sermons be mostly eternal truths, and let the timeliness come in the illustration of those truths by, and their application to, the events of current life. So you will make the thinking of your hearers larger, and not smaller, as you preach to them.

The Present Age

So much in general. But now let us come to this most interesting age in which we live and in which we are set to preach. I want to point out two or three of its broadest characteristics and see how they affect the preacher's work. I do not undertake any such task as a general estimate of the character of our strange century and country. I only want to indicate some points in it which come directly home to you and me, and to see, if we can, how we shall treat them. Let me speak of the feeling of our time about truth and life in general, about the ministry and about the Bible.

In the first place, then, there are certain vaguely conceived but real difficulties lying in people's minds today against which the Gospel that we preach strikes. We meet them in a great variety of forms. We find their spirit appearing in regions of intelligence where there cannot be any understanding of their intellectual statements. The most common, the most wonderfully subtle and pervasive of all these is the notion of Fate, with all the consequences which it brings with it to the ideas of responsibility and even to the fundamental conceptions of personal Life. We are so occupied with watching the developments of fatalistic philosophy in its higher and more scientific phases that I think we often fail to see to what an extent and in what unexpected forms it has found its way into the common life of men and is governing their thoughts about ordinary things. The notion of fixed helplessness, of the impossibility of any strong power of a man over his own life , and, along with this, the mitigation of the thought of responsibility which, beginning with the sublime notion of a man's being answerable to God, comes down to think of him only as bound to do his duty to society, then descends to consider him as only liable for the harm which he does to himself, and so finally reaches the absolute abandonment of any idea of judgment or accountability whatever—all this is very much more common than we dream. It runs down through all the degrees of lessening consciousness.

There is nothing stranger than to watch how the intelligent speculations of the learned become the vague prejudices of the vulgar. You can shut up nothing within the scholar's study-door. For good or for mischief all that the wisest are thinking becomes in some form or other the basis upon which the ignorant live. Partly this, and partly a power which works just the other way. Partly that the learned are led on by their oneness with all their brethren to take for the subjects of their study those things to which the interest of the unlearned has been turned, and to reduce to philosophical expression those ideas by which the rudest are shaping their lives. Whatever the interaction of the two causes may have been, the result is here in a certain suspicion of fatalism all around us. With it come the inevitable consequences of hopelessness and restraint pervading all society and influencing all action, different in different natures, hard and defiant in some, soft and luxurious in others, but in all their various forms unfitting men for the best happiness, or the best growth, or the best usefulness to fellowmen.

This is what we find scattered through the society in which we live. This is what you have got to preach to, my young friends. You will not escape it by ministering to one class of people rather than to another, for it runs everywhere. You will leave it in the study only to find it in some new form in the workshop. You will silence it in the dull querulous discontent of the boor only to hear it in the calm and resigned and lofty philosophy of the sage.

What preaching can you meet it with? Certainly one may point out the broadest features of the preaching which alone can meet it. It must be positive preaching. There never was an age when negative preaching, the mere assertion of what is not true, showed its uselessness as it does today. It does no good to show the fatalist that fatalism is untenable. He does not really believe it; it is only that he seems to be unable to believe anything else. You disprove it, and that only adds another to the heap of things that are incredible. You must preach positively, telling him what is true, setting God before his heart and bidding it know its Lord. And it must be preaching to the conscience. The conscience is the last part of our personality that dies into the death of fatalism. It must be the first part of us that wakens to the privileges and obligations of personal life. Make a man know that he is wicked and that he may be good, and his self and God's self will be realities to him which no juggle of words can make him believe do not exist. And thirdly, there never was an age that so needed to have Christ preached to it—the personal Christ. In His personality the bewildered soul must refind its own personal life. In the service of Him it must rediscover the possibility and the privilege of duty. The haunting skepticism must be invaded by preaching such as this. The doubt which has grown up so vaguely and will give no account of itself must be overshadowed and undermined, overshadowed by the vivid majesty of God in Christ, undermined by the sense of sin and the necessity of righteousness. The only hope of its complete dispersion is to produce the Christian life which is its own assurance, declares its own freedom, and prophesies its own possibilities.

The Preacher and Science: Three Classes

I speak of this tendency to doubt concerning spiritual and personal forces principally as it appears all through the movements of society and the lives of common men. I have not much to say here about the way in which the preacher meets it in the theories of science, the guesses at the philosophy of the universe which the philosophers of our time have made so plentifully. But nobody can listen to sermons nowadays and not be struck by seeing how confusedly the purpose of preaching and the function of the preacher seem to be apprehended by those who preach.

Among the preachers who busy themselves with what modern science is doing and saying, we can easily discern several classes. *One class claims competently to criticise the work of specialists and to revise their judgments*, even about those subjects on which they ought to be authorities. It attempts to pronounce with competence upon the results of scientific inquiry in a summary way which it would never tolerate with reference to its own peculiar subjects of study. It is needless to say how this class puts itself into the power of those whom it criticises. It can get the material for its criticism only from them. So soon as it leaves the field of general reasoning and attempts to touch the question of scientific fact, it must look for its facts to those who, for the time, it is treating as its adversaries. It is reduced to something of the helplessness to which the Israelites were brought when the Philistines who had conquered them compelled them to come to their smiths to sharpen every man his share, and his coulter, his axe, and his mattock.

Another class seems to stand ready, not merely to disown the power of competent criticism, but to accept with headlong zeal every momentary conclusion of modern science, even before the scientific world itself has learned to treat it as more than a probable hypothesis; and seems to be all the more eager to accept it the more entirely it seems to be in conflict with the faith of Christianity. No one will deny, I think, that there are among the disciples of natural science today some men who curiously repeat on their own ground every offensive and arrogant peculiarity of the priestcraft whose historical enormities they so fondly and truly upbraid. It is an interesting illustration of how human nature is the same at heart, and, if it be bad, will show the same kind of badness whether it wear the priest's surplice or the professor's gown. To this overbearing assumption this second class is always in great haste to prostrate itself.

Surely the spirit of both of these classes is not good. Either is bad, either the competence with which some clergymen attempt to pronounce upon the value of scientific theories, or the panic in which other clergymen seem to be waiting only to surrender to the first man with a hammer or a microscope who challenges them. There is another class still which seems to be merely frightened. A sense of vague inevitable danger is continually haunting *those who feel how wholly incompetent they are to master or even to comprehend the thing they fear. They hate and dread the very name of science.* They would really, literally, silence its investigations if they could. As the best thing which they can do, they are very apt to devise or to adopt some exceedingly fantastic and exaggerated form either of church government, or of ritual, or of doctrine, which they clothe with artificial sacredness, and then set it up to keep the advancing monster back, as they said that Chinese piled their most sacred crockery upon the track to stop the progress of the first locomotive that came thundering through their land. All fanaticism is closely bound to fear.

A Suggested Alternative

These are the dispositions with which some ministers meet the spirit of the day. These are the various classes. Among these classes comes some new minister, and stands and says, To which shall I belong? Is there not something better than either? Indeed there is. It is possible for you and me, taking the facts of the spiritual life, to declare them with as true a certainty as any preacher ever did in what men call the "ages of faith." They are as true today as they ever were. Men are as ready to feel their truth. The spiritual nature of man, with all its needs, is just as real a thing, and Christ is just as truly and richly its satisfaction. To speak to it and offer Him is your privilege and mine. And yet not to be unregardful of what men are thinking by our side, to watch it, so far as we may to understand it all, but always to watch it with a desire to see, not what it will say to overthrow, but what it will say to strengthen and enlarge the truth we preach; to watch it with a feeling that it may modify our conception and statement of the truth, but with no fear at all that it ever can destroy the truth itself; this does seem to me to be the temper for the preacher of today. Our truth stands on its own evidence, but it has its connections with all the truth that men are learning so wonderfully on every side. To listen to what they learn, not that we may see whether our truth of the soul and of God is true, but that we may come to truer and larger ways of apprehending it—this is our place. If we can take this place, it will give us both firmness and freedom; it will free us alike from the uselessness of doubt and the uselessness of bigotry.

I seem to see strange panic in the faces of the ministers of today. I have seen a multitude of preachers gathered together to listen to one who expounded scientific theories upon the religious side, and making the hall ring with vociferous applause of statements which might be true or not, but certainly whose truth they had not examined, and in which it certainly was not the truth but the tendency to help their side of the argument that they applauded. I think that that is not a pleasant sight for any one to see who really cares for the dignity and purity of his profession.

The preacher must mainly rely upon the strength of what he does believe, and not upon the weakness of what he does not believe. It must be the power of spirituality and not the feebleness of materialism that makes him strong. No man conquers, no true man tries to conquer merely by the powerlessness of his adversary.

I think the scene which I just described was principally melancholy because it suggested a lack of faith among the ministers themselves. And one feared that that was connected with the obstinate hold upon some untenable excrescences upon their faith which they chose to consider part of the substance of their faith itself. So bigotry and cowardice go together always.

But after all, in days like these, one often finds himself falling back upon the simplest truths concerning the whole matter of belief. If there be disproof or modification of what we Christians hold, the sooner it can be made known to us the better. We are Christians at all, if we are Christians worthily, because we are first lovers of the truth. And if our truth is wholly true, it is God's before it is ours, and we may at least trust Him with some part of its care. We are so apt to leave Him out.

And there is one strong feeling that comes out of the extravagant unbelief of our time which has in it an element of reassurance. The preacher and pastor sees that in human nature which assures him of the essential religiousness of man. He comes to a complete conviction that only a religion can overthrow and supplant a religion. Man wholly unreligious is not even conceivable to him. And so, however he may fear for single souls, the very absoluteness of much of the denial of the time seems to offer security for the permanence of faith.

But the main thing is to know our own ground as spiritual men, and stand on its assured and tested strength. And that strength can be tested only by our own experience; and so once more we come round to our old first truth, that the man is behind the ministry, that what is in the sermon must be in the preacher first.

Here must come what useful work we can do for those who are bewildered and faithless in these trying times. If you are going to help men who are materialists, it will not probably be by a scientific disproof of materialism. It will be by a strong live offer of spiritual realities. It is not what the minister knows of science, but how he grasps and presents his spiritual verities, that makes him strong. Many ignorant ministers meet the difficulties of men far wiser than themselves. I may know nothing of speculative atheism. It is how I know God that tells.

I do not disparage controversy. Theology must be prepared to maintain her ground against all comers. If she loses her power of attack and defence, she will lose her life, as they used to say that when parted with his sting he parted with his industry and spirit. Only not every minister is made for a controversialist, and the pulpit is not made for controversy. The pulpit must be positive, telling its message, trusting to the power of that message, expecting to see it blend into harmony with all the other truth that fills the world; and the preacher, whatever else he may be elsewhere, in the pulpit must be positive too, uttering truth far more than denying error. There is nothing that could do more harm to Christianity today than for the multitude of preachers to turn from preaching Christ, whom they do understand, to the discus-

sion of scientific questions which they do not understand.
Hear the conclusion of the whole matter.

- Preach positively what you believe.

- Never preach what you do not believe or deny
  what you do believe.

- Rejoice in the privilege of declaring God.

- Let your people frankly understand, while you
  preach, that there is much you do not know, and
  that both you and they are waiting for completer
  light.

I must not linger longer on this topic. May God help you,
as you meet it constantly, to be wise and true.

The Preacher and Tolerance

Another of the questions which belong to this time of ours
in some peculiar ways is the question of toleration, the relation
of truth to partial truth and error. This again, like every deep
pervading question, has its form for the learned and for the
unlearned. To the scholar it comes with the speculations, for
which the enlarged acquaintance with other lands and times
has furnished such abundant food, about comparative
religion. To the unscholarly it offers itself in the prevailing
disposition to exalt conduct above belief, and ask not what
views a man holds, but what sort of life he lives. In both
these cases the tendency of our time is no doubt toward
tolerance. The scholar and the ignorant man alike are both
content that their neighbors should think differently from
them about religion. The very desire for the stake has died
away.

We look back to the sixteenth and seventeenth century
and wonder at the enormities of bigotry. We are all thankful
for the progress; but often as we read the books of the time,
often as we talk with our friends, there is a misgiving which
intrudes. How much of this toleration is indifference? How
many of these people that are kindly to their neighbors' faiths
are careless about their own? How much of the difference
between us and the zealots of the seventeenth century has
come from our weakened hold on truth? They believed with
all their hearts, and were intolerant; we have grown tolerant,
but then we do not believe as they believed. We must realize

their intensity before we presume to sit in judgment on their intolerance. So often we are only trying to be mutually harmless.

We are like steamers lying in the fog and whistling, that we may not run into others nor they into us. It is safe, but commerce makes no great progress thereby, and it shows no great skill in navigation. And then there comes the picture of a higher state than either the seventeenth or nineteenth century has reached. We see that here, as everywhere, mankind has been advancing in a halting and awkward way, first dragging one side forward, and only gradually dragging the other side along to meet it. There was a time when men were standing with their love of truth in advance of their love of personal liberty. We see that we are standing now with our love of personal liberty in advance of our love for truth. We anticipate a time when the love of truth shall come up to our love of liberty, and men shall be cordially tolerant and earnest believers both at once. When that comes it will be a new thing in the world. It has been seen in beautiful or splendid individuals scattered all through the ages, but there has been no age in which the mass of thinkers were at once strong in positive belief and tolerant of difference of opinion.

The Two Kinds of Parishioners

Now it is certainly the minister's duty to inculcate positive belief. We rejoice that it has also been recognized as the minister's duty to foster charity and tolerance. In the minister, then, would seem to rest the hope of that better time to come when both of these together are to bless the world. As he goes about among his people he is perpetually saddened by their unnatural divorce. He hears some member of his church talk about truth. He listens to clear statements of the Gospel; wise, sound discriminations; true scriptural explanations of the mysteries of God and man and grace. And all uttered with a deep fervor which shows how the man loves the truth he knows. The preacher says, "What clearness!" "What faith!" and rejoices over his disciple. And just then some stray word drops from the glowing lips which shows with what a strangeness, amounting almost to antipathy, this believer looks upon other people who hold truth differently from himself; with what a sense of narrow and exclusive privilege he treasures his orthodox belief. Or, just the opposite. Some hearer of your preaching delights you with his ardent charity for all religions, until you find that he has no real religion of his own. He upbraids the bigot without ever having dreamed of the intense belief which has made the bigot what he is. In either case there is a disappointment in the result of your work as it appears in these two men. Belief and charity are not yet in their true association. Mercy and truth have not yet met together. And you set yourself, as you walk home from your two parish calls, to think what you can do to bring about their union.

Creating Union

What the minister can really do is this. I give it in no special rules. I know none. If I did I should not think it worth my while or yours to come here and repeat the little methods of my working which would not help you. I only give here, as I have tried to all along, the principles for which the grace of God and your good sense, if you have both, will find for you the applications. The preacher can, first, always insist on looking and on making his people look on doctrines not as ends but means; and so, if other men less perfectly reach the same ends by means of other doctrines, he will be able to rejoice in their attainment of the end without doing dishonor to or valuing one whit the less the truth which, as it seems to him, leads much more directly and fully to the great attainment. "Master," said John, "we saw one casting out devils in Thy name; and we forbade him, because he followeth not with us." And Jesus said, "Forbid him not; for there is no man which shall do a miracle in My name, that can lightly speak evil of Me. For he that is not against us is on our part." I suppose the day is past when people strengthened their sense of the importance of the Gospel and of their privilege in hearing it, and of their duty to carry it to the heathen, by asserting that no heathen could be saved who had not heard it. But something of the same spirit lingers still at home. The grosser forms of an error will often disappear before its milder ones. And many men, many ministers, are apt to emphasize the value of the truth to themselves by asserting or at least implying consequences which they do not really think would follow on its rejection by their neighbors. The abandonment of such a way of thinking and talking would be a great step forward towards the desired union of belief and charity.

And, again, the preacher may industriously and discriminately set himself to discern what there is good in the heart of the system that he tolerates, and, tolerating it *for that good*, may so keep his absolute standards and his love for his own truth unimpaired. The weakness of a large part of our tolerance for other systems than our own is that it is not discriminating. It is a mere sentiment. It thinks that it is narrow not to tolerate, and so it says, "Come now and let us tolerate;" but it never dissects out that soul of goodness in things evil or only half good which should make it possible to tolerate them cordially and be glad of their existence; and so, while it wastes its cheap and unmeaning compliments upon them, it often has no real sympathy with them, and either despises or hates them underneath its compliments.

This is the kind of tolerance that haunts the anniversary platforms where sects are met together, where men seem to have forgotten that there are any differences between them, and from which they go back to their pulpits without a perceptible mitigation in the blindness with which they misapprehend the whole position of their neighbor who is preaching in the next street to them. Toleration as a mere fashion and sentiment is very feeble. It must study and appreciate that which is good in what it tolerates. To see the positive truths that underlie the Roman Catholic errors, that is the only way to be cordially tolerant of Romanism and yet keep clearly and strongly one's own Protestant belief.

It is possible for earnest belief to be united with ardent charity, and it is for us who preach the Gospel of Christ to show the possibility in all our life and preaching. Value the ends of life more than its means, watch ever for the soul of good in things evil, and the soul of truth in things false, and beside the richer influence that will flow out from your life on all to whom you minister, you will do something to help the solution of that unsolved problem of the human mind and heart, the reconciliation of hearty tolerance with strong positive belief.

Other Concerns of the Day

I have been speaking of some of the intellectual characteristics of our time which the preacher must encounter. They are very prominent. But there are other characteristics of a different sort that force themselves upon us almost as much. We talk about the scientific character of our age. We think of it as wholly given up to the search after knowledge. But after all there is a vast preponderance of the activity of our time which is in no sense scientific. The commercial and social and political movements which go on about us cannot be said, I think, to have any more of the scientific spirit, to show any more tendency to revert to facts and trust to established principles, than those same movements have always manifested. The trouble with these great continuous and universal interests of life no doubt has its connections with the danger which besets the study of science.

Ignoring God for Second Causes

What we have to fear is the magnifying of second causes to the forgetfulness of the first cause and the final cause of things. We need to remember as we preach with what enormous urgency this danger is pressing upon the lives of the men and women to whom our preaching is addressed. The men and women are living in the midst of the intense but superficial excitement which comes of the unnatural and exclusive vividness of second causes. It seems to the business man as if wealth were the king of everything; as if it made reputation, made happiness, almost made character. It seems to the man or woman of society as if fashion, in some supreme reserve of queenship where she sits and whence her undisputed mandates come, were the supreme arbiter of destiny. It is the frankness with which men own that their views of the forces which govern things stop with these immediate causes, wealth and fashion and the pleasure of the senses that appalls us now. They do not even go through the form of recognizing some spiritual force further back. "Alas, there are no more hypocrites now," cried the Abbé Poulle in France in the last century. And it was indeed a symptom. As humanity is constituted, when men no longer give themselves the trouble to make an imitation, it proves how little the reality is honored; and the very carelessness of men about affecting any thought of higher causes is an indication of how the lower causes have absorbed the attention and are trying to satisfy the needs of men.

Preaching the First Cause

This is the world to which we have to bring the Gospel, the story that begins with "God created the heaven and the earth," and goes on with the record of God's power and love until it comes to the prophecy of the spiritual judgment day. What can we do to get that story of the one first cause home to the heart of this eager, feverish age worshiping in its Pantheon of second causes?

First, O my brothers, who are to be pastors of the Church, we can take watchful care that the Church herself is true to her belief in God as the source of all power. One of the most terrible signs of how the spirit of sordidness has filled the world is the lamentable extent to which it has pervaded the Church.

The Church is constantly found trusting in second causes as if she knew of no first cause. She elaborates her machineries as if the power lay in them. She goes, cap in hand, to rich men's doors, and flatters them and dares not tell them of their sins because she wants their money. She lets her officers conduct her affairs with all the arts of a transaction on the street or an intrigue in politics, or only shows her difference of standards and freedom from responsibility by some advantage taken which not even the conscience of the exchange or of the caucus would allow. She degrades the dignity of her grand commission by puerile devices for raising money and frantic efforts to keep herself before the public which would be fit only for the sordid ambitions of a circus troupe.

You must cast all that out of the church with which you have to do, or you will make its pulpit perfectly powerless to speak of God to our wealth-ridden and pleasure-loving time. You must show first that His Church believes in Him and trusts Him and is satisfied in Him, or you will cry in vain to men to come to Him. To do this you must not only cast out at your doors the disreputable tinsel of church life of which I have been speaking you must believe in man as the child of God enough to preach to him at once the highest spiritual truth about his Father.

Many a well-meaning preacher is all wrong here, I think. He says, "You must take men as you find them. You must speak to such faculties and perceptions as are awake in them." And so because he sees the economical perceptions very acute in our commercial time, he preaches the economy of goodness. He shows men how holiness will pay. He knows there is a higher truth, but he cannot trust men to hear it. He hopes to lead them on to it by and by. Ah, that is all wrong. There is in every man's heart, if you could only trust it, a power of appreciating genuine spiritual truth; of being moved into unselfish gratitude by the love of God. Continually he who trusts it finds it there.

A hundred men stand like the Spanish magnates on the shore and say, "You must not venture far away. There is no land beyond. Stay here and develop what we have." One brave and trustful man like Columbus believes that the complete world is complete, and he sails for a fair land beyond the sea and finds it. The minister who succeeds is the minister who in the midst of a sordid age trusts the heart of man who is the child of God, and knows that it is not all sordid, and boldly speaks to it of God his Father as if he expected it to answer. And it does answer; and other preachers who have not believed in man, and have talked to him in low planes and preached to him half gospels which they thought were all that he could stand, look on and wonder at their brother-preacher's unaccountable success. There have always been illustrations of this.

There never were more striking ones than in our time. With all the sordidness of our time, the preachers that have been the most powerful have been the most spiritual. His theology has something of the taint of mercenariness about it, but of all the great revivalists I do not know where we shall find any one who has preached more constantly to the good that there is in man, and assumed in all men a power of spiritual action, than Dwight L. Moody. There is nothing finer than to see a soul, which amazes the men in whom it rises, rise up in men, when he who trusts it to answer to the highest call speaks to it of the love of God. In all your preaching echo the ministry of Jesus, who spoke to the lowest and most sensual people directly of the everlasting love, and by the trust He had in them brought them to His Father.

The Danger of Sentimentality

I do not think that one could rightly suggest the characteristics of our time which a minister encounters without naming a tendency to sentimentalness which shows itself in a great deal of our religion, and which, both directly and indirectly, does our work great harm. It is connected, with the other features of the time, with the prevalence of doubt and unbelief. It is most natural that when a multitude of men have more or less deliberately taken up the idea that the foundations of faith are shaken, when they are afraid to say that they hold the truths of religion to be literally and absolutely true, when even the authority of religion as the lord of morality is disturbed, and men are looking somewhere else than to God for a constant reason why they should do right, and when yet, with all this, the impulses of reverence and worship remain strong, it is inevitable then that a certain religion of sentiment should grow up, of which it is impossible to say how much it believes, but which delights in glowing and vague utterances of feeling.

No one can read our hymns, whether they be of the rudest revival sort or the translated medievalisms of ritualism, without feeling what I mean. They are very beautiful often, but, compared with the hymns that our fathers sang, they are weak. They lack thought, and no religion that does not think is strong. It may be in reaction from the way in which many of the old hymns were made to labor with a process of reasoning that struggled on most unlyrically from verse to verse that the favorite hymn of today discards connected thought and seems to try only to utter moods of mystic feeling, or to depict some scene in which the spiritual parable is apt to be lost in the brightness of the sensuous imagery. I think that the same thing is true of prayers. A prayer must have thought in it. The thought may overburden it so that its wings of devotion are fastened down to its sides and it cannot ascend. Then it is no prayer, only a meditation or a contemplation. But to take the thought out of a prayer does not insure its going up to God. It may be too light as well as too heavy to ascend. I saw once in a shop-window in London a placard which simply announced "Limp Prayers." It described, I believe, a kind of Prayer Book in a certain sort of binding which was for sale within; but it brought to mind many a prayer to which one had listened, in which he could not join, out of which had been left the whole backbone of thought, and to which he could attach none of his own heart's desires.

I know that there have always been sentimentalists in religion. Mysticism, which at its best is a very high and thorough action of the whole nature in apprehending spiritual truth, is always degenerating into sentimentalism. But it is dangerous today because it so frankly claims for itself that it is religion. Disowning doctrine and depreciating law, it asserts that religion belongs to feeling, and that there is no truth but love. You will meet it surely in your first parish at the very door. Some of the sweetest and noblest natures there are sure to be full of it, and show it to you very winningly. Others will set it before you as mere weak self-indulgence. You will find many of the strongest brains and consciences in town separated entirely from the church because they consider it, as they would say if they spoke their whole minds out to you, to be the very shop and banquet room of sentimentalism. You cannot ignore this as you preach. You cannot help struggling against its influence upon yourself. The hard theology is bad. The soft theology is worse. You must count your work unsatisfactory unless you waken men's brains and stir their consciences. Let them see clearly that you value no feeling which is not the child of truth and the father of duty. And to let them see that you value no other feeling you must value no other feeling either in yourself or them.

It is natural for sentimentalism and skepticism to go together, like the fever and the chill, and the same mixture of deeper faith and more conscientious duty must be medicine for both.

How the Preacher Is Regarded

We ministers cannot help noting with interest among the symptoms of our time the way in which the preacher himself is regarded. To remark the changed attitude which the people generally hold towards ministers is the most familiar commonplace; to mourn over it as a sign of decadence in the religious spirit is the habit of some people. But the reasons of it are plain enough and have been often pointed out. The preacher is no longer the manifest superior of other men in wit and wisdom. That deference which was once paid to the minister's office, upon the reasonable presumption that the man who occupied it was better educated, more large in his ideas, a better reasoner, a more trustworthy guide in all the various affairs of life than other men, if it were paid still would either be the perpetuation of an old habit, or would be paid to the office purely for itself without any presumption at all about the man. This latter could not be long possible; no dignity of office can secure men's respect for itself continuously unless it can show a worthy character in those who hold it.

I am glad that the mere forms of reverence for the preacher's office have so far passed away. I am not making a virtue of necessity. I rejoice at it. Nothing could be worse for us than for men to keep telling us by deferential forms that

we are the wisest of men when their shelves are full of books
with far wiser words in them than the best that we can preach;
or that we are the most eloquent of men when there are
better orators by the score on every side; or that we are the
best of men when we know of sainthoods among the most
obscure souls before which we stand ashamed. No manly
man is satisfied with any *ex-officio* estimate of his character.
Whether it makes him better or worse than he is, he cares
nothing for it. And so the nearer that ministers come to being
judged like other men just for what they are, the more they
ought to rejoice, the more, I think, they do rejoice.

But what then? Is the minister's sacred office nothing? Does
not his truth gain authority and his example urgency from
the position where he stands? Indeed they do. It seems to me
that the best privilege which can be given to any man is a
position which shall stimulate him to his best and which
shall make his best most effective. And that is just what is
given to the minister. An official position which should
substitute some other power for the best powers of the man
himself, and should make him seem effective beyond his real
force, would be an injury to him and ultimately would be
recognized as an empty sham itself. I quarrel with no man
for his conscientious belief about the high and separate
commission of the Christian ministry. I only quarrel with the
man who, resting satisfied with what he holds to be his high
commission, is not eager to match it with a high character.
The more you think yourself different from other men because
you are a minister, the more try to be different from other
men by being more fully what all men ought to be. That is a
high churchmanship of which we cannot have too much.

I hold, then, that the Christian ministry has still in men's
esteem all that is essentially valuable, and all that is really
good for it to have. It has a place of utterance more powerful
and sacred than any other in the world. Then comes the
question, What has it to utter? The pedestal is still there. Men
will not gather about it as they once did, perhaps, without
regard to the statue that stands upon it. But if a truly good
statue stands there the world can see it as it could if it stood
nowhere else.

There are two great faults of the ministry which come, one
of them from ignoring, the other from rebelling against, this
change in the attitude of the minister and the people towards
each other. *The first is the perpetual assertion of the minister's*

authority for the truth which he teaches. To claim that men should believe what we teach them because we teach it to them, and not because they see it to be true, is to assume a place which God does not give us and men will not acknowledge for us. Many a Christian minister needs to be sent back to him whom we call the heathen Socrates, to read these noble words in the "Phaedo"—which whole dialogue, by the way, is itself no unworthy pattern of the best qualities of preaching: "You, if you take my advice, will think little about Socrates, but a great deal about Truth."

And *the other fault is the constant desire to make people hear us who seem determined to forget us*. This is the fault of the sensational preacher. A large part of what is called sensational preaching is simply the effort of a man who has no faith in his office or in the essential power of truth to keep himself before people's eyes by some kind of intellectual fantasticalness. It is a pursuit of brightness and vivacity of thought for its own sake, which seems to come from a certain almost desperate determination of the sensational minister that he will not be forgotten. I think there is a great deal of nervous uneasiness of mind which shows a shaken confidence in one's position. It struggles for cleverness. It lives by making points. It is fatal to that justice of thought which alone in the long run commands confidence and carries weight. The man who is always trying to attract attention and be brilliant, counts the mere sober effort after absolute truth and justice dull. It is more tempting to be clever and unjust than to be serious and just. Every preacher has constantly to make his choice which he will be. It does not belong to men, like angels, to be "ever bright and fair" together. And the anxious desire for glitter is one of the signs of the dislodgment of the clerical position in our time.

There is a possible life of great nobleness and usefulness for the preacher who, frankly recognizing and cordially accepting the attitude towards his office which he finds on the world's part, preaches truth and duty on their own intrinsic authority, and wins personal power and influence because he does not seek them, but seeks the prevalence of righteousness and the salvation of men's souls.

The Bible and Our Time

The relation of our time to the Bible is another subject which must interest a preacher very deeply. The Bible is the authority by which we preach; and to find the people whom our preaching interests so largely uninterested in and ignorant of the source from which our truth is drawn must awaken some questions as to whether our preaching is wholly right. I do not speak now of the prevalent doubts about the Bible, though they are, of course, connected very closely, both as cause and effect, with men's ignorance about it. I speak merely of the fact of that undoubted ignorance. Who is there among our people who knows the Old Testament? Where are the people that in any real sense know the New?

Why Is There Biblical Ignorance?

If we look for the reasons of such ignorance about a book which lies on everybody's table, and whose name is on everybody's lips, they are not hard to find. *First, there is in our time a great reaction from the belief that men once had in the saving power of the Bible.* Men who have read a book not because it was true or because they wanted to get at its lessons, but because they thought it was safe to read it and unsafe not to read it, just as soon as the notion of safety is loosened from it, will be less ready to care for its truth and to feel its power than that of other books. This is human nature. The stronger feeling about the Bible has kept down the more familiar feeling which attaches us to other books.

Another reason is, of course, the crowd of other books, their cheapness and their apparent pressingness. Even the man who knows that the Bible is the best of books will read the last new treatise on religion instead of the Bible, because he knows the Bible belongs to all ages, and can never pass out of date, while with this "latest publication" it is today or never.

And yet another reason is the prevalent disposition to consider the Bible the clergy's book. We wonder at the pusillanimity with which the people of the Middle Ages and the Romanists of today have submitted to restrictions on the reading of the Bible, and to the acceptance of whatever account of it their preachers chose to give. The real truth is that they like this state of things; and many of our Protestants like it too, and of their own free will treat the Bible so exactly as the Medieval Christian was compelled to trust it that it ought not to seem strange.

And another reason is that the clergy, by their unreal fantastic treatment of the Bible, often do what they can to make the people think that it is indeed unintelligible except to one who holds a very complicated key, and so that it is not for the like of them to touch it. This is the evil of all unreal exegesis. It throws an unreal air about the book of God. I heard of a sermon on the first verse of the Forty-first Psalm which declared it to be a statement of the mission of Christ and the scheme of the Atonement. Imagine a believing disciple going home after that sermon and reading his Bible with the slightest hope of knowing what it meant!

And another reason still is our unbiblical preaching. I mean our preaching about all topics with various degrees of wisdom but with nothing which would suggest that what we give men is only a few drops out of a spring of truth and life, and so would send them eagerly to the fountain to drink their fill.

Against these tendencies to make the Bible unreal and uninteresting there has come the protest of the new way of treating it and the new books about it. I know the danger of superficialness which attends the realistic treatment of the Bible. I know how apt it is to carry the mind up to a certain point of amateur interest and leave it there. Certainly no one can praise it except as an introduction to a spiritual richness which is far deeper than itself, but in our day it is something to be very glad of that Milman and Stanley, and Farrar and the author of *Ecce Homo*, in literature, and Holman Hunt and Bida, in the region of art, have made the outer life of the Bible live anew, and by sweeping aside the mist of unreality that hung about its door have opened the way for a deeper entrance into its spirit than man has yet attained.

There is need of every special effort to make men know the Bible. The Bible class, the expository lecture, the illustrative picture, none of them can do too much. But there is yet greater need that you and I who preach should let the people see that we are men of the Bible, that we know its letter and are possessed by its spirit, that out of it directly comes the support of our own religious life and the food which we offer in our preaching.

I must not let my lecture grow any longer. I have tried to point out to you some of the peculiarities of our time which we as preachers must encounter. I must not close without begging you not to be ashamed or afraid of the age you live in, and least of all to talk of it in a tone of weak despair. In the beginning of the last century many men talked of Christianity as if it were an effete superstition. And yet behold the new life which has come forth since from that which men then called dead. The state of things which then existed may seem to be renewed, though it is not possible for men to be as wholly unbelieving in the nineteenth century as they were in the eighteenth. But out of what men now call a slow death new life will come. In many ways we can see clearly that it is not death, but some strange change and progress of the methods of life by which we are surrounded. To be thoroughly in sympathy with the age, to admire everything in it that is admirable, to rejoice in its great achievements, to see the beauty of the superb material structure which it is building for the better spirituality which is to come to dwell in it, to love to trace the strange nomadic currents of spiritual desire which run, often grotesquely or frantically, through its tumultuous life, to see with joy how its new needs bring out new sides of helpfulness in the ever helpful Gospel of Christ; this is the true culture of a preacher for our time. He believes in it and loves it, and sees its great strong faults against the background of its noble qualities. He thanks God, who sent him here to work; for he is sure that while there have been many centuries in which it was easier, there has been none in which it was more interesting or inspiring for a man to preach.

8

THE VALUE OF A HUMAN SOUL

There is a power which lies at the center of all success in preaching, and whose influence reaches out to the circumference, and is essential everywhere. Without its presence we cannot imagine the most brilliant talents making a preacher of the Gospel in the fullest sense. Where it is largely present it is wonderful how many deficiencies count for nothing. It has the characteristics which belong to all the most essential powers.

It is able to influence the whole life as one general and pervading motive; and it can also press on each particular action with peculiar force. Under its compulsion a man first becomes a preacher, and every sermon that he preaches is more or less consciously shaped by the same laws. Without this power preaching is almost sure to become either a struggle of ambition or a burden of routine. With it preaching is an ever fresh delight. The power is the value of the human soul, felt by the preacher, and inspiring all his work.

The power of that motive has been assumed in all that I have said to you. But it seems to me to be so supremely important; the ministry which is full of it is so rich; the ministry which lacks it is so poor, that I determined, when I undertook the duty which I complete today, that this last lecture should be given to a serious consideration of the importance and value of this mainspring, which lies coiled up within all the complicated machinery of the ministry, the realized value of the human soul.

As to its importance, we get our clearest impression if we look at the earthly ministry of Jesus. There are many accounts to be given of His wondrous work. People may say many ingenious things about it, and many of them are true. But we are sure that he has put his hand most certainly upon the central power of Christ's ministry who holds up before us the intense value which the Savior always set upon the souls for which He lived and died. It shines in everything He says and does. It looks out from His eyes when they are happiest and when they are saddest. It trembles in the most loving consolations, and thunders in the most passionate rebukes which come from His lips. It is the inspiration at once of His pity and His indignation. And it has made the few persons on whom it chanced to fall, and in whose histories it found its illustrations, the men and women who represented humanity about Him in Palestine—Nicodemus, Peter, John, the Pharisees, the Magdalen, the woman of Samaria, and all the rest—luminous forever with its light. That power still continues wherever the same value of the human soul is present.

If we could see how precious the human soul is as Christ saw it, our ministry would approach the effectiveness of Christ's. "I am not convinced by what you say. I am not sure that I cannot answer every one of your arguments," said a man with whom a preacher had been pleading, "but one thing which I confess I cannot understand. It puzzles me, and makes me feel a power in what you say. It is why you should care enough for me to take all this trouble, and to labor with me as if you cared for my soul." It is a power which every man must feel. It inspires the preacher; and his hearers, catching its influence, become soft and ready to receive the truth. It is strength in the arm which strikes, and tenderness in the rock which receives the blow.

The other motives of the minister's work seem to me to stand around this great central motive as the staff officers stand around a general. He needs them. They execute his commands. He could not do his work without them. But he is not dependent upon them as they are upon him; any one of them might fall away and he could still fight the battle. The power of the battle is in him. If he falls, the cause is ruined. So stand the subordinate motives of the ministry around the commanding motive, the realized value of the human soul. They are the motives which I have had occasion to dwell on one by one in the course of these lectures. They are the pleasure of work, the mere delight in the exercise of powers, which is natural to any man who is healthy both in body and mind; the love of influence, that gratification in feeling our life touch another life for some good result, which is also natural and healthy; the perception of order, that love of regulated movement, of the rhythm of righteousness in the lives and ways of men, which in its higher forms is noble, though in the lower it degenerates into routine.; and lastly the pure concern for truth, the pleasure in seeing right ideas take the place of wrong ideas, which may be quite separate from any regard for the interest of the person in whom the change takes place. These are the nobler members of the staff of the great general.

There are more ignoble ones who volunteer their services and wear something like his uniform and cannot always be distinguished from his true servants; such as emulation, and the love of fame, and the pride of opinion, and the enjoyment of congenial society. I will not dwell on those.

These others are the real staff of the general. But when we look at their group, how the commanding motive whom they serve towers up far above them all. They get their highest dignity from serving him. For in his service each of them, which is abstract in itself, comes into actual contact with man; and no abstract principle has shown its full power or given its full pleasure until it has opened the essential relations which exist between it and human nature. It is the great privilege of the ministry that it is kept in constant necessary contact with mankind. Therein lies its healthiness. Man in his mystery and wonderfulness is more full of the suggestion of God than either abstract truth or physical nature, And so the "truth preacher," in spite of his imperfect opportunities for study, in spite of his separation from the beauty of the natural world, has the chance to know more of God than the profoundest speculative philosophy or the most exquisite scenery of earth could reveal to him.

The Effects of Reaching the Soul

Let us try, then, to point out to you what some of the effects will be in a man's preaching from a true sense of the value of the human soul, by which I mean a high estimate of the capacity of the spiritual nature, a keen and constant appreciation of the attainments to which it may be brought. And first of all it helps to rescue the Gospel which we preach from a sort of unnaturalness and incongruity which is very apt to cling to it. This is, I think, very important.

Consider what it is that you are to declare week after week to the men and women who come to hear you. The mighty truths of Incarnation and Atonement are your themes. You tell them of the birth and life and death of Jesus Christ. You picture the adorable love and the mysterious sacrifice of the Savior. And you bind all this to their lives. You tell them that in a true sense all this was certainly for them. I do not know what you are made of, if sometimes, as you preach, there does not come into your mind a thought of incongruity. What are you, you and these people to whom you preach, that for you the central affection of the universe should have been stirred? You know your own life. You know something of the lives they live. You look into their faces as you preach to them. Where is the end worthy of all this ministry of almighty grace which you have been describing? Is it possible that all this once took place and, by the operation of the Holy Spirit, is a perpetual power in the world, merely that these machine-lives might run a little truer, or that a series of rules might be established by which the current workings of society might move more smoothly? That, which men sometimes make the purpose of it all, is too unworthy. The engine is too coarse to have so fine a fire under it.

You must see something deeper. You must discern in all these men and women some inherent preciousness for which even the marvel of the Incarnation and the agony of Calvary was not too great, or it is impossible that you should keep your faith in those stupendous truths which Bethlehem and Calvary offer to us. Some source of fire from which these dimmed sparks come, some possible renewal of the fire which is in them still, some sight of the education through which each soul is passing, and some suggestion of the special personal perfectness to which each may attain—all this must brighten before you, as you look at them; and then the truths of your theology shall not be thrown into confusion nor faded into unreality by your ministry to men. The best thing in a minister's life is the action of his works and his faith on one another; his experience of the deeper value of the human soul making the wonders of his faith more credible, and the truths of his faith always revealing to him a deeper and deeper value in the soul.

I think that nobody can preach with the best power who is not possessed with a sense of the mysteriousness of the human life which he preaches to. It must seem to him capable of indefinite enlargement and refinement. He must see it in each new person as something original and new. This must be something which belongs to his whole conception of man as the child of God. It must not be the mere inspiration of his whim, attributed in great richness to some lives which chance to take his fancy, but ignored in others. He must see it in all men simply as men. When he undertakes to lead them he must feel the mystery and spontaneity of the lives that he takes under his teaching. He must be a careful student of the characters he trains. He cannot carry people over the route of his ministry as a ferryman carries passengers across the river, always running his boat in the same line and never even asking the names of the people whom he carries. He must count himself rather like the tutor of a family of princes, who, with careful study of their several dispositions, trains the royal nature of each for the special kingdom over which he is to rule.

The Preacher As Poet

Here is where the preacher and the poet touch. Every true preacher must be a poet, at least in so far as to see behind all the imperfections of men a certain ideal manhood from which they have never separated, which underlies the life and lends its value to the blurred and broken character of every one. A belief in the Incarnation, in the divine Son of Man, makes such poets of us all. It is interesting to see in how many ministers the hopefulness of this ideal poetic view of human life overcomes the tendencies of natural temperament, the discouragement of poverty and disease, and the disenchanting influence of relationship with men, and keeps ministers the most hopeful class of men. They are always standing where, if they will, they may listen for the bells that shall "ring in the Christ that is to be." I have seen ministers try to crush back this noble tendency of their vocation and to assume a cynicism and a hopelessness which they did not feel, so that other men might not call them childish. And I have seen men of the world disappointed when they came to such ministers and did not find in them the childlike hope and trust that they expected, but only false and despairing thoughts of human nature like their own; as if the ice came up to the fire to warm itself, and found the fire ashamed of being warm and trying hard to make itself as cold as ice.

The Pleasure of Preaching

I might dwell, also, on this value of the human soul for its own sake, as constituting the constant reserve of pleasure in the ministry. There are other pleasures in our work, as I have recounted to you already; but they are all, to a certain extent, dependent upon circumstances. A parish uproar which reveals the bad reality of life may scatter some of them. Poverty, which deprives you of the means of culture, and takes away the power of carrying out your plans, may rob you of others. But the mere pleasure of dealing with man as man, as a being valuable in himself; for this no peculiar happiness of circumstances is needed. Wherever men are, you may have it. Nobody but Robinson Crusoe is shut out from it, and even to him the man Friday is sure to come.

And herein lies the real fellowship of the ministry. There are no fellowworkers who come so close together as fellow-workers in the ministry of the Gospel; and their companionship is closest when they most deeply know this truth of the essential value of the human soul. A preacher comes to me from Africa, or from some church of another denomination in the next street, which often seems farther off than Africa. It depends upon what the power of our preaching is, how near we come together. If we are both given to machineries, each of us valuing only what a certain sort of people may become under the peculiar culture of the denomination which he represents, then we talk together, however pleasantly, only over our fences, and shake hands, however cordially, only through the slats. If we both really value the soul of man, we understand each other; the different methods of our work do not keep us apart, but bring us together, for they are the means by which we manifest to one another the deep motive which is the power of both our lives. The fences are turned into bridges.

Certainly, Christian union, whenever it comes, must come thus; not by compromise and the adjustment of various forms of government and worship, but by the development in all preachers of all kinds of that value for man in Christ which burrows far beneath the differences of forms and flies far above them. It may be given to some people in these days to take direct steps toward organic Christian union. I bid them Godspeed. But if that is not our task let us know, and let us rejoice in knowing, that we are doing, perhaps, as much as they for the millennium, if, in ourselves and those who hear us, by whatever partial name we and they may be called, we are doing what we can to make strong that sense of the value of the human soul which, by its very nature, is universal, and cannot be partial. Here is where the zealous partisan, who is at the same time an earnest Christian, is often working better than he knows. He is like a jealous farmer who prays for rain to water his field that it may be richer than his neighbor's; but the heaven is too broad for him, and will not limit its bounty by the intention of his prayer. It will rain, but it cannot rain between fences; and so his selfish prayer brings refreshment for the alien acres for which he does not pray.

And as this power in the ministry lies deepest, so it lasts longest. The veteran preacher, I think, keeps the enjoyment and tries to keep the practice of his work later in life than the veteran in almost any other occupation. That always seems to me a touching and convincing proof of the excellence of our calling. It shows better and better as it grows older. The delightful French artist, Millet, used to say to his pupils; "The end of the day is the proof of a picture"—"*La fin du jour, c'est l'epreuve d'un tableau.*" He meant that the twilight hour, when there is not light enough to distinguish details, is the most favorable time to judge a picture as a whole. And so it is with the ministry. When the cross lights of jealous emulation and the glare of constant notoriety are softening towards the darkness in which lies the pure judgment of God and the peace of being forgotten by mankind, then that which has been lying behind them all the time comes out, and the old preacher who has ceased to care whether men praise or blame him, who has attained or missed all that there is for him of success or failure here, preaches on still out of the pure sense of how precious the soul of man is, and the pure desire to serve a little more that which is so worthy of his service, before he goes.

Flippance, Flattery, or Respect

Let me follow still further the enumeration of the qualities which grow up in the preacher from his value for the human soul. Courage is one of its most necessary results. The truest way not to be afraid of the worst part of a man is to value and try to serve his better part. The patriot who really appreciates the valuable principles of his nation's life is he who most intrepidly rebukes the nation's faults. And Christ was all the more independent of men's whims because of His profound love for them and complete consecration to their needs. There come three stages in this matter; the first, a flippant superiority which despises the people and thinks of them as only made to take what the preacher chooses to give to them, and to minister to his support; the second, a servile sycophancy which watches all their fancies, and tries to blow whichever way their vane points; and the third, a deep respect which cares too earnestly for what the people are capable of being to let them anywhere fall short of it without a strong remonstrance. You have seen all three in the way in which parents treat their children. I could show you each of the three today in the relation of different preachers to their parishes. Believe me, the last is the only true independence, the only one that is worth while to seek, or indeed that a man has any right to seek. An actor may encourage himself by despising or forgetting his audience, but a preacher must go elsewhere for courage. The more you prize the spiritual nature of your people, the more able you will be to oppose their whims. There must be the fountain of your independence.

Conscience and Good Taste

And here, too, is the power of simplicity and absolute reality. All turgid rhetoric, all false ornament, all doctrinal fantasticalness must disappear in the presence of a supreme absorbing value for the souls of men. The conscience and the taste, when both are pure, will coincide. Every divorce which separates them is a parting of what God has joined together. The two are most essentially united in the functions of our sacred office. The man whose eye is set upon the souls of men, and whose heart burns with the desire to save them, chooses with an almost unerring instinct what figure will set the truth most clearly before their minds, what form of appeal will bring it most strongly to their sluggish wills. He takes those and rejects every other.

The mere unwarlike citizen goes lounging through the Tower of London, and among the old armor there he praises that which he calls beautiful. The soldier walks through the same halls, and, with a soldier's instinct, thinks no armor beautiful which will not kill the enemy or protect the man who wears it. That is the final principle of all right choice, the touchstone of good taste. The sermon is to be sacrificed to the soul, the system of work to the purpose of work always. It strikes at the root of all clerical fastidiousness and the tyranny of order. It is wonderful how the character of all ornament in a sermon declares itself.

That which really belongs to the purpose of the sermon is always good. That which is there for its own sake every pure taste, however untrained, instantly feels to be bad. The one is like the sculpture on an old cathedral which, however rude, was meant to tell a story. The other is like the carving on our house-fronts which is meant merely to look pretty, and so fails of even that. There are some men born to positions of such dignity that they are doomed to be either illustrious or ridiculous. And so ornament when it is applied to a sermon must either do the lofty work of making truth plain and glorious or it fails of everything. It cannot be allowed simply to amuse or please as may the ornament of an essay or a poem.

Developing a Broad View

But our principle goes deeper than this. This controlling value of the human soul must save a preacher, also, from a narrow treatment of the souls under his care. If he values them more than any theory of his own about how souls generally are to be treated, he will be broad and try only to lead each into that entire obedience to God which results in such different experiences for us all. The ascetic theorist values self-sacrifice for its own sake and would enforce it indiscriminately. The theorist of self-indulgence says, "No, pain is a curse. Pleasure is good. Shun pain. Do what is pleasant." The teacher who values the souls which he teaches more than any theory says something different from either. He says, "Not enjoyment and not sorrow, but the meeting of your will with the will of God, whatever it may bring, is the purpose of all discipline. Be ready for any way which God shall choose to bring your will to His." But to this large wisdom no teacher can be brought except by a true sense of the preciousness of the soul of man.

A Danger Signal

It cannot be denied, and it must not be forgotten, that this

absorbing conviction of the value of the human soul has its
besetting danger. That danger is not slight nor casual. It is
important and essential. The danger is lest, in our eagerness
to help the spiritual nature which we so highly value, we
should be led to judge of the truth of any idea by what we
think might be its influences on the soul for which we are so
anxious. The tendency to estimate and treat ideas according
to what appear their probable effects on human character
has been, no doubt, a great besetting sin of spiritual teachers
always. I suppose that it cannot be wholly separated from
any vocation which is bound at once to seek for truth and to
educate character. This is the way in which a great deal of
half-believed doctrine comes to be clinging to and cumbering
the church.

Men insist on believing and on having other people believe
certain doctrines, not because they are reasonably
demonstrated to be true, but because, in the present state of
things, it would be dangerous to give them up. This is the
way in which one man clings to his idea of verbal inspiration,
and another to his special theory of the divine justice, and
another to his material notion of the resurrection, and yet
another to his notion of the church's authority and the
minister's commission. It is a very dangerous danger, because
it wears the cloak of such a good motive; but it is big with all
the evil fruits of superstition. It starts with a lack of faith in
the people and in truth and in God. Jesus bids us not to cast
pearls before swine, but He does not bid us to feed even
swine on pebbles. "God forbid," says Bishop Watson, "that
the search after truth should be discouraged for fear of its
consequences. The consequences of truth may be subversive
of systems of superstition, but they can never be injurious to
the frights or well-founded expectations of the human race."

There is nothing that one would wish to say more earnestly
to our young and ardent ministers than this: *Never sacrifice
your reverence for truth to your desire for usefulness.* Say nothing
which you do not believe to be true because you think it may
be helpful. Keep back nothing which you know to be true
because you think it may be harmful. Who are you that you
should stint the children's drinking from the cup which their
father bids you to carry to them, or mix it with error because
you think they cannot bear it in its purity? We must learn in
the first place to form our own judgments of what teachings
are true by other tests than the consequences which we think

those teachings will produce; and then, when we have formed our judgments, we must trust the truth that we believe, and the God from whom it comes, and tell it freely to the people. He is saved from one of the great temptations of the ministry who goes out to his work with a clear and constant certainty that truth is always strong no matter how weak it looks, and falsehood is always weak, no matter how strong it looks.

But if we bear this danger in our minds, and are upon our guard against it, then the value for our brethren's souls will help us to avoid many false standards. It will give interest to many people whom otherwise we should find very uninteresting. There is much in the minister's training to make him value purely intellectual companionships. There is a tendency in many ministers, whose disposition leads them to value truth more than men, to let themselves be drawn almost exclusively into the society of those whose ways of thought are like their own. I think it is a wonder to many people who are not ministers, how one man who is the pastor of a great parish can be genuinely interested in so many people of such various characters and lives. A good many people, and even some clergymen, take it for granted that it is not possible, and treat the appearance of such universal interest as a pretence, necessary in order to keep up the parish feeling, and so a very valuable accomplishment in a minister. But it is not so. No man ever did it successfully, year after year, as a pretence. The secret of it all is simply the great sense of the value of the human soul brought home and individualized upon these human souls committed to our care, as a magistrate sees all the dignity of the law represented in the settlement of the petty quarrel that is brought before his court.

The large conception of the value of humanity must go before the special value of one's own parishioners, otherwise the pastoral relation softens into mere personal fondness, or else hardens into a rigid and formal treatment of the people according to arbitrary classifications which lose both alike their general humanity and their personal distinctness. There is a ministry which is all the more personal because of its broad humanness; a ministry which, beginning with the sacredness of man, counts all men sacred, and touches, with its own peculiar pressure upon each, the lives of strong men and little children, of women and boys and girls, of working people and people of idle lives, of saints and sinners, as the rain and dew of God which water the earth feed both the oak-tree and the violet; a ministry which makes its care for every soul dearer and more sacred to that soul because it is evidently no mere personal fondness, but one utterance of that Christlikeness which deeply feels the preciousness of the souls of all God's children.

The Preacher's Reward

I have not time to dwell upon the help which a perpetual value for the souls of men must render to our own spiritual life, and so to our efficiency as preachers. Indeed, it is the great power by which our souls must grow. This is the ministry of the people to the preacher, which is often greater than any ministry that the preacher can render to the people. I assure you that the relation between the pastor and his parish is not right if the pastor thinks the obligation to be all upon one side; if while he lives with them and when he leaves them he is not always full of gratitude for what they have done for him. A pastor who is insensible to this cannot do the best good to his people. And the sort of help which a minister gets from his congregation whose souls he values is a direct complement of the good which he gets from his study. He needs them both. His study furnishes him with ideas, with intellectual conceptions, and his congregation furnishes him with an atmosphere in which these ideas ripen to their best result. The minister as he grows older changes some of the opinions which he used to hold. The new opinions, it is to be hoped, are truer than the old ones. But greater than all such changes are the deepening convictions about all spiritual things which come from the long years of dealing with men's souls and which color every opinion whether new or old. The conviction that truth and destiny are essential and not arbitrary, that Christianity is the personal love and service of Christ, and that salvation is positive, not negative; convictions such as these fill and enrich the preacher's maturer years; and they are convictions whose clearness and strength he owes to that occupation which has both demanded and cultivated a value for the souls of men.

Don't Stop at Rescue

As to the nature of this value for the human soul, notice, I beg you, that it is something more than the mere sense of the soul's danger. It is a deliberate estimate set upon man's spiritual nature in view of its possibilities. The danger in which that nature stands by sin intensifies and emphasizes the value which we set upon it, but it does not create that value. I think that this is important. I think that we are sometimes apt to let our anxiety for the salvation of souls degenerate into a mere pity for the misery into which they may be brought by sin; and the result of such a low thought is that when we have been brought to believe that a soul is, as we say, "safe," that it has been forgiven and will not be punished, we are satisfied. The thought of rescue has monopolized our religion and often crowded out the thought of culture. I think that the tone of the New Testament is different from this. I know how eminently there the truths of danger and rescue always appear. I know that Christ "came not to call the righteous but sinners to repentance," and that He was called Jesus because He should "save His people from their sins."

But all the time behind the danger lies the value of that spiritual nature which is thus in peril. It is not solely or principally the suffering which the soul must undergo; it is the loss of the soul itself, its failure to be the bright and wonderful thing which, as the soul of God's child, it ought to be. That is the reason why the process of salvation cannot stop with the removal of penalties and the forgiveness of sins. It must include all the gradual perfection of the soul by faith and love and obedience and patience. This is the reason too, why those who have taken only a half view of the complete salvation are apt to be severe on those who have seen only the other half. Half a truth is often more jealous of the other half than of an error.

This larger and deeper value for the human soul, I think, is seen in all the sermons of the greatest preachers. It is not mere pity for danger that inspires them to plead with men. That might move them to a sort of supercilious exertion, no matter how intrinsically worthless was the thing in peril, as one might start up to pluck even an insect from the candle's flame. But it is a glowing vision of how great and beautiful the soul of man might be, of what great things it might do if it were thoroughly purified and possessed by the love of God and so opened free channels to His power.

Why We Don't Value the Soul

There are special causes which make this great power of which I have been speaking, the sense of the value of the soul, more difficult to win and keep in this age of ours than it has been in many other times. There are two characteristics of our time which have their influence upon it. One is the tendency of philosophy to divert itself from man and turn towards other nature, and in its study of man to busy itself least with his spiritual nature, most with his physical history. The other is the strong philanthropic disposition which prevails about us, the desire to relieve human suffering and to promote human comfort and intelligence. The first of these tendencies would certainly make it more than usually hard to realize the spiritual value of humanity; and the second, while it makes much of man, cares mainly for his material well-being and is always disposed to treat the individual as subservient to the interests of the mass. The general result is one of which I think that there can be no doubt, a difficulty in the real, vivid perpetual sense of the worth of man's spiritual nature such as has very rarely beset those in other ages who have tried to serve their fellow men. At such a time we need to hold very strongly to the constant facts of human life which lie below all such temporary changes, and to be very sure of their reappearance. We need a keen, quick-sighted faith which shall discover the first signs of what must surely come, a reaction from the partial tendencies of the time. We need a generous fairness to discover thought and feeling which is really spiritual, but which has cloaked itself, even to its own confusion, in the forms and phrases of the time.

How Can We Value the Soul?

But, more than all of these, we who are preaching in such days as these need to understand these methods by which in any time we must acquire and preserve the sense of the preciousness of the human soul. What are these methods? First of all, *before a man can value the souls of other men, he must have learned to value his own soul.* And a man learns to value his own soul only as he is conscious of the solemn touches of the Spirit of the Lord upon it. Ah, my friends, here is the real reason why he who preaches to the inner life of others must himself have had an inner life. Not that he may take his own experience and narrowly make it the type to which all other experiences must conform, but that having learned how God loves him, having felt in many a silent hour and many a tumultuous crisis the pressure of God's hands full of care and wisdom, he may know, as he looks from his pulpit, that

behind every one of those faces into which he looks there is a
soul for which God cares with the same thoughtfulness. In
his closet he has first seen the light which from his closet he
carries forth to illuminate the humanity of his congregation
and bring out all its colors. The personal desire to be pure
and holy, the personal consciousness of power to be pure
and holy through Christ, reveals the possibility of other men.

Again, *a preacher's view of all theology ought to be colored with
the preciousness of the human soul*. It is possible for two men to
hold the same doctrine and yet to differ very widely in this
respect. To one of them the Christian truths reveal much of
the glory and mercy of God, to the other they shine also with
the value of the spiritual manhood. To this last the Incarnation
reveals the essential dignity of that nature into union with
which the Deity could so marvelously enter. The Redemption
bears witness of the unspeakable love of God, but also of the
value underneath the sin of man, which made the jewel worth
cleaning. And all the methods of sanctification, all the
disciplines of the Spirit, open before the watchful minister
new insight into the possibilities of that being upon whom
such bounty of grace is lavished. I think that we ought to
distrust at least the form in which we are holding any
theological idea, if it is not helping to deepen in us the sense
of the preciousness of the human soul, first impressing it as a
conviction and then firing it into a passion. There is not one
truth which man may know of God which does not
legitimately bear this fruit. I beg you, more and more to test
the way in which you hold the truth of God by the power
which it has to fill you with honor for the spiritual life of
man.

It is evident as we look at the ministry of Jesus that He
was full of reverence for the nature of the men and women
whom He met. There was nothing which He knew of God
which did not make His Father's children precious to Him.
We see it even in His lofty and tender courtesy. How often I
have seen a minister's manners either proudly distant and
conscious of his own importance, or fulsome and fawning
with a feeble affectionateness that was unworthy of a man,
and have thought that what he needed was that noble union
of dignity and gentleness which came to Jesus from His divine
insight into the value of the human soul.

One other source from which the knowledge of this value
comes let me mention in a single word. *It is by working for the*

soul that we best learn what the soul is worth. If ever in your ministry the souls of those committed to your care grow dull before you, and you doubt whether they have any such value that you should give your life for them, go out and work for them; and as you work their value shall grow clear to you. Go and try to save a soul and you will see how well it is worth saving, how capable it is of the most complete salvation. Not by pondering upon it, nor by talking of it, but by serving it you learn its preciousness. So the father learns the value of his child, and the teacher of his scholar, and the patriot of his native land. And so the Christian, living and dying for his brethren's souls, learns the value of those souls for which Christ lived and died.

And if you ask me whether this whose theory I have been stating is indeed true in fact, whether in daily work for souls year after year a man does see in those souls glimpses of such a value as not merely justifies the little work which he does, but even makes credible the work of Christ, I answer, surely, yes. All other interest and satisfaction of the ministry competes itself in this, that year by year the minister sees more deeply how well worthy of infinitely more than he can do for it is the human soul for which he works.

I do not know how I can better close my lectures to you than with that testimony. May you find it true in your experience. May the souls of men be always more precious to you as you come always nearer to Christ, and see them more perfectly as He does. I can ask no better blessing on your ministry than that.

And so may God our Father guide and keep you always.

APPENDICES

THE TEACHING
OF RELIGION

An address to the Divinity School of
Yale University, February 28, 1878.

A year has passed away since I had the satisfaction of meeting you here before—a year in which we have all been busy in doing or preparing to do the work of the Christian ministry. At its close I come back to you with a deepened sense of what a privilege it is to be a preacher, and with a renewed pleasure and gratitude in being allowed to address those who are making ready to preach.

I come at the kind invitation of your faculty to speak to you on the teaching of religion. But I want to say at once that I should not venture to come unless I might be allowed to stand in precisely the same position toward you in which I stood last year. I am no professor dealing wisely with the philosophy of a great subject; nor scholar to interpret to you its history. I am simply a working minister, ready and glad, if they care to listen, to tell those who are almost ministers how the problems of religious teaching have presented themselves to my experience. I rely entirely upon the sympathy of our common work. It is more in suggestions than in continuous and systematic treatise that I shall give you what I have to say, and I can only promise you in recompense for your courteous attention that I will tell you frankly and honestly just how the work of teaching religion has seemed to me as I have labored in it.

What Is Religion?

And we must begin with definitions which need not detain us very long. I am to speak about the teaching of religion. What is religion? Religion, I hold to be *the life of man in gratitude and obedience and gradually developing likeness to God.* There are no doubt more subtle definitions to be given, but that is the sum of it all, as it stands out in the experience of men. For a man to be religious is for him to be grateful to God for some mercy and goodness, to be obedient as the utterance of his gratitude, and to be shaped by the natural power of obedience into the likeness of God whom he obeys. And the Christian religion—using the term not as the title for a scheme of truth but as the description of a character—the Christian religion is the life of man in gratitude and obedience and consequent growing likeness to God in Christ.

A Christian, when I look to find the simplest definition of him which any thoughtful man can understand, is a man who is trying to serve Christ out of the grateful love of Christ, and who by his service of Christ is becoming Christ-like. It is not simply service, for service may be the mere slavery of fear, and that is superstition, not religion. It is not simply grateful love, for that may exhaust itself as a mere sentiment. It is gratitude assured by obedience, obedience uttering gratitude, and both together bearing witness of themselves and accomplishing their true result in character. The life of man in gratitude, obedience, and growing likeness to Jesus Christ, as simple as that let us make and keep the definition of the religion in which we live ourselves, to which we tempt, in which we try to instruct our fellow men. And now, upon this essential character of the religion which we wish to teach must depend, of course, the possibility and the way of teaching it.

Four Views of Teaching Religion

But notice first how out of vague or partial ideas about what religion is, there have grown up and have been always present among religious men various views about the possibility of teaching religion and the general method by which, if such teaching were possible, it must proceed. Such views in general are four.

Disbeliever's View: Skepticism

First, there is the disbeliever's view. I do not mean the man who disbelieves in religion, but *the man who disbelieves in teaching it*. Of the disbeliever in religion itself we can say nothing. He does not come in here. Of course, he cannot believe in teaching that which is to him a fraud or a mistake. But there are many men, themselves religious, to whom it seems a full impossibility to teach religion. Many of such men are thoroughly devout and earnest souls. Sometimes, I think, the very intenseness of their personal experience makes it seem to them incapable of being shared. It seems as if every man's religion must come to him as theirs has come to them, direct from God Himself.

In times like these, of ours in which the institutional and traditional methods of religion are shattered and disturbed, there are many, I think, who, driven inward from the tumult and distress around them, realizing supremely the personalness of their own life with Christ, feeling how little they were led to it or upheld in it by any outward influence, distrust such outward influence for any man. There are parents who feel so about their children. "Let them find out for themselves," says the undevout father. "I cannot teach them," says each, "religion is unteachable. It is too personal. It is not like history or arithmetic. There is a notion of fate about it. The soul seems to be like the seashore rock at whose feet the tide is rising. No hand can bend the rock to drink the water. No hand can lift the water to the rock. Only the appointed time of the full tide can bring the two together."

I must not stop now to speak about this first conviction of despair. It would not certainly be hard to point out the fallacy of such an exaggeration of the personal responsibility as would forbid any most kindly and sympathetic hand to help it see the task it has to do. It is like saying that you must not feed a child gratuitously because the full-grown man is bound to earn his own bread. The result is that he dies a baby.

Intellectual View: Dogmatism

But pass on and see what are the suggestions which come from various persons who do believe that religion is teachable, and who undertake to teach it. One man, one class of men, taking the intellectual idea which belongs preeminently to that word "teaching," *think of religious teaching as something purely intellectual.* It is the hard method of the hard sort of Protestantism. It is the method of the catechism and the doctrinal sermon. We shall come in a few minutes to the description of what part it has to play in the full religious teaching of a man. Notice now simply that it is partial, that it involves a very partial notion of what religion is. The idea that religion has been taught when certain truths have been imparted, that the church is a school room in the narrowest sense; this idea, with the consequences that follow from it of the saving power of the tenure of right beliefs, was far more common once than it is now. It belongs to every era of confessions when special conditions lead to the making of minute creeds.

The very dislike which this idea excites in some men's minds, the violence with which they rail against it, is one sign that it is passing away. There is a certain condition of the ocean which is neither storm nor calm. It shows that there has been a storm where we are sailing and that it is over. And there are persons who suffer more with seasickness there upon the dying swell of an old storm than when the fury of the gale is all about them. So there are many writers on religion who grow more excited over the honors or errors of some system of thought that is in decay than they do over the system which is vigorous and live around them. They are always full of indignation about the shade or aspect of orthodoxy which is just passing out of sight. And you can tell that an idea is obsolescent when it begins to vigorously stir those men's dislike. So it is now with the abuse of purely dogmatic teaching which we often hear.

Emotionalist View: Revivalism

Next to the conception of religious teaching which thinks of it solely as the imparting of knowledge comes *that teaching which dwells entirely on the creation of feeling.* This is the soft Protestant method as the other is the hard Protestant method. This is the method of the revivalist as the other is the method of the dogmatist.

Two parish churches stand side by side in one of our great cities. In their pulpits are two men, both teachers of religion, both teachers of Christianity. In those churches are gathered two congregations, two bodies of men and women who have become assigned to those two churches by the curious, inexplicable, seemingly accidental processes which do decide at what table different men shall eat the bread of life. In those two churches two distinctly different works are going on. In one, week after week, year after year, men are being taught certain ideas as if the work for which the church was built was done when they had learned them. In the other, week after week, year after year, men are being stirred up to feel certain feelings as if the work was done when they had felt them. Two Christian parents training their children, two Sunday school teachers teaching their classes, two missionaries going out to India—everywhere there are these two conceptions, the intellectual and the emotional, side by side.

Activist View: Legalism

And then another. With his eye fixed peculiarly on action, looking supremely at the outward life, more or less clear in his perceptions of its strong and subtle relations with the unseen but always cognizant first of that which is seen, comes the third teacher. *To him the teaching of religion means the government of action.* His method is drill. No longer the lecture room or the prayer-meeting, but now the practical sermon, the confessional, the scene of spiritual directorship, where one man tells another man just what he ought to do. You see how far we have come now from him whom we saw first so cognizant of the personal rights and privileges of his brother's soul that he thought it impossible for man to teach his fellowman religion at all. We have come now to another man who does not mind taking the delicate machinery of his brother's life into his meddlesome hands and moving it as he thinks he has learned from his own experience that human lives were made to move. Each successive method has blended a little more the personality of the scholar with the personality of the teacher than the one that went before it. You overwhelm a man more when you flood him with your emotion than when you enlighten him with your wisdom. But you claim him most completely away from himself when you give him a law and say, "Do this," "Do that," neither showing him the deep reason nor firing him with the warm impulse for doing it.

These are the various conceptions that men have of what it is to teach religion. I must pass by the idea of those who think that it is totally impossible, though I venture to hope that it may come out as we go along how even their supreme and often beautiful regard for the separate personal rights of every soul is wholly consistent with what we shall find that the teaching of religion really is.

But take only the three who do believe that it is possible and who attempt it in their various ways. They stand everywhere side by side. The dogmatist, the revivalist, and the ecclesiastic, as we may freely call them. One trying to teach religion as truth, another trying to excite religion as feeling, and another trying to enforce religion as law or drill. There is no age where all three efforts are not all at work; though every age has its preference and stamps itself with some peculiar character, is supremely dogmatic or emotional or legal. There is no church which, however it may be known by the one spirit, has not the others present in it in some less degree. They so belong together that they never can be wholly separated. And yet they are always getting out of perfect harmony and union, and the faults and failures of the teaching of religion come of the partial conceptions of what religion is, of its conception either as simply truth, or as simply emotion, or as simply law.

And what is religion? We come back once more to our definition: *"Religion is the life of man in gratitude and obedience and consequent growing likeness to Jesus Christ."* Now see how out of each of these words a line starts out and runs to something behind itself, and see how all those lines meet in a *person*, Jesus Christ—"gratitude to," "obedience to," "likeness to *Jesus Christ*." Gratitude, obedience, resemblance—these are the windows through which the personality of Jesus Christ comes to the personality of men. After all, then, our definition of religion is but a description of methods and processes. There is something yet more essential, that to which the methods will minister, that for which they exist. The purpose at least of the awakening of gratitude and obedience is the bringing of Christ to men. Religion, the Christian religion— once again to give it a simpler and a profounder definition— is the life of Christ in the life of man, and the teaching of religion, of the Christian religion, in its largest statement, is the bringing of the life of Christ into the life of man.

A Controlling Idea

I speak from the point of view not of theory, but of practice. I speak as a working minister who has sought, as every working minister must seek, for some conception of his work which should most completely cover all of its demands and most constantly summon all his powers to do it. Every man in every work needs some such controlling idea under which all details of method can be harmonized. It keeps the largeness of a man's labor. It saves him from the danger of first thinking there is only one way to do his work, and then narrowing his work to the possibilities of that single method.

Now what is this primary comprehensive conception of the religious teacher's work which grows in the mind of the Christian minister through many years of work? I answer without hesitation. *It is the personal conception: the notion that his task consists in bringing the personal Christ to the personal human nature, to the human soul.* I am sure that the highest delight and the highest effect of a man's preaching comes just in the degree in which all the circumstances of his work— first its great perpetual departments, the instruction in doctrine, the awakening of feeling, the enforcement of law; and then all its minute details, the methods of preaching, the habits of study, the ways of parish government, the relationships to individuals—all find their dignity, their interpretation, their urgency, and their harmony with one another by being included in one simple conception of the total mission of the preacher, a conception that is never lost and never allowed to grow dim, the conception of a personal introduction of person to person, of the teacher by every means in his power making real and influential the personality of Jesus Christ upon the personalities of the men whom he is teaching.

Forgive me if I dwell on this, and try, by mere reiteration, to make you feel how important it seems to me. It is what I have come here to urge upon you. It is what to me makes the whole secret of a happy, earnest, and successful ministry.

The minister who has reached and holds always the simplest picture of what his ministry means, that he is to make the personal Christ known to men, in the same way, in the same sense, only with infinitely more of responsibility and joy than that with which one man makes his brother know another man who has helped him and who he knows may help them both. He is the minister to whom this picture of his work in life is always clear, to whom all the duties and circumstances of his ministry play within this picture, giving it vividness, but never making it confused and dim—he is the preacher in every land, in every age, who really teaches men religion. It is that picture lying distinct in the preacher's mind that gives to many a sermon which seems most abstract its vividness and power. It is the absence of that picture that weakens and scatters the force of the ministry of many an able and earnest man, makes his careful arguments wearisome, and makes his impassioned appeals like so much very distant thunder.

The Personal Christ in the Gospels

Look at the ministry of the Lord Himself, and see how clear this is. Jesus preached Himself, not in the secondary, modern sense of giving definitions of His nature, and theories of His history. He set His self before men and bid them feel the power that came out from Him to all who were receptive with that personal receptiveness which He called faith. All that was dimly but majestically real to men in what they knew of God's personal creatorship and personal governorship of the world, all that was familiar to them in their daily domestic experience of friendship, all this came to its clear and consummate exhibition when Jesus stood forth on that pedestal of Jewish life which seemed so obscure, and has proved to be so high, and uttered those sublime personal announcements of himself: "I am the Light of the world;" "I am the Bread of Life;" "I am the Way, and the Truth, and the Life;" "Come unto Me."

We wonder sometimes at what there is in Christianity which there is not in the four gospels. What is the difference between our Christianity and that of Christ's disciples? Doctrines, types of feeling, and standards of conduct have been made tests of Christian life to such degree that it seems almost certain that the apostles of Jesus, for all that we know of them in the gospels, could only dubiously and by a stretch of charity be admitted as members of an evangelical church in America today. But the main difference is not in what has been added but in what has been lost. It is the weakening and dimming of the personal picture of the gospels, with the consequent loss of the idea of loyalty as the test of Christian condition, that has allowed the doctrinal, the emotional, and the legal aspects of Christian life, which all have their place within the personal idea, and, under it, live in absolute harmony, to come up into a prominence and often into a conflict which is nowhere in the gospels.

And when we pass outside the gospels, when we come to the earliest Christian teachers, St. Peter, St. Stephen, St. Paul, the same character is there as clear as possible. They declare truth, they appeal to feeling, they challenge the conscience, they play on the whole range of human nature, but always everything is within the circuit and comprehension of the friendship, the mastery, the brotherhood of Jesus Christ. It is always the "simplicity that is in Christ" that blends the multiplicity which is in Christian teaching. The range and freedom of thought, emotion, action, is secured by the perpetual assured preeminence of the personal Christ. It is where the Spirit of the Lord is that there is liberty. Back and forth over land and ocean, up and down from beggar to prince, from prince to beggar, they go, telling men of Jesus and summing up all their appeals in that one exhortation which no amount of cant and vulgar ignorance has ever yet succeeded in robbing of its fine and beautiful attraction, "Come to Him," "Come to Jesus."

Conveying the Personal Nature of Christ

It would be interesting to trace the history of the teaching of Christianity and see how it pales or brightens according as this personal character of it all is obscure or vivid. That I must not undertake to do, but all the history of preaching would sustain the truth of the essentialness of this personal element in Christianity. Indeed, the peculiar feeling with which in the best days of the ministry Christian people have regarded their ministers, so different from that with which the superstitious savage honors the priest he fears, or that with which the scholar regards the teacher to whom he listens, that confidence blending of respect and love which, so far as I know, is unlike what any other disciple has for any other teacher through the world. This seems to me to be one indication of the personalness of the religion which the minister teaches.

He who brings me a truth has himself something of the sacredness of the truth he brings. He who kindles a feeling must always have something of the brightness or the sadness of the emotion he excites. He who enforces duty must have some of the dignity of the task which he declares. But he who makes me know a gracious and great Person who is to me thenceforth truth, love, and law together, has something of the mystery and dearness and infiniteness of the Person whom he has made me know. And this has made the singular power which has belonged, among all true ministries of men to men, to the ministry of the Incarnation and the Cross. I am sure, if we could trace it, that the degree of the best feeling of various people toward various ministers would correspond very exactly with the degree to which those different ministers realized themselves, and made real to their people the first great truth of Christianity, that Christianity is Christ.

If you have this in your ministry, my friends, your ministry must be strong, whether its strength be of a sort that men will recognize and praise or not. Without this, it cannot be strong, however rigid or however persuasive it may seem. It is the necessity of the preacher's work that it should know its best motive. In all works it is good, in ours it is essential. A man will dig his ditch better if he knows and cares for the great plan of giving the thirsty city water. Still, he can dig his ditch for his dollar a day. But a man cannot really preach at all unless he knows why he preaches, unless he is in some degree eager to make men know the Christ whom he knows.

I have dwelt long on this general first truth, because it is essential to all that I have to say. Indeed, I am not sure but it is all that I have to say. But now let us go back again. We saw the different views which different men took of the whole work of teaching religion. One class of men believed that it was impossible; another class comprehended it all in the teaching of doctrine; another in the excitement of emotion; another in the regulation of life. The skeptic, the dogmatist, the revivalist, and the ecclesiastic or the legalist—these are the four. And now we want to see what effect it will have upon each of them if what we have seen to be the true character of Christian teaching, the bringing of Christ to men and of men to Christ, be wholly recognized.

Skepticism and the Personal Christ

It certainly must touch the skepticism of those who, religious themselves, doubt whether it is possible in the nature of things for one man to really teach another man religion. That doubt, as I pointed out, comes from the strong sense of individuality in the way in which the believer holds also the individuality of others. These are its best motives. I think it is impossible for any man to be earnest and thoughtful today and not feel their force. I think there can be no more interesting condition, no condition in some ways more painful to behold, than that in which many very true and noble people in our day are standing. They are believers. Their belief is everything to them. They would do anything, give anything, to make their brethren share their belief. But the very earnestness of their belief makes them feel the distinctiveness of their faith. It seems, as it indeed is true, that no other believer ever believed just as they do. The doctrines are to them different from any definitions they have ever read; they have heard from no other penitent of a repentance, from no other forgiven soul of a rapture, that exactly matches what they have felt. And duty is to them something peculiar, and their own, struck out from the contact of their own character, full of its own needs and temptations, against this, their own world.

No wonder they are puzzled. How can they teach another? How can they bid them believe and feel and act as they do when they seem to believe and act and do like no other soul? I think that these are questions that haunt many a pulpit. I think that in them there must lie the explanation of what puzzles us so often, the sight of a minister of deep, true, characteristic personal religion who preaches empty commonplaces. He does not expect these men and women to be just the Christians that he is, and no other type of Christianity has any reality to him. Must it not save this man if he can clearly, strongly comprehend that the essence of Christian character is loyalty to a personal Christ? When he cannot bring men to his doctrine and say, "Believe just that," nor to his emotional experience and say, "Feel just that," nor to his way of living and say, "Live just so," he can still bring them to Christ and Christ to them and say, "Love Him," and look to see them know Him, obey Him as He shall lead them. He does not disown or dishonor his own individuality, nor does he invade and overpower theirs when he does that. He teaches them that religion which he knows belongs to him and them alike, and yet he satisfies himself and honors them by more than readiness, by a sincere desire that Christ shall make it theirs for them as He has made it his for him.

Dogmatism, Revivalism and Legalism

And now we have to ask how, with this fundamental conception of Christianity always in mind, we shall deal with the three ideas of those who *do* believe that it is possible to teach religion. Religion as doctrine, as feeling, and as law — those were the three ideas. The difficulty with them, as we saw, lay in their separation. The true, complete religious teaching, that which you and I as ministers are arriving at, comprehends them all. And this unity of what is so often separated is secured by the presence behind them all of that which is greater than either of them, as the purpose is always greater than the means, the personal idea of Christianity. When doctrine, emotion, and conduct cease to be counted as valuable for themselves and are valued as the avenues through which Christ, the personal Christ, may come to the souls that He is seeking to renew, then each of them is rightly understood in itself and comes to the souls that He is seeking to renew, then each of them is rightly understood in itself and comes into its true harmony and union with the others.

Doctrine and the Personal Christ

In what is left of this lecture I want to speak of the teaching of doctrine as a means by which the soul of man may be brought to know Christ. I have before defined doctrine as truth considered with reference to its being taught, and the taught truth about any person or anything is like a glass through which that person or thing is to be seen. Two things are necessary; one is that the glass should be clean and pure; the other is that it should be held in the right place at the right angle, squarely between the man who is to see and the person or thing which is to be seen. And these two things are necessary about doctrine—these two things are to be studied by every man whose business it is to teach truth about God: one is that the truth which he teaches should be purely, simply true; the other is that it should be properly presented, held squarely between the eye of the man and God, so that the eye of man shall see God through the truth about Him. If the truth be held aslant you *see the truth*, and not God *through* the truth, as, if a sheet of glass is held not squarely between you and a picture, you see the glass, and not the picture through the glass.

Two Tendencies Among Teachers

Among the teachers of truth there seem to me to be two tendencies, both of which, so far as they are indulged, interfere with this primary and fundamental purpose for which truth is taught at all. There are two classes of preachers: one, of those who disregard the first of the necessities, the *cleanness* of the glass; the other, of those who forget the second of the two necessities, the right *position* of the glass. There are both kinds today, and the young preacher finds himself sorely puzzled among them.

One kind of preacher simply insists that the statement of truth shall be self-consistent, that it shall be absolutely a perfect system as far as he can make it. The other is perpetually trying to modify and pare down truth to meet men's wants as shown in their demands. I suppose that in all times there have been these two kinds of teachers, and that always the question of how far truth was to be adapted to men in its selection and in its forms of presentation has been one that has been answered in part according to the different temperaments of different men, and that has given continual anxiety to anxious, conscientious teachers.

Christ as the Answer

And yet some answer to the question is not hard. No most earnest and affectionate desire to make Christ dear to men can justify us in saying anything which we do not hold to be absolutely and purely true concerning Him, in changing, or, as we dare to say sometimes, "softening" the truth about Him. *The best safeguard against that tendency is the profound conviction, wrought out and wrought into us by our own experience of Christ's work for our souls, that Christ is perfectly what the human soul needs*, that if He only reaches it, He must save it with complete salvation. The more thoroughly I honor and love a picture the more I shall be above any temptation to put any color into the glass which I hold before it; the more I shall revolt against any suggestion that I may soften or brighten its colors to make men like it more. I trust the thing which I completely love. The only real assurance against unreal, fantastic, sensational, indulgent teaching about Christ is in the teacher's own complete conviction, from his own experience, of the perfection and sufficiency of Christ, just as Christ is.

No doubt, in times like these, when men's power of believing seems to be weak and sickly, many a preacher with the purest motive feels a desire to make the truth he has to tell and ask men to believe as easy as he can. He thinks he must not quench the smoking flax, nor break the reed that is already sorely bruised. But, not to speak of the essential restraint which there must always be on such an impulse, that, if the truth we utter is not wholly true, it will not be really Christ that men see through it, and so the power of it all which is in Christ will be so far lost, there is another conviction which grows strong as we watch preachers and congregations. It is that men are not won by making belief seem easy, nor are men alienated by the hardness of belief, provided only that the hardness seems to be something naturally belonging to the truth, and not something gratuitously added to it.

Indeed, the natural history of belief would seem to show that men at large are fascinated rather than repelled by difficulty. *Credo quia impossible* is the expression of no rare experience. It is the religion of most demands that have most ruled the world. The easy faiths have been the weak faiths. Men like to feel heroic in their faith; and always it has been easier to excite fanaticism than to build up a quiet, reasonable belief. It would be a wretched falsehood, and one which would no doubt defeat itself if a preacher tried to take advantage of this fact of human nature; but it may at least come in to help us to resist the disposition to omit or soften truths in order that men may receive the truth more easily. The hope of a large general belief in Christian truth, more general than any that any past age has witnessed, does, no doubt, involve a more reasonable and spiritual presentation of it than the past has seen, but it will never be attained by making truth meager. The Christ whom the world shall at last believe in will be the whole Christ, seen through all the depth of all His truth.

Needed Truth

And yet, no doubt, there is something real and pressing in the cry which we hear everywhere for the curtailing of doctrine. It is very ignorant and blind. The minister must find out what it means more wisely than it knows itself. If he takes it at its word and tries to satisfy it by making doctrine slight and easy, he will, as I have said, defeat his own well-meant but foolish effort. It seems to me that what he really is to hear in it underneath the mistaken expression of itself which it makes, is a great general desire to reach the more spiritual meaning of truths whose presentation has grown unspiritual. Not easiness nor hardness of belief is what men really want in what they are taught, but *truth*, whether it be hard or easy. Not greater ease is what we are to seek in order to conciliate more belief, but more spiritually, which means more truth.

For instance, when men cry out against the teaching of an everlasting hell to which they have long listened, nothing could be more mistaken than to try to win their faith by a mere sweeping aside of the whole truth of retribution; nothing could be more futile than to try to make them believe in God by stripping the God we offer them of His divine attributes of judgment and discrimination. But if there comes, as there must come, out of the tumult a deeper sense of the essential, the eternal connection between character and destiny; if men looking deeper into spiritual life are taught to see that the wrath of God and the love of God are not contradictory but the inseparable utterances of the one same nature; if punishment be fastened close to sin as the shadow to the substance, able to go, *certain* to go, where sin can go *and nowhere else* — then the tumult will bring a peace of deeper and complete faith. But surely it will not be easier for a man to believe the new and deep than the old crude doctrine. It will lay an even deeper and more awful burden on his conscience. It will make life more and not less solemn, when men come to see and feel the punishment in the sin than when they listened for the threats of punishment as men at sea listen for the breakers on the shore while they are sailing in smooth waters, which give them no intimation of how far away or near the breakers are.

Men really serious, men in a condition where they are capable of being taught religion, do not *dread*, they *want* to find life solemn. They will turn aside from any teaching which fritters its solemnity of ghosts who haunt and scare them with incoherent cries, whose threatening they do not see how to escape, and whose beckoning fingers they do not see how to follow.

Object: Bring Them to Christ

I turn to another point in which the teaching of Christianity as doctrine is helped by the clear sight and constant recollection of our first principle, that the object of all the teaching is to bring Christ to men. It will direct us in our choice of the truth that we shall teach. It will inspire truth with timeliness. For, after all, all divine truth is one. What we call different truths are different aspects of truth. They are the different ways in which we hold the glass between man and the Christ whom we want him to see. Now when a man comes to me and says "Why do you not preach this truth more?" and I reply to him, "Why should I?" and he answers, "Because it is a truth which many men are denying and many other men are forgetting," I venture to think that he has not given me a satisfactory or sufficient reason. It may be that I ought to preach that truth, but his reason is not enough to make me think I ought. It may very possibly be that the fact to which he points me, that it is a truth on which the minds of men are careless now, may prove that it is not the truth for me to preach just now. It may be true, but not the truth which men are needing now. The instinct with which men have turned away from it just as the present moment may be a healthy instinct. Certainly the disposition which some preachers have always shown to decide what truths they ought most to emphasize by seeing what truths the people most disliked to hear cannot be sensible or sound. It is firing your shot where the ranks of the enemy are thinnest. Nor can the desire to preserve the symmetry of truth, to rekindle in the great circle of doctrines those lights which for the moment are burning dim, furnish you a safe and sufficient rule. That desire has been the secret of the weakness of many a conscientious, able, and wholly ineffective ministry.

Tell Them What They Want to Hear

But, on the other hand, it is quite as true under our definition of what it is to teach religion that the mere desire of people that a certain truth should be *magnified* cannot be taken as a certain indication that it is the truth for us to preach. I do believe that it is a better indication than the other. I would rather be guided, on the whole, by what the people want to hear than by what the people hate to hear. But neither is a worthy guide for a man who is a student of humanity and a servant of Christ, bringing the two together. If I am trying to bring the seed and the ground together, I shall be sure that the time to sow the seed must be when the ground is soft and welcomes it, and not when it is hard and refuses it. But I shall know that it is possible for the ground to be too soft as well as for it to be too hard for the seed's best reception, and so the people's desire for the preaching of a certain truth may indicate not a healthy sense of need, but a morbid craving. They may want to hear about it just because it is antiquated and unpractical and does not trouble their consciences, and can be treated purely as a subject of curiosity and speculation. Its attraction for them may be like the unnatural sweetness of an apple which has been frozen and is no longer nutritious.

This applies to the whole question of the minister's relation to those strange outbreaks of interest in some special doctrine which are so frequent and sometimes seem so unaccountable. Such outbreaks are not so unaccountable as they appear; if they are not artificial, if they come naturally, without sensational intention, they are only the breaking out of a fire which has been brewing under the crust at some point where the crust is thinnest. But it may well be questioned whether the moment of such sudden interest in some great truth of Christianity is the moment when the preacher can best preach upon it. There is much, I know, to make men think it is. That interest which it is often so hard to stir is stirred already.

Men are eager to listen. Every newspaper stimulates their interest. Every platform speech is seasoned with the theological controversy of the hour. Boys sell tracts and sermons along with the journals of the day. Doctrinal novelettes shine in the monthly magazines, and stately symposia sit in the solemn banquet-chambers of the quarterlies.

Of the preacher's duty in connection with such times there are two things to say. First, this: *he must decide his duty by the great, final object of his ministry.* If the object of his ministry is a large congregation, here is the time, here is the way to get it. If the object of his ministry is to impress his ideas about eternal punishment or any other topic upon the people, probably there could be no better time than this. If the object of his ministry is to show God to men, the danger is that an intense interest in some one side, the magnitude of some one bit of truth, will distort the medium through which he shows Him. If you will forgive me for returning once more to the figure which I used, the danger is less if some one component of the glass be in undue proportion, the glass shall be muddy and show its own muddiness instead of the picture that it is trying to display. And the second thing is this: *if a preacher sees it right to take advantage of a temporary interest in some religious truth and make that truth his topic, he is bound to treat it always with reference to the great purpose of his preaching.* If he preaches about everlasting punishment, he is bound to let men see, to *make* men see, that whether the wicked are to be everlastingly punished or not, at least the gospel, the good news, cannot be the tidings that they are. To represent the Christian faith as consisting in a right belief as to what will be done to men if they are wicked, and not a clear sight of the regenerating grace by which the vilest sinner may become good, is to misrepresent it and dishonor it.

It seems to me, as if I were a layman in the days when some doctrine had got loose as it were into the wind and was being blown across the common land up and down the streets, I should go to church on Sunday, not wanting my minister to give me an oracular answer to all the questions which had been started about it, which I should not believe if he did give it, but hoping that out of his sermon I might refresh my knowledge of Christ. I would hope to get Him, His nature, His work, and His desires for me once more clear before me, and go out more ready to see this disputed truth of the moment in His light and as an utterance of Him.

I do not plead for shirking. Incidentally it may be wise to declare yourself upon the question of the hour just in order that your people may know that you are frank and have nothing to conceal from them. If a preacher holds anything to be true and knows that his people think he is unwilling to speak his mind upon that point, he had better preach on it next Sunday morning. But that is incidental; that is to assure their confidence in him and make them trust his honesty whenever he shall speak to them. But whether that is the best moment to show them Christ through that special truth is quite another question.

Handling Controversy

And here comes in another point, our duty with regard to religious controversy. It seems to me that controversy which has in it any element of bitterness or personal antagonism is like war, a necessary evil in an imperfect state of things, whose worst harm is only to be obviated by its being continually remembered that it is not the ideal method of religious life and progress. I dare not wish that all the great controversial voices of the past or of the present could be silenced, any more than I could desire that all the great warriors of history could be swept off the pedestals where the admiration of mankind has set them. I may feel my heart beat faster at the challenge of a disputant as I may own to the thrill of the bugle and the enthusiasm of the flag, and yet all the while I may feel sure that there is a higher way for the soul of man to reach truth than by fighting over it, as the general himself leading his army into battle may own that the perfect condition of man shall be peace, not war, and pray for peace through the smoke and thunder of the war that he delights in now. Controversy is a means. The end is greater than the means. The end is always claiming for itself purer and more perfect means. Controversy conducted with real reference to God and man, with a real wish to make God more real to man and man more near to God, may be legitimate, may be a duty, like war that is truly carried on for the advance of civilization. But the moment that controversy is waged for its own sake, the moment that it is asserted as a duty, and any preacher is reproached because he loves to build up truth more than beat down error, it becomes like a mere war of spite or conquest, which is always hideous. But there are conditions of the public mind when a man has to set his face against and steadfastly resist the summons to such controversies. There are times that make artificial sins and artificial heresies, lest they should find no enemies to fight with. It is bad to cry, "Peace, peace!" when there is no peace. It is just as bad, in some ways it is worse, to cry, "War, war!" when there is no war.

In general, the terrors of bad doctrine cannot be made the safeguard of truth, any more than the terrors of sin can be made the safeguard of righteousness. Terror has its place in the teaching of religion as in the government of life, but it is always preliminary, always arousing and awaking only, never creative. You do not plant a field by pulling out the rocks. You only make it fit for planting. You do not make a man believe truth by making him disbelieve error. That is where the danger of all the controversialists has always lain.

The Person of Christ in Various Situations

There remain some points of detail in the preacher's work of which I wish to speak in connection with the relation of doctrine to the fundamental purpose of religious teaching, which is the showing of Christ to men. I must allude to them very briefly. The first is the duty which the preacher feels to take advantage, not merely of certain conditions of the public mind, but also of certain conditions of individuals to impress the truth he has to teach. A man is softened by sickness or bereavement; some shock has broken down his confidence in life and in himself. You or I as his minister go to help him if we can. It is a God-given opportunity. But everything depends on how we go, on how, in going, we conceive of what we have to do; if we go thinking that now is a good time to make this crushed and frightened man accept our doctrine, our visit is a failure. He either throws us off indignantly or wearily, or else he takes our doctrine in some narrow form, and forever after holds it in some special way in which he happened to take refuge in it in his exigency. But if you go simply desiring to get Christ and that soul together, that the soul may rest in Christ, that Christ may satisfy the soul, then your doctrine, not abstract but personal, becomes the declaration of the facts of Christ. Through the facts he lays hold of the Person, and however different afterward the facts may seem to him, the Person he will hold always with the intensity of gratitude. Many a man's religious life has suffered, as many another's has been blessed, by the fact that he became religious in some critical, exigent, exceptional hour of his life. Such hours are not good for learning doctrine, but they are good for laying hold on Christ. And according to whether the religion of a man converted in such an hour was of the first or second sort will be the harm or blessing.

The same is true of the preacher's attempt to suit his teaching to different classes in his congregation, to old and young, to men and women, to the ignorant and learned. Christ's doctrine is the same for all. Christ Himself touches each with its own needed help. He whose idea of Christianity stops short in doctrine will weakly preach one truth to one class and another to another in his desire to suit them all. He who, behind and through doctrine, always feels Christ, will tell the self-same truth forever, and trust the endlessly adapted love of the Savior to make it to each soul what that soul needs.

I find, too, in this principle the key to that much discussed institution, the Sunday school. It is easy to praise our Sunday schools, and easy to blame them. Just now I think the blame inclines to outrun the praise and no doubt they have faults enough. But first of all, we must have some clear standard to judge them by, and that can come only from a clear idea about the nature of religious teaching. If to teach religion is primarily and fundamentally to impart knowledge, the schools are failures. With their limited time, their changing administration, their voluntary attendance, they must be failures. But if the teaching of religion is the bringing of Christ to men, then I can see great cause for hope, congratulation, and gratitude in what the Sunday schools are doing, where men and women to whom Christ is dear are in their different ways making Him known to hosts of boys and girls. I can be sure that there is very much crude and wrong teaching, and yet be thankful for the simple-hearted and gracious work.

Preaching With Humility and Sincerity

I think, then, in a clear, strong hold of our truth there lies the only hope for a minister's *humility*, which is the crown and jewel of his ministry. It is a great deal easier to grow proud of the thoroughness and faithfulness with which you hold a doctrine than of the completeness with which you understand Christ. The doctrine you may squeeze so small that you can hold it all in your hand and feel that you have comprehended it. The divine Savior we know, however we may talk competently of Him, is past our comprehension, wiser, dearer, truer than we have begun to know. Your pride in doctrine requires a doctor wiser and more orthodox than you to shake it. Your pride in Christ any poor saint nearer to Him than you have ever dreamed of being, or some wretched beggar bringing Him in some new shape of appealing misery to your weak love, may overturn in a moment. "The man is thrice welcome to whom my Lord has reprimanded me," said Mohammed one day most nobly, but he said it not of a theologian who had beaten him in argument, but of a blind wretch whose supplication he had rejected, and thereby learned how far he still was from God. If you want to protect your religious pride, make your religion consist in knowing truth. If you want to be humble in your religion, make your religion begin and end in knowing Christ.

The sister-jewel of humility is *sincerity*. Insincerity comes either from falsehood or from fear. It is either because I want men to believe something which I do not believe, or because I do not really trust the strength of what I believe, that I am insincere. The first is the ground of all insincerity in the matter of teaching. The second is the ground of all insincerity in the manner of teaching. There is enough of both. The minister whose own soul is doubtful, preaching some doctrine which he does not believe, and the minister who believes, but will not let his truth rest for his people on the grounds on which it rests with him, but bolsters it with arguments and sanctions which he does not think are true and sound, both of these ministers are insincere. I know that such insincere ministers are rare. I believe, in the freedom of Christian teaching which prevails today, they are rarer today than they have ever been. I believe they are rarer in Christian pulpits than in the preaching-places of any other faith, mainly because Christianity is an essentially personal religion; mainly because Christian truth has not to be guarded, like a woven cloth, by a hem of prejudice that it may not ravel out, but is kept complete like a live tree by the living principle which gives it life and value. Oh, beware of being insincere, but be sure that the natural and true salvation from insincerity is in *preaching* Christ! That old phrase, which has been so often the very watchword of cant — how it still declares the true nature of Christian teaching! Not Christianity, but Christ! Not a doctrine, but a Person! Christianity only for Christ! The doctrine only for the Person! Preach not Christianity but Christ, and so be saved from sacrificing the spiritual necessity of truthfulness to the seeming needs of what you call the truth—for in making that sacrifice good men grow almost conscientiously insincere.

Newness Comes From Christ

I add but one word more. The burden that weighs down many a man's ministry is the sense of triteness and commonplaceness. Oh, the wretchedness of feeling how often this has been said which I am going to say next Sunday! Oh, the struggles and contortions to shake off that misery and say something new and be original! But that is all as if the glass reproached itself with colorlessness and tried to stain itself with red and green that men might look at it. No; the white glass is saved from commonplaceness by the glory of the picture that looks through it. And the redemption of our sermons as of our characters from insignificance into dignity and worth must come not from fantastic novelties which they invent for themselves, but from their bearing simple and glorious witness to their Lord. Do not fear triteness. Only really hold your own new life honestly up to Christ in thoughtful and loving consecration, and men will see through you something of that Master and Savior who is forever new.

The preacher's work is the best work in the world. Let us believe that fully, but let the lives of all the preachers teach us that its glory is not in it, but in the Christ whom it is its privilege to declare. There is no study of the famous and successful preachers which does not bear testimony to that truth.

THE FIRE AND THE CALF

This message, an example of Phillips Brooks' pulpit oratory, was delivered in London on May 27, 1883 (Publisher's note).

"So they gave it me: then I cast it into the fire and there came out this calf." —*Exodus 32:24*

In the story from which these words are taken we see Moses go up into the mountain to hold communion with God. While he is gone, the Israelites begin to murmur and complain. They want other gods, gods of their own. Aaron, the brother of Moses, was their priest. He yielded to the people, and when they brought him their golden earrings he made out of them a golden calf for them to worship.

When Moses came down from the mountain, he found the people deep in their idolatry. He was indignant. First, he destroyed the idol, "He burnt it in the fire, and ground it to powder, and strawed it upon the water, and made the children of Israel drink of it." Then he turned to Aaron. "What did this people unto thee," he said, "that thou hast brought so great a sin upon them?" And Aaron meanly answered, "Let not the anger of my lord wax hot: thou knowest the people, that they are set on mischief. For they said unto me, Make us gods, which shall go before us. . . . And I said unto them, Whosoever hath any gold, let them break it off. So they gave it me: then I cast it into the fire, and there came out this calf" (Exod. 32:20-24). That was his mean reply. The real story of what actually happened had been written earlier in the chapter. When the people brought Aaron their golden earrings, "he received them at their hand, and fashioned it with a graving tool, after he had made it a molten calf; and they said, These be thy gods, O Israel, which brought thee up out of the land of Egypt" (32:4). That was what really happened, and this is the description which Aaron gave of it to Moses: "So they gave it me: then I cast it into the fire, and there came out this calf."

Aaron was frightened at what he had done. He was afraid of the act itself, and he was afraid of what Moses would say about it. Like all timid men, he trembled before the storm which he had raised. And so he tried to persuade Moses, and perhaps in some degree even to persuade himself, that it was not he that had done this thing. He lays the blame upon the furnace. "The fire did it," he declares. He will not blankly face his sin, and yet he will not tell a lie in words. He tells what is literally true. He had cast the earrings into the fire, and this calf had come out. But he leaves out the one important point, his own personal agency in it all; the fact that he had moulded the earrings into the calf's shape, and that he had taken it out and set it on its pedestal for the people to adore. He tells it so that it shall all look automatic. It is a curious, ingenious, but transparent lie.

Let us look at Aaron's speech a little while and see what it represents. For it does represent something. There never was a speech more true to one disposition of our human nature. We are all ready to lay the blame upon the furnaces. "The fire did it," we are all of us ready enough to say.

People Like Aaron

Here is a man all gross and sensual, a man still young who has already lost the freshness and the glory and the purity of youth. He is profane; he is cruel; he is licentious; all his brightness has grown lurid; all his wit is ribaldry. You know the man. As far as a man can be, he is a brute. Suppose you question that man about his life. You expect him to be ashamed, to be repentant. There is not a sign of anything like that! He says, "I am the victim of circumstances. What a corrupt, licentious, profane age this is in which we live! When I was in college, I got into a bad set. When I went into business, I was surrounded by bad influences. When I grew rich, men flattered me. When I grew poor, men bullied me. The world has made me what I am, this fiery, passionate, wicked world. I had in my hands the gold of my boyhood which God gave me. Then I cast it into the fire, and there came out this calf." And so the poor, wronged, miserable creature looks into your face with his bleary eyes and asks your pity.

Another man is not a profligate, but is a miser, or a mere business machine. "What can you ask of me," he says, "this is a mercantile community. The business man who does not attend to his business goes to the wall. I am what this intense commercial life has made me. I put my life in there, and it came out this." And then he gazes fondly at his golden calf, and his knees bend under him with the old long habit of worshiping it, and he loves it still, even while he abuses and disowns it.

And so with the woman of society. "The fire made me this," she says of her frivolity and pride. And so of the politician and his selfishness and partisanship. "I put my principles into the furnace, and this came out." And so of the bigot and his bigotry, the one-sided conservative with his stubborn resistance to all progress, the one-sided radical with his ruthless iconoclasm. So of all partial and fanatical men. "The furnace made us," they are ready to declare. "These times compel us to be this. In better times we might have been better, broader men; but now, behold, God put us into the fire, and we came out this." It is what one is perpetually hearing about disbelief. "The times have made me skeptical. How is it possible for a man to live in days like these and yet believe in God and Jesus and the resurrection. You ask me how I, who was brought up in the faith and in the church, became a disbeliever. Oh, you remember that I lived "five years here," or "three years there." "You know I have been very much thrown with this set or with that. You know the temper of our town. I cast myself into the fire, and I came out this."

One is all ready to understand, my friends, how the true soul, struggling for truth, seems often to be worsted in the struggle. One is ready to have tolerance, respect, and hope for any man who, reaching after God, is awed by God's immensity and his own littleness, and falls back crushed and doubtful. His is a doubt which is born in the secret chambers of his own personal conscientiousness. It is independent of his circumstances and surroundings. The soul which has truly come to a personal doubt finds it hard to conceive of any ages of most implicit faith in which it could have lived in which that doubt would not have been it. It faces its doubt in a solitude where there is none but it and God. All that one understands and the more he understands it, the more unintelligible does it seem to him, that any earnest soul can really lay its doubt upon the age, the set, or the society it lives in. No, our age, our society is what, with this figure taken out of the old story of Exodus, we have been calling it. It is the furnace. Its fire can set and fix and fasten what the man puts into it. But, properly speaking, it can create no character. it can make no truly faithful soul a doubter. It never did. It never can.

Casting Off Responsibility

Remember that the subtlety and attractiveness of this excuse, this plausible attributing of power to inanimate things and exterior conditions to create what only man can make, extends not only to the results which we see coming forth in ourselves. It covers also the fortunes of those for whom we are responsible. For example the father says of his profligate son whom he has never done one wise or vigorous thing to make a noble and pure minded man: "I cannot tell how it has come. It has not been my fault. I put him into the world and this came out." The father whose faith has been mean and selfish says the same of his boy who is a skeptic. Everywhere there is this cowardly casting off of responsibilities upon the dead circumstances around us. It is a very hard treatment of the poor, dumb, helpless world which cannot answer to defend itself. It takes us as we give ourselves to it. It is our minister fulfilling our commissions for us upon our own souls. If we say to it, "Make us noble," it does make us noble. If we say to it, "Make us mean," it does make us mean. And then we take the nobility and say, "Behold, how noble I have made myself." And we take the meanness and say, "See how mean the world has made me."

Why the Excuses?

You see, I am sure how perpetual a thing the temper of Aaron is, how his excuse is heard everywhere and always. I need not multiply illustrations. But now, if all the world is full of it, the next question is, What does it mean? Is it mere pure deception, or is there also delusion, self-deception in it? Take Aaron's case. Was he simply telling a lie to Moses and trying to hide the truth from his brother whom he dreaded, when he said, "I cast the earrings into the fire, and this calf came out"? Or was he in some dim degree, in some half-conscious way, deceiving himself? Was he allowing himself to attribute some power to the furnace in the making of the calf? Perhaps as we read the verse above in which it is so distinctly said that Aaron fashioned the idol with a graving tool, any such supposition seems incredible. But yet I cannot but think that some degree, however dim, of such self-deception was in Aaron's heart. The fire was mysterious. He was a priest. Who could say that some strange creative power had not been at work there in the heart of the furnace which had done for him what he seemed to do for himself. There was a human heart under that ancient ephod, and it is hard to think that Aaron did not succeed in bringing himself to be somewhat imposed upon by his own words and in hiding his responsibility in the heart of the hot furnace.

However it may have been with Aaron, there can be no doubt that in almost all cases this is so. Very rarely indeed does a man excuse himself to other men and yet remain absolutely unexcused in his own eyes. When Pilate stands washing the responsibility of Christ's murder from his hands before the people, was he not feeling himself as if his hands grew cleaner while he washed?

When Shakespeare paints Macbeth with the guilty ambition which was to be his ruin first rising in his heart, you remember how he makes him hide his newborn purpose to be king even from himself. He pretends that he believes that he is willing to accept the kingdom only if it shall come to him out of the working of things, for which he is not responsible, without an effort of his own.

> If chance will have me king,
> Why, chance may crown me,
> Without my stir.

That was the first stage of the growing crime which finally became murder.

Sailing With the Current

Often it takes this form. Often the way to help ourselves achieve a result that we have set before ourselves is just to put ourselves into a current which is sweeping on that way, and then lie still and let the current do the rest. In all such cases it is so easy to ignore or to forget the first step, which was that we chose that current for our resting place, and so to say that it is only the drift of the current which is to blame for the dreary shore on which at last our lives are cast up by the stream.

Suppose you are today a scornful man, a man case-hardened in conceit and full of disbelief in anything generous or supernatural, destitute of all enthusiasm, contemptuous, supercilious. You say the time you live in has made you so. You point to one large tendency in the community which always sets that way. You parade the specimens of enthusiastic people whom you have known who have been fanatical and silly. You tell me what your favorite journal has been saying in your ears every week for years. You bid me catch the tone of the brightest people whom you live among, and then you turn to me and say, "How could one live in such an atmosphere and not grow cynical? Behold, my times have made me what I am."

What does that mean? Are you merely trying to hide from me, or are you also hiding from yourself the certain fact that you have chosen that special current to launch your boat upon, that you have given your whole attention to certain kind of facts and shut your eyes to certain others, that you have constantly valued the brightness which went to the depreciation of humanity and despised the urgency which a healthier spirit has argued for the good in man and for his everlasting hope? Is it not evident that you yourself have been able to half forget all this, so when the stream on which you launched your boat at last drives it upon the beach to which it has been flowing all the time, there is a certain lurking genuineness in the innocent surprise with which you look around upon the desolate shore on which you land, and say to yourself, "How unhappy I am that I should have fallen upon these evil days, in which it is impossible that a man should genuinely respect or love his fellowmen"?

There are always currents flowing in all bad directions. There is a perpetual river flowing toward sensuality and vice. There is a river flowing perpetually toward hypocrisy and skepticism and infidelity. And when you once have given yourself up to one of these rivers, then there is quite enough in the continual pressure in that great movement like a fate beneath your keel to make you lose the sense and remembrance that you are there by your own will. You think only of the resistless flow of the river that is always in your eyes and ears.

A Confusion of Blame

This is the mysterious, bewildering mixture of the consciousness of guilt and the consciousness of misery in all our sin. We live in a perpetual confusion of self-pity and self-blame. We go up to the scaffolds where we are to suffer, half like culprits crawling to the gallows and half like martyrs proudly striding to their stakes. When we think of what sort of reception is to meet us in the other world as the sum and judgment of the life we have been living here, we find ourselves ready, according to the moment's mood, either for the bitterest denunciation, as of souls who have lived in deliberate sin; or for tender petting and refreshment, as of souls who have been buffeted and knocked about by all the storms of time, and for whom now there ought to be soft beds in eternity. The confusion of men's minds about the judgments of the eternal world is only the echo of their confusion about the responsibilities of the life which they are living now.

Suppose there is a man here this morning who committed a fraud in business yesterday. He did it in a hurry. He did not stop to think about it then. But now, here, in this quiet church, with everything calm and peaceful round him, with the words of prayer which have taken God for granted sinking into his ears, he has been thinking it over. How does it look to him? Is he not certainly sitting in the mixture of self-pity and self-reproach of which I spoke? He did the sin, and he is sorry as a sinner. The sin did itself, and he is sorry as a victim. Nay, perhaps in the next pew to him, or perhaps in the same pew, or perhaps in the same body, there is sitting a man who means to do a fraud tomorrow. In him too is there not the same confusion? One moment he looks it right in the face and says, "Tomorrow night I shall despise myself." The next moment he is quietly thinking that the sins will do itself and give him all its advantage, and he need not interfere. Macbeth's words affirm it:

> If chance will make me cheat,
> Why, chance may crown me,
> Without my stir.

Both thoughts are in his mind, and if he has listened to our service, it is likely enough that he has found something in it

—something even in the words of the Bible—for each thought
to feed upon.

The Incompleteness of Self-deception

Such self-deception almost never is absolutely complete.
We feel its incompleteness the moment any one else attempts
to excuse us with the same excuse with which we have
excused ourselves. Suppose one of the Israelites who stood
by had spoken up in Aaron's behalf and said to Moses, "Oh,
he did not do it. It was not his act. he only cast the gold into
the fire, and there came out this calf." Must not Aaron as he
listened have felt the wretchedness of such a telling of the
story, and been ashamed, and even cried out and claimed his
responsibility and his sin? Very often it is good for us to
imagine someone saying aloud in our behalf what we are
silently saying to ourselves in self-apology. We see its thinness
when another hand holds it up against the sun, and we stand
off and look at it.

If I might turn again to Shakespeare and his wonderful
treasury of human character, there is a scene in Hamlet that
illustrates exactly what I mean. The king has determined that
Hamlet must die, and he is just sending him off upon the
voyage from which he means that he is never to return. The
king has fully explained the act to his own conscience, and
accepted the crime as a necessity. Then he meets the courtiers,
Rosencrantz and Guildenstern, who are to have the execution
of the base commission. And they, as courtiers do, try to
repeat to the king the arguments with which he has convinced
himself. One says,

> Most holy and religious fear it is
> To keep those many many bodies safe
> That live and feed upon your majesty.

And the other takes up the strain and says,

> The single and peculiar life is bound,
> With all the strength and armor of the mind,
> To keep itself from 'noyance; but much more
> That spirit upon whose weal depend and rest
> The lives of many.

They are the king's own arguments. With them he has
persuaded his own soul to tolerate the murder. But when

they come to him from these other lips, he will have none of them. He cuts them short. He cannot hear from others what he has said over and over to himself.

> Arm you, I pray you, to this speedy voyage.

So he cries out and interrupts them. Let the deed be done, but let not these echoes of his self-excuse parade before him the way in which he is trifling with his own soul.

So it is always, I think of the mysterious judgment day, and sometimes it appears to me as if our souls would need no more than merely that voices outside ourselves should utter in our ears the very self-same pleas and apologies with which we, here upon the earth, have extenuated our own wickedness. They of themselves, heard in the open air of eternity, would let us see how weak they were, and so we should be judged. Is not that partly the reason we hate the scene of some old sin? The room in which we did it seems to ring forever with the sophistries by which we persuaded ourselves that it was right, and which will not let us live in comfortable delusion. Our life there is an anticipated judgment day.

I doubt not that this tendency to self-deception and apology with reference to the sins which they commit differs exceedingly with different men. Men differ, perhaps, nowhere else more than in their disposition to face the acts of their lives and to recognize their own personal part in and responsibility for the things they do. Look, for instance, at this Aaron and his brother Moses. The two men are characterized and illustrated by their two sins. The sin of Aaron was a denial or concealment of his own personal agency. "I cast it into the fire, and there came out this calf." As he stood with his thirsty people in front of the rock in Horeb, he intruded his personal agency where it had no right. "Hear now, ye rebels; must we fetch you water out of this rock?" To be sure, in the case of Moses it was a good act of mercy to which he put in his claim, while in Aaron's case it was a wicked act whose responsibility he desired to avoid. And men are always ready to claim the good deeds in which they have the smallest share, even when they try to disown the sins which are entirely their own. But still the actions seem to mark the men. Moses is the franker, manlier, braver man. In Aaron the priest there is something in that oversubtle, artificial, complicated character, that power of becoming morally confused even in the midst of pious feeling, that lack of simplicity, and of the disposition to look things frankly in the eye; in a word, that which has often in the history of religion made the very name of priestcraft a reproach. Moses is the prophet. His distinct mission is the utterance of truth. He is always simple; never more simple than when he is most profound; never more sure of the fundamental principles of right and wrong, of honesty and truth, than when he is deepest in the mystery of God; never more conscious of himself and his responsibilities than when he is most conscious of God and His power.

Looking for a Cure

And this brings me to my last point, which I must not longer delay to reach. If the world is thus full of the Aaron spirit, of the disposition to throw the blame of wrong-doing upon other things and other people to represent to others and to our own souls that our sins do themselves what is the real spiritual source of such a tendency, and where are we to look to find its cure? I have just intimated what seems to me to be its source: It is a vague and defective sense of personality. Anything which makes less clear to a man the fact that he, standing here on his few inches of the earth, is a distinct separate being, in whom is lodged a unit of life, with his own soul, his own character, his own chances, his own responsibilities, distinct and separate from any other man's in all the world; anything that makes all that less clear demoralizes a man and opens the door to endless self-excuses. And you know, surely, how many tendencies there are to-day which are doing just that for men.

Every man's personality, his clear sense of himself, seems to be standing today where almost all the live forces of the time are making their attacks upon it. It is like a tree in the open field from which every bird carries away some fruit. The enlargement of our knowledge of the world, the growing tendency of men to work in large companies, the increased despotism of social life, the interesting studies of hereditation, the externality of a large part of our action, the rush and competition for the prizes which represent the most material sort of success, the spread of knowledge by which at once all men are seen to know much, and, at the same time, no man is seen to know everything; all these causes enfeeble the sense of personality. The very prominence of the truth of a universal humanity, in which our philanthropy justly glories, obscures the clearness of the individual human life. Once it was hard to conceive of man, because the personalities of men were so distinct. Once people found it hard, as the old saying was, to see the forest for the trees. Now it is just the opposite. To hundreds of people it is almost impossible to see the trees for the forest. Man is so clear that men become obscure. As the laureate of the century sings of the time which he so well knows: "The individual withers and the race is more and more." These are the special causes, working in our time, of that which has its general causes in our human nature working everywhere and always.

Finding the Cure

And if this is the trouble, where, then, is the help? If this is the disease, where is the cure? I cannot look for it anywhere short of that great assertion of the human personality which is made when a man personally enters into the power of Jesus Christ. Think of it! Here is some Aaron of our modern life trying to cover up some sin which he has done. The fact of the sin is clear enough. There is no possibility of concealing that. It stands out wholly undisputed. It is not by denying that the thing was done but by beclouding the fact that he did it with his own hands, with his own will; thus it is that the man would cover up his sin. He has been nothing but an agent, nothing but a victim; so he assures his fellowmen, so he assures himself.

Suppose that while he is doing that, the great change comes to that man by which he is made a disciple and servant of Jesus Christ. It becomes known to him as a certain fact that God loves him individually, and is educating him with a separate personal education which is all his own. The clear individuality of Jesus stands distinctly out and says to him, "Follow me!" Jesus stops in front of where he is working just as evidently, with just as manifest intention of calling him as that with which He stopped taxes, and says, "Follow me." He is called separately, and separately he does give himself to Christ. Remember all that is essential to a Christian faith. You cannot blur it all into indistinctness and generality. In the true light of the redeeming incarnation, every man in the multitude stands out as every blade of grass on the hillside stands distinct from every other when the sun has risen. In this sense, as in many another, this is the true light which lighteneth every man that cometh into the world.

The Bible calls it a new birth, and in that name too there are many meanings. And among other meanings in it must there not be this—the separateness and personality of every soul in Christ? Birth is the moment of distinctness. The meanest child in the poorest hovel in the city, who by and by is to be lost in the great whirlpool of human life, here at the outset where his being comes as a new fact into the crowded world, is felt in his distinctness, has his own personal tending, and excites his own personal emotion. When he is born and when he dies, but perhaps most of all when he is born, the commonest, most commonplace and undistinguished of mankind asserts the fact of privilege of his separateness. And so when the possession of the soul by Christ is called the "New Birth," one of the meanings of that name is this, that then there is a reassertion of personality, and the soul which had lost itself in the slavery of the multitude finds itself again in the obedience of Christ.

And now what will be the attitude of this man, with his newly-awakened selfhood, towards that sin which he has been telling himself that his hands did, but that he did not do? May we not almost say that he will need that sin for his self-identification?

Who is he? A being whom Christ has forgiven, and then in virtue of that forgiveness made His servant. All his new life dates from and begins with his sin. He cannot afford to find his consciousness of himself only in the noble parts of his life, which it makes him proud and happy to remember. There is not enough of that to make for him a complete and continuous personality. It will have great gaps if he disowns the wicked demonstrations of his selfhood and says, "It was not I," wherever he has done wrong. No! Out of his sin, out of the bad, base, cowardly acts which are truly his, out of the weak and wretched passages of his life which it makes him ashamed to remember, but which he forces himself to recollect and own, out of these he gathers the consciousness of a self all astray with self-will, which he then brings to Christ and offers in submission and obedience to His perfect will.

You try to tell some soul rejoicing in the Lord's salvation that the sins over whose forgiveness by its Lord he is gratefully rejoicing, were not truly his; and see what strange thing comes. The soul seems to draw back from your assurance as if he were true, he would be robbed of all his surest confidence and brightest hope. You meant to comfort the poor penitent, and he looks into your face as if you were striking him a blow. And you can see what such a strange sight means. It is not that the poor creature loves those sins or is glad that he did them, or dreams for an instant of ever doing them again. It is only that through those sins, which are all the real experience he has had, he has found himself, and finding himself has found his Savior and the new life.

So the only hope for any of us is in a perfectly honest manliness to claim our sins. "I did it, I did it," let me say of all my wickedness. Let me refuse to listen for one moment to any voice which would make my sins less mine. It is the only honest and the only hopeful way, the only way to know and be ourselves. When we have done that, then we are ready for the gospel, ready for all that Christ wants to show us that we may become, and for all the powerful grace by which He wants to make us be it perfectly.

Inspirational Reading From Great Pulpit Masters

The *Classic Sermons Series*, compiled by Warren W. Wiersbe:

Classic Sermons on the Attributes of God. These classic sermons by highly acclaimed pulpit masters lay a solid foundation for a study of God's attributes. Provides new insights into such attributes of God as His sovereignty, jealousy, omnipresence, immutability, mercy, omniscience and love. Gleaned from the past are the messages of such famous preachers as Henry Ward Beecher, J.D. Jones, C.H. Spurgeon, D.L. Moody, John Wesley, and others.

4038-6	160 pp.	paperback

Classic Sermons on Faith and Doubt. A collection of 12 carefully selected sermons, the goal of which is to stimulate the growth and maturity of the believer's faith. Among the preachers represented are: A.C. Dixon, J.H. Jowett, D. Martyn Lloyd-Jones, G. Campbell Morgan, and Martin Luther.

4028-9	160 pp.	paperback

Classic Sermons on Prayer. Fourteen pulpit giants present the need, the how-to, and the results of a life permeated with prayer. These sermons, by such famous preachers as Dwight L. Moody, G. Campbell Morgan, Charles H. Spurgeon, Reuben A. Torrey, Alexander Whyte, and others, will energize your prayer life, show you how to expect great things from God, and help you experience the strength and power of God in your everyday life.

4029-7	160 pp.	paperback

Classic Sermons on Suffering. Sermons by such illustrious preachers as C.H. Spurgeon, Phillips Brooks, John Calvin, Walter A. Maier, George Truett, and others that will uplift the depressed, comfort the heartbroken, and be especially useful for the preacher in his pulpit and counseling ministries.

4027-0	204 pp.	paperback

Classic Sermons on Worship. In these classic sermons by pulpiteers such as C.H. Spurgeon, John A. Broadus, James S. Stewart, Frederick W. Robertson, G. Campbell Morgan, and Andrew A. Bonar, we discover the true meaning and practice of worship.

4037-8	160 pp.	paperback

Available from your Christian bookstore, or

KREGEL *Publications*

P.O. Box 2607 • Grand Rapids, MI 49501